The IDEA MAGAZINE FOR TEACHERS®
MAILBOX®

The Education Center®

3 1526 03579791 6

2007–2008 YEARBOOK

The Education Center, Inc.
Greensboro, North Carolina

The Mailbox® 2007–2008 Grades 2–3 Yearbook

Managing Editor: *The Mailbox* Magazine: Jennifer Bragg

Editorial Team: Becky S. Andrews, Debbie Ashworth, Diane Badden, Kimberley Bruck, Karen A. Brudnak, Kitty Campbell, Jenny Chapman, Kathy Coop, Chris Curry, Lynette Dickerson, Sarah Foreman, Margaret Freed (COVER ARTIST), Theresa Lewis Goode, Karen Brewer Grossman, Tazmen Hansen, Marsha Heim, Lori Z. Henry, Sherry McGregor, Dorothy C. McKinney, Sharon Murphy, Jennifer Nunn, Gerri Primak, Mark Rainey, Greg D. Rieves, Kelly Robertson, Hope Rodgers, Eliseo De Jesus Santos II, Rebecca Saunders, Barry Slate, Hope Taylor Spencer, Zane Williard

ISBN10 1-56234-856-6
ISBN13 978-156234-856-4
ISSN 1088-5544

Printed in the United States of America.

The Education Center, Inc.
P.O. Box 9753
Greensboro, NC 27429-0753

Look for *The Mailbox® 2008–2009 Grades 2–3 Yearbook* in the summer of 2009. The Education Center, Inc., is the publisher of *The Mailbox*®, *Teacher's Helper*®, *The Mailbox*® BOOKBAG®, and *Learning*® magazines, as well as other fine products. Look for these wherever quality teacher materials are sold, call 1-800-714-7991, or visit www.themailbox.com.

Contents

Math Units

Teacher Resource Units

ARTS & CRAFTS

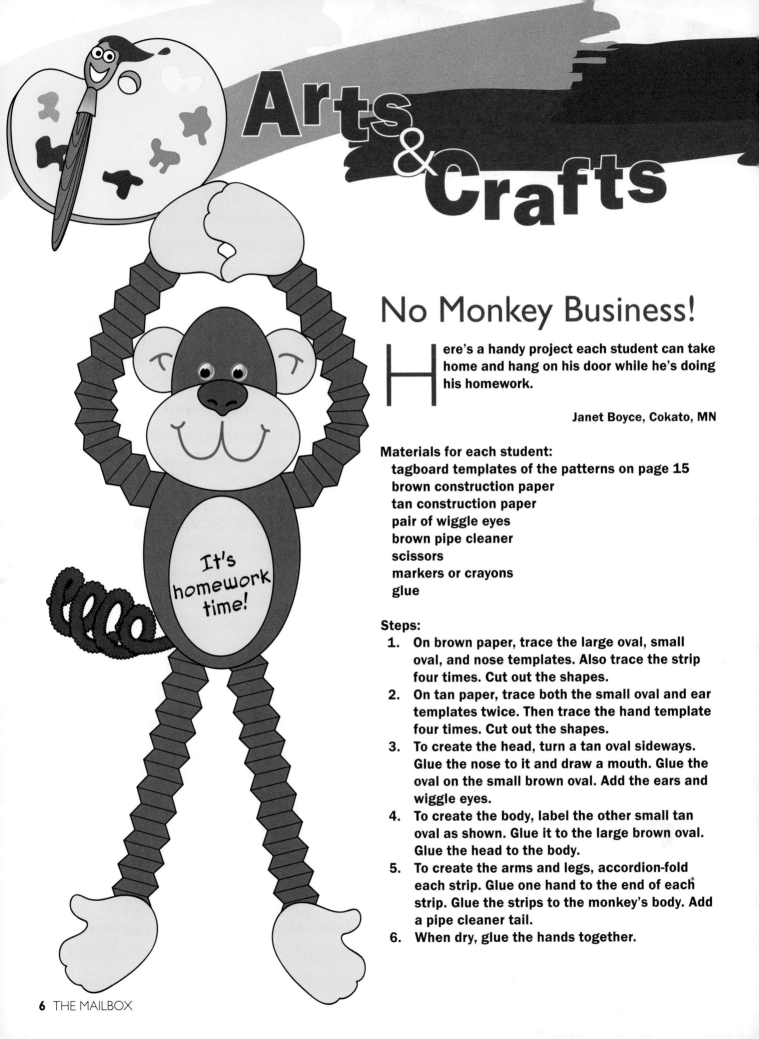

Arts & Crafts

No Monkey Business!

Here's a handy project each student can take home and hang on his door while he's doing his homework.

Janet Boyce, Cokato, MN

Materials for each student:
tagboard templates of the patterns on page 15
brown construction paper
tan construction paper
pair of wiggle eyes
brown pipe cleaner
scissors
markers or crayons
glue

Steps:

1. On brown paper, trace the large oval, small oval, and nose templates. Also trace the strip four times. Cut out the shapes.
2. On tan paper, trace both the small oval and ear templates twice. Then trace the hand template four times. Cut out the shapes.
3. To create the head, turn a tan oval sideways. Glue the nose to it and draw a mouth. Glue the oval on the small brown oval. Add the ears and wiggle eyes.
4. To create the body, label the other small tan oval as shown. Glue it to the large brown oval. Glue the head to the body.
5. To create the arms and legs, accordion-fold each strip. Glue one hand to the end of each strip. Glue the strips to the monkey's body. Add a pipe cleaner tail.
6. When dry, glue the hands together.

It's homework time!

Dinner Chime

After students make these turkey bells, they'll have a surefire way to call their families to the Thanksgiving dinner table!

Valerie Wood Smith, Morgantown, PA

Materials for each student:
  jingle bell
  small foam cup
  brown tissue paper squares
  red, orange, and yellow construction paper
  pipe cleaner
  black marker
  scissors
  glue
  tape
  stapler

Steps:
  1. Use the pipe cleaner to poke a small hole in the bottom of the cup.
  2. Glue the tissue paper squares to the upside-down cup, leaving the hole open.
  3. While the glue is drying, cut several feathers from the construction paper. Staple the feathers together and tape them to the cup as shown.
  4. Use the marker to add eyes. Cut out a beak and a wattle from the construction paper and then glue them below the eyes to make a turkey face.
  5. Push the pipe cleaner through the hole and thread the bottom of the pipe cleaner through the bell. Form the top of the pipe cleaner into a handle. Twist the ends around the pipe cleaner to secure them.

Arts & Crafts

In the fall, I like to make jack-o'-lanterns.

Devin

Fall Wreath

Highlight students' favorite fall activities with easy-to-make wreaths! In advance, use the patterns on page 16 to make several tagboard templates. To make a wreath, fold a paper plate in half, cut out the center, and unfold the resulting wreath and circle. Trace chosen templates on construction paper, cut out the tracings, and add details. Then glue the cutouts around the wreath. Next, draw on the circle (cut from the center of the plate) a picture of a favorite fall activity and write a caption. To complete the wreath, trim around the picture and caption and then use a piece of yarn to suspend the art inside the wreath.

Dawn Hanson, Cornerstone Christian School, Olympia, WA

Stitched Sampler

To practice sewing skills—a common activity during colonial times—many Pilgrim children stitched pictures, their names, or other meaningful phrases on small squares of cloth to make *samplers*. To have students make mock samplers, give each student a manila tagboard square and access to colorful fine-tip markers. Have her use the markers to make designs or words out of small Xs (stitches) on her square. If desired, display the completed samplers together in the form of a quilt.

Jill D. Hamilton, Ephrata, PA

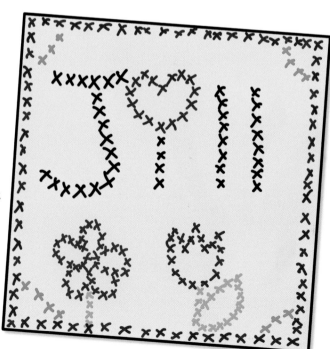

From the Heart

This easy-to-make gift is sure to be treasured. To make a gift, a student uses markers or paint to decorate the front of a legal-size envelope so it resembles holiday gift wrap. When it's dry, he glues on ribbon and a bow. Then he colors and cuts out a gift tag and selected coupons from a copy of page 17. (If desired, use more than one copy of the coupons.) On each coupon he writes a heartfelt task, chore, or object that he could give to a chosen loved one. After he places the completed coupons inside the envelope, he fills out the gift tag and glues it by the bow. When he gives his loved one the special gift, he encourages her to redeem the coupons as desired.

adapted from an idea by Elizabeth Searls Almy
Greensboro, NC

Warm Winter Wishes
This coupon is good for one night of dish duty.

Happy Holidays!
This coupon is good for extra hugs and kisses.

To: Mom
From: Deron

Arts & Crafts

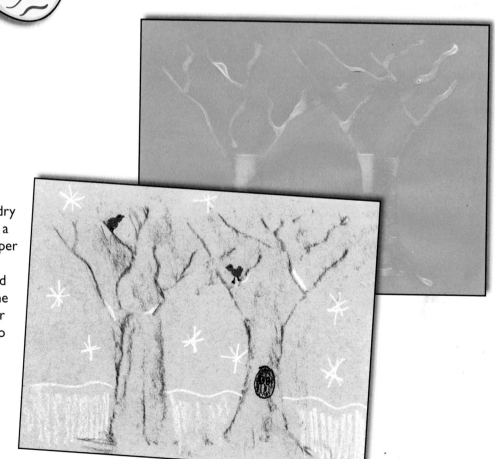

Scrimshaw Necklace

With this craft, students perform an art technique similar to that of some Inuit whalers of 200 years ago! Explain to youngsters that to stay busy during long voyages, the sailors often carved designs in whale teeth and bones to make scrimshaw art. To make a necklace, form a ball of white self-hardening modeling clay or dough into a whale tooth shape. Then use the point of a paper clip or a toothpick to etch a design or pattern into the tooth. After adding a hole at the top for stringing, set the project aside to dry. If desired, use water-colors to paint over the tooth. To complete the necklace, thread a length of ribbon through the hole.

Cindy Schumacher, Prairie Elementary School, Cottonwood, ID

Winter Wonderland

To make a winter scene, squeeze thick lines of glue on a sheet of construction paper to make two bare trees. Set the paper aside to dry for several hours. Then lightly tape a sheet of light blue construction paper atop the paper. Rub over the glue lines with the side of an unwrapped brown crayon. Carefully remove the blue paper and then use crayons or paint to add other winter details to the rubbing.

adapted from an idea by Cindy Barber
Fredonia, WI

Views of Spring

With this project, students use creativity and craft supplies to create four different outdoor images of spring. In advance, gather a variety of craft materials, such as tissue paper, pipe cleaners, craft foam, construction paper, sequins, doilies, and pompoms. To make a project, a student uses desired craft materials to create a different spring image in each window on a copy of page 18. Then he adds descriptive captions. To complete his project, he mounts his paper on a colorful sheet of construction paper.

Spring is a time for...

pretty flowers

colorful butterflies

bright sun

tall grass

Arts & Crafts

Lovebug
Students and their loved ones are sure to go buggy over this valentine!

adapted from an idea by Julie Lewis, J. O. Davis Elementary, Irving, TX

Materials for each student:
individual student photo
2 wiggle eyes
2 heart cutouts
4 pipe cleaner pieces

large craft stick
fine-tip marker
glue
tape

Steps:
1. Glue the photo to one heart and then glue the wiggle eyes over the eyes.
2. Write on the other heart a Valentine's Day message like the one shown.
3. Fold a pipe cleaner piece in half and tape it behind the photo heart so it resembles antennae.
4. Tape the craft stick to the back of the photo heart.
5. Glue the backs of the hearts together.
6. Twist three pipe cleaner pieces around the craft stick so they resemble legs.

Going Buggy Over You! Happy Valentine's Day! Love, Adam

Animal Windsock
Prior to making a windsock, a child chooses an animal to research and lists five facts about it on a large index card. To make a windsock, she uses a variety of art materials to create the animal and its habitat on a 9" x 12" sheet of construction paper. The child also writes the animal's name in the top center of the paper. She staples the paper to form a tube and glues paper strips to the bottom. Then she punches two holes at the top of the windsock and ties on a yarn hanger. She suspends the windsock and displays the index card nearby.

adapted from an idea by Rita Skavinsky, Minersville Elementary Center, Minersville, PA

Tracey
Cheetah
Cheetahs are large cats.
Cheetahs are yellowish-brown with black spots.
Cheetahs live on grassy plains.
Cheetahs are the fastest land mammal.
Cheetahs hunt and eat antelope.

Rain Forest Rain Stick

Transform a potato chip canister into a decorative rain stick!

Tracie Watson, P. H. Craig Elementary, Augusta, GA

Materials for each child:
clean, empty potato chip canister with lid
five aluminum foil strips
¼ c. rice
9" x 12" sheet of construction paper
tape
crayons or markers

Directions:
1. In the center of the paper, draw and label the different layers of a rain forest. Add rain forest animals if desired.
2. Wrap the paper around the canister and tape it in place.
3. Roll the aluminum foil strips into snake shapes and then form each one into a spiral.
4. Place the foil spirals and rice in the canister. Secure the lid.
5. Slowly turn the resulting rain stick upside down to hear the sound of rain.

Symmetrical Butterfly

To make a butterfly, a student folds a 6" x 9" sheet of construction paper in half. Then he cuts a butterfly wing shape in the paper, leaving the fold intact. Next, he opens his paper and glues a flat wooden clothespin to the center to make the butterfly body. Then he draws or paints a symmetrical design on the wings. To complete the project, he draws a face on the clothespin and tapes pipe cleaner antennae to the back of the butterfly.

adapted from an idea by Susan A. Chuey, Poland, OH

Arts & Crafts

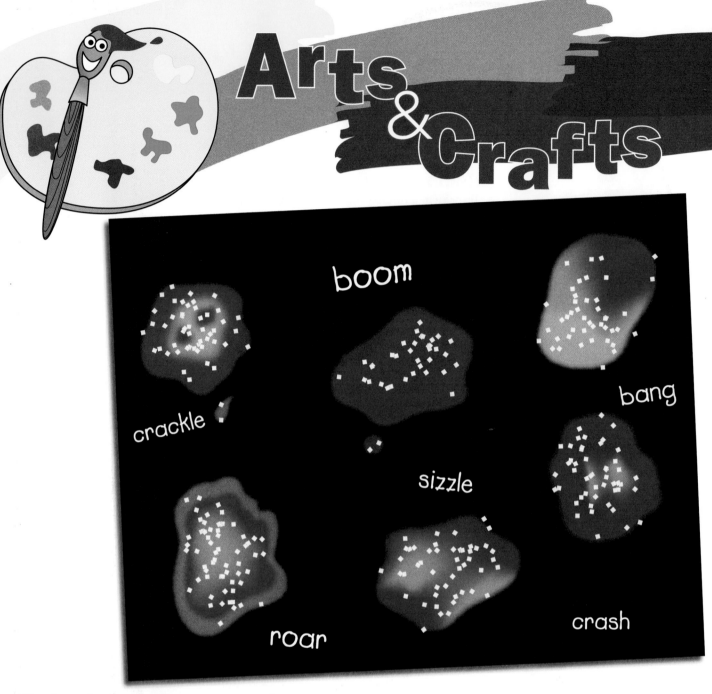

boom

crackle

bang

sizzle

roar

crash

Fabulous Fireworks

The sight and sounds of fireworks on a summer night are the inspiration for this project! To make a fireworks project, a student squeezes a small amount of brightly colored paint onto a sheet of black construction paper. Next, she holds a straw over the center of the paint and blows through the straw toward the paint until a desired effect is achieved. Then she adds a different color of paint to the center of the resulting firework and blows toward the paint to create a multicolor effect; or she places two colors of paint next to each other and blows through the straw to create a blended effect. After she makes several fireworks in this manner, she sprinkles glitter over the wet paint and shakes off the excess glitter. When the paint is dry, she uses a white colored pencil to write several words that describe the sounds of fireworks.

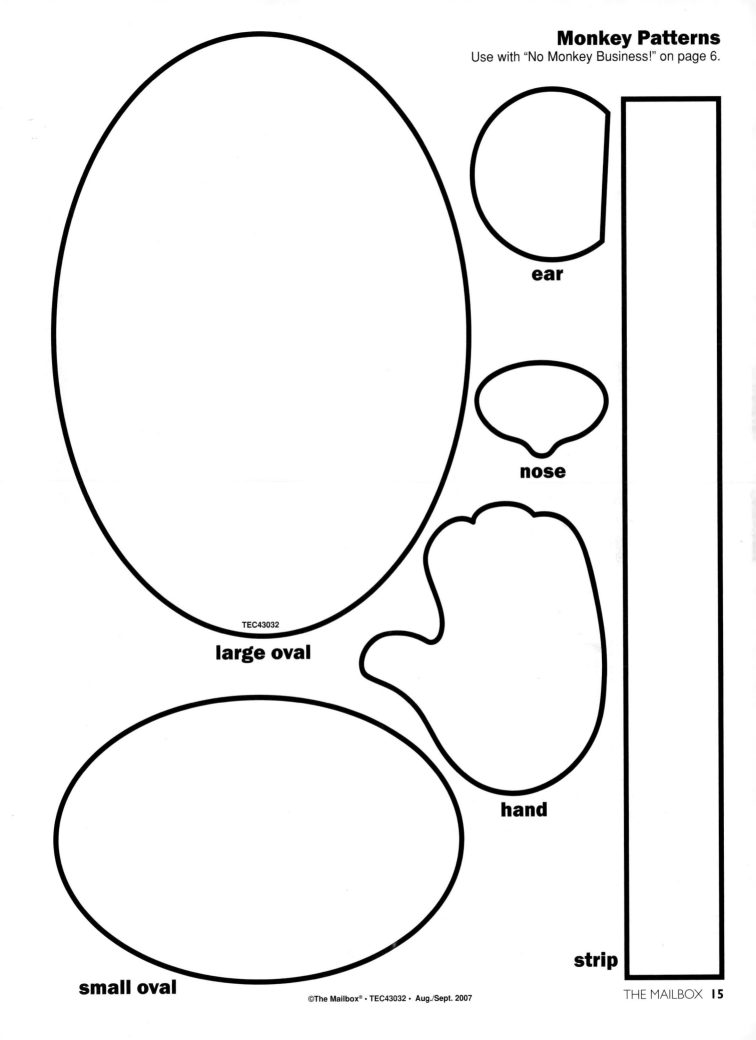

ear

nose

TEC43032

large oval

hand

strip

small oval

Leaf, Bat, Pumpkin, and Acorn Patterns
Use with "Fall Wreath" on page 8.

TEC43033

TEC43033

TEC43033

TEC43033

TEC43033

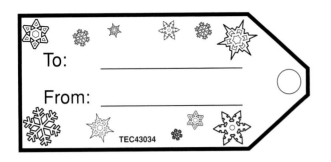

To: _____

From: _____

TEC43034

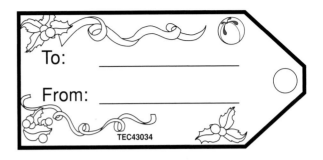

To: _____

From: _____

TEC43034

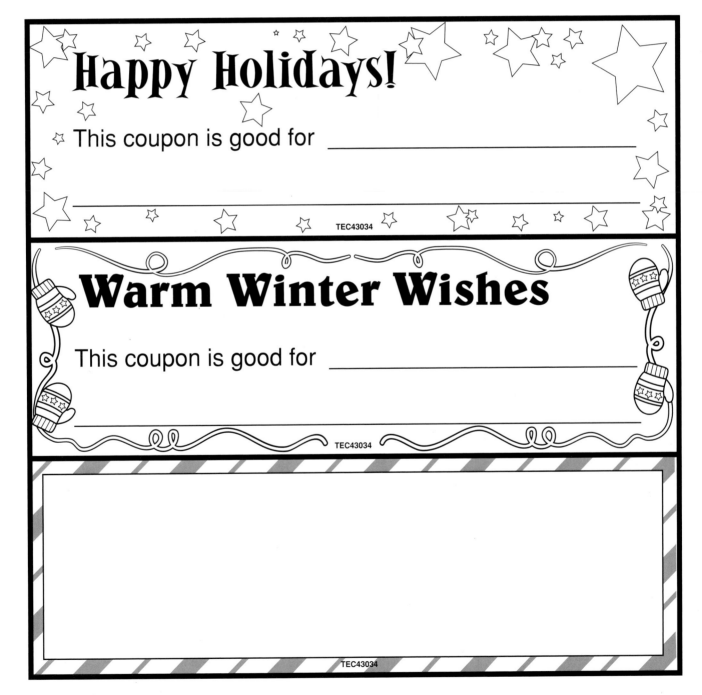

Happy Holidays!

☆ This coupon is good for _____

_____

TEC43034

Warm Winter Wishes

This coupon is good for _____

_____

TEC43034

TEC43034

Spring is a time for...

Note to the teacher: Use with "Views of Spring" on page 11.

CELEBRATE THE SEASON!

Celebrate the Season!

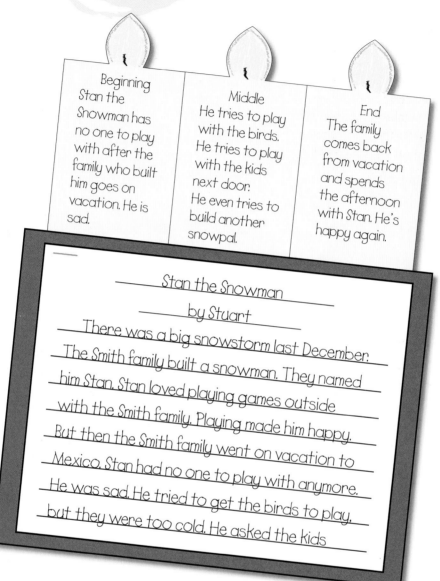

Beginning
Stan the Snowman has no one to play with after the family who built him goes on vacation. He is sad.

Middle
He tries to play with the birds. He tries to play with the kids next door. He even tries to build another snowpal.

End
The family comes back from vacation and spends the afternoon with Stan. He's happy again.

Stan the Snowman
by Stuart

There was a big snowstorm last December. The Smith family built a snowman. They named him Stan. Stan loved playing games outside with the Smith family. Playing made him happy. But then the Smith family went on vacation to Mexico. Stan had no one to play with anymore. He was sad. He tried to get the birds to play, but they were too cold. He asked the kids

Lighting the Way
Prewriting

Lead students to better writing with this festive organizer. First, guide each student to accordion-fold an 8½" x 11" sheet of yellow paper into thirds. Next, have him place a cutout copy of the candle pattern from page 28 on top of the folded paper and trace it. The student cuts around the pattern and unfolds his paper. He then writes in each section ideas for the beginning, middle, and end of a seasonal story or facts about how candles are used in different holiday celebrations. Finally, he uses his organizer to write his final draft, glues it to a large sheet of construction paper, and attaches the organizer to the top.

Bonnie Gaynor, Franklin, NJ, and Vicki Dabrowka, Palm Harbor, FL

Trimming a Tree
Rounding numbers

To prepare this partner activity, make a supply of paper stars and program a different multiple of ten on each. Then have each student pair trim a triangle shape (tree) from a large sheet of green construction paper. Give each duo a star and have the pair glue it to the top of the tree. Next, have the students use paper scraps to cut ornament shapes, writing on each ornament a different number that could be rounded to the number on the star. After the pair glues the ornaments to the tree, post the completed projects on a display titled "Rounding Around the Tree."

Allysa Lombardo, Washington School, Waterbury, CT

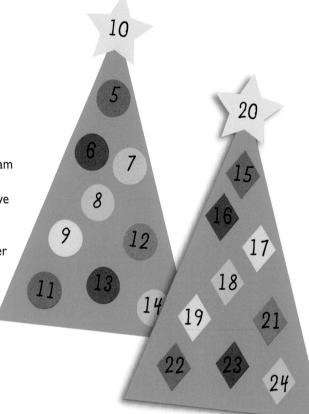

Snowy Sort
Spelling long o words

For this quick review, each child draws three wide snowmen on a large sheet of paper and labels their hats as shown. Next, she cuts out the picture cards from a copy of page 28. She softly names each picture and then sorts the cards according to the word's long o spelling. When all the cards have been sorted, she glues each one to the body of the corresponding snowman and writes the word for each picture next to its card. If desired, have students write additional words that use the designated spelling pattern listed on each snowman.

Happy New Year!
Researching, using a map

Assign each small group a different country or foreign city. Provide access to research materials and challenge students to find an interesting fact that tells how citizens from that area celebrate the New Year. Next, have a group member fold a sheet of paper in half and rewrite the fact as a question on the front of the folded paper. Then have another group member write the answer on the inside section, adding illustrations if desired. Post the completed projects with a world map on a display titled "Where in the World?" Encourage students to read and answer the questions and then find the location on the map.

inspired by an idea by Bonnie Gaynor, Franklin, NJ

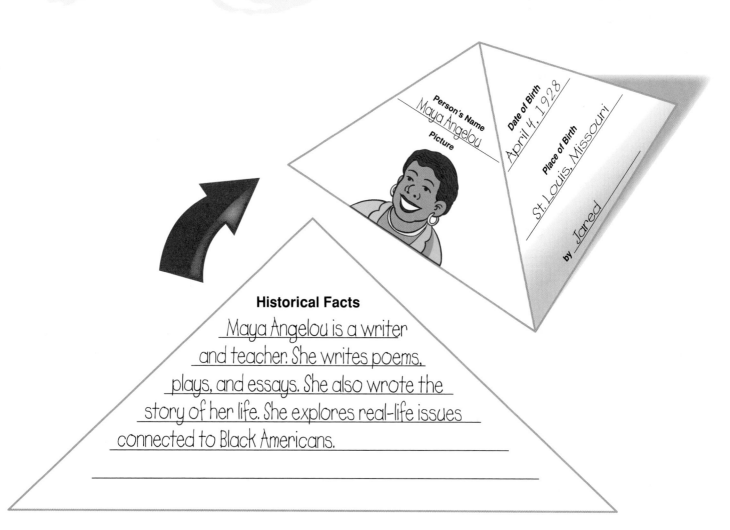

Person's Name
Maya Angelou
Picture

Date of Birth
April 4, 1928

Place of Birth
St. Louis, Missouri

by Jared

Historical Facts
Maya Angelou is a writer and teacher. She writes poems, plays, and essays. She also wrote the story of her life. She explores real-life issues connected to Black Americans.

Just the Facts
Researching

Celebrate Black History Month with this informative project. Provide access to research materials and give each student a copy of page 29. Instruct each student to choose a famous Black American and guide him to use the research materials to gather information about his chosen individual. Then have him record the appropriate information on his copy of page 29. Instruct each student to cut out the pattern and fold along the dotted lines. Finally, have him glue the tab to make a pyramid. Display the completed projects around the room.

Julie Hamilton, The Da Vinci Academy, Colorado Springs, CO

Seasonal Word Search
Word skills, making a line plot

To begin, write a phrase such as "Happy Saint Patrick's Day!" on the board. Then challenge each student to list on a sheet of paper as many words as she can make using the letters in the featured phrase. After a predetermined amount of time, have each student count the number of letters in each of the words she made. Then have her make a line plot to display her results.

inspired by an idea by Debra Miller, Sherman Elementary, Warwick, RI

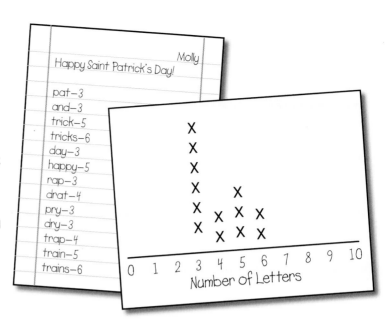

Molly
Happy Saint Patrick's Day!

pat—3
and—3
trick—5
tricks—6
day—3
happy—5
rap—3
drat—4
pry—3
dry—3
trap—4
train—5
trains—6

Number of Letters
0 1 2 3 4 5 6 7 8 9 10

My Spelling Words Made the Headlines!

HURRY   Better
TODAY
Only

Spelling List

1. about
2. better
3. choose
4. could
5. hurry
6. laugh
7. only
8. search
9. someone
10. today

Breaking News
Spelling

Here's an activity for Newspaper in Education Week, the first full week in March. Give each child a sheet of construction paper and have him add a title similar to the one shown. Then have him look for examples of his spelling words in various newspapers. When he finds a spelling word, have him cut it out and glue it to the construction paper. For an alternate version, direct students to look for examples of vocabulary words or high-frequency words.

Rita Skavinsky, Minersville Elementary Center, Minersville, PA

100th Day Snack Bags
Problem-solving strategies

For a tasty activity for the 100th day of school, give each small group a 100-calorie snack package and a sheet of construction paper. Direct each group to count the number of pieces inside the package, guiding students to combine broken pieces as needed to equal one piece. Pose the question, "If each package had the same number of snack pieces, how many bags would you need to have 100 pieces?" Next, have each group fold its paper in half and record on the left side the steps they followed to answer the question. Challenge students to check their work by showing a different strategy on the right side of the paper. Provide time for groups to share their answers and compare strategies used.

adapted from an idea by Anna Annunziata
Mildred Barry Garvin Microsociety School, East Orange, NJ

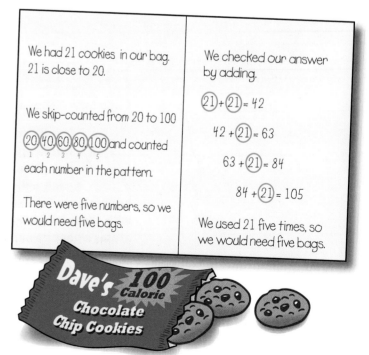

We had 21 cookies in our bag. 21 is close to 20.

We skip-counted from 20 to 100
20 40 60 80 100 and counted
 1   2   3   4   5
each number in the pattern.

There were five numbers, so we would need five bags.

We checked our answer by adding.

(21) + (21) = 42

42 + (21) = 63

63 + (21) = 84

84 + (21) = 105

We used 21 five times, so we would need five bags.

Dave's 100 Calorie Chocolate Chip Cookies

Celebrate the Season!

You're a smart cookie, Mom! Thanks for always helping me with my homework. Happy Mother's Day!

Love, Thomas

Mother's Day Memento
Figurative language

After discussing similes and metaphors, have each student list words and phrases that describe his mother or a special loved one. Give each child one of the items listed below and have each child determine how the item relates to his mother and her actions. For example, a packet of sugar may lead a child to respond with "Your love is as sweet as sugar," or "You are as sweet as sugar because you always wash my clothes." Guide each student to write his reply on a piece of construction paper cut to resemble a gift tag and attach the tag to the item.

Jackie Roberts, Venice Elementary, Venice, FL

Possible Items
sugar packets
prepackaged cookies
highlighters
rubber bands
Life Savers candies

Earth Day Basics
Science vocabulary

To create this informative booklet, a child cuts apart the booklet pages from a copy of page 30. She uses the words listed on the cover to complete the remaining booklet pages. Then she adds an illustration to match each description and staples the pages in order.

Honor the Earth

conserve
Earth Day
recycle
reduce
reuse

Name Lizzy

May 16, 2008

Dear U.S. Armed Forces,
Thank you for all you do to keep our country safe. Also, thank you for helping people in other countries have freedom. You do a good job every day!

Your fellow citizen,
Andrew

"Bear-y" Thankful
Letter writing

This activity is just right for Armed Forces Day! First, discuss with students the different sacrifices military service people make for our country. Next, have each student write on an index card a brief note of thanks to our military. Direct the student to then color and cut out a copy of the bear pattern from page 31. Then have him tape his index card to a straw and tape the straw to the back of his bear. Display the completed projects on a display titled "On Armed Forces Day, We're 'Bear-y' Thankful."

adapted from an idea by Natalie McGregor, Grenada Upper Elementary, Grenada, MS

Scrambled Eggs
Number sense

Here's a hands-on activity for springtime review. Program each of ten plastic egg halves with a different digit from 0 through 9. Place the eggs at a center with a supply of paper. A student chooses three eggs and arranges them on her workspace to build six different three-digit numbers. She records each number on her paper, and when she has recorded all six, she draws an egg shape around the set. Then she chooses another three eggs and repeats the process. **To make the activity more challenging,** have students choose four or five eggs to build larger numbers.

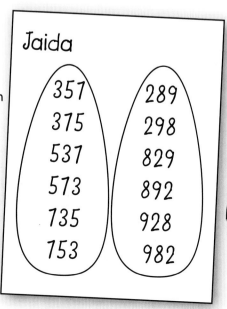

Jaida

357	289
375	298
531	829
573	892
735	928
753	982

9 2 8

Sail Into Summer

Making a glyph

I n advance, cut from tagboard a boat and a sail pattern. To make a sailboat glyph, a child refers to a copy of the instructions from page 32 as he uses construction paper and the tagboard patterns to make a set of sailboat pieces. After he makes the pieces, he cuts a paper strip to use as a mast. Next, he glues the portholes on the boat and glues one end of the mast to the middle of the boat. Then he glues the sail and the flag to the mast. Post the completed projects on a display titled "Sailing Into Summer."

Jennifer S. Graf, St. Paul Lutheran School, Chicago, IL

Summer Stepping
Narrative writing

A child starts a story with the phrase "My summer shoes will take me…" and then writes about a place she would like to visit during the summer. To publish her story, the child traces a copy of the flip-flop pattern from page 32 twice onto construction paper and cuts out the tracings to make two covers. Next, she traces the pattern on lined paper, cuts it out, and copies her story onto the page, making more pages as needed. She stacks her story between the covers and punches a hole through all the layers near the top center. Then she hole-punches the top cover two more times—once on each side, about a third of the way down—as shown. She tapes the end of a piece of ribbon to the back cover and threads it through the top hole and then down to the left hole. She trims it and tapes the end to the back of the front cover. She repeats the steps on the right side and then titles and personalizes her cover as shown. Provide time for students to share their stories.

Kelli Higgins, P. L. Bolin Elementary, East Peoria, IL

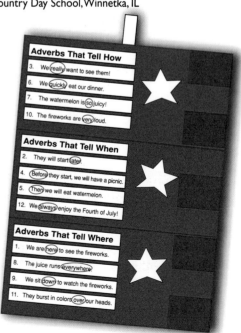

My summer shoes will take me to the zoo. I like to look at the bears. The polar bears are my favorite. They are playful. They dive in the water. They are huge! I love to watch them. They make me laugh.

Summer Shoes by Taylor

A Chilly Matchup
Math fact review

For this refreshing partner game, prepare several ice-pop cutouts, each with a slit cut toward the bottom as shown. Write a different math fact on the front of each cutout. On the back, write the problem's answer; then label a craft stick with the same number. Place the sticks, number-side down, in a container. To play, one student lays the ice pops, problem-side up, in rows. Player 1 draws a craft stick and finds the matching ice pop. To check his answer, he turns over the ice pop. If he is correct, he slips the stick inside the slit and lays the ice pop near him; then his turn is over. If he is incorrect, he leaves the ice pop and stick in play and his turn is over. Players continue taking turns until each stick is matched to an ice pop. The player with more ice pops is the winner.

David Green, North Shore Country Day School, Winnetka, IL

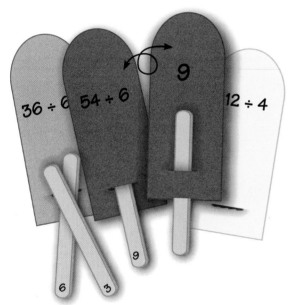

$36 \div 6$ $54 \div 6$ 9 $12 \div 4$

Stars, Stripes, and Fireworks
Adverbs

A child folds a sheet of blue construction paper to make three equal sections. Next, he cuts apart the adverb heading strips from a copy of page 33 and glues one at the top of each section. Then the child reads each sentence strip, circles the adverb in each sentence, cuts apart the strips, and glues each one under the appropriate heading. To make a firecracker, he trims a small piece of white paper so it resembles a wick and glues it to the top of his paper. Then he uses red and white construction paper scraps to decorate his firecracker.

Adverbs That Tell How
3. We really want to see them!
6. We quickly eat our dinner.
7. The watermelon is so juicy!
10. The fireworks are very loud.

Adverbs That Tell When
2. They will start later.
4. Before they start, we will have a picnic.
5. Then we will eat watermelon.
12. We always enjoy the Fourth of July!

Adverbs That Tell Where
1. We are here to see the fireworks.
8. The juice runs everywhere.
9. We sit down to watch the fireworks.
11. They burst in colors over our heads.

Candle Pattern
Use with "Lighting the Way" on page 20.

TEC43034

Vowel Picture Cards
Use with "Snowy Sort" on page 21.

TEC43034	TEC43034	TEC43034	TEC43034	TEC43034
TEC43034	TEC43034	TEC43034	TEC43034	TEC43034

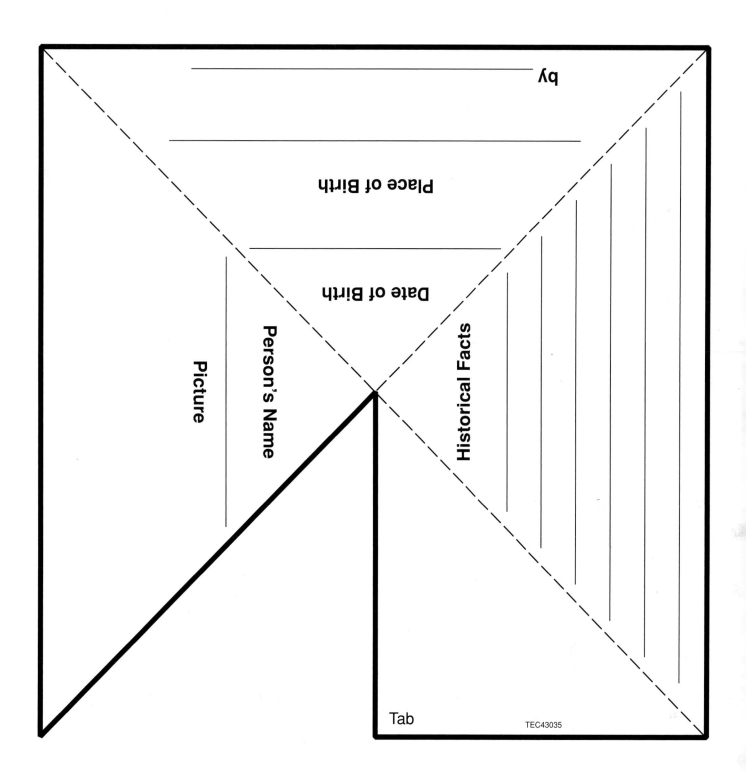

by

Place of Birth

Date of Birth

Person's Name

Picture

Historical Facts

Tab

TEC43035

Booklet Cover and Pages

Use with "Earth Day Basics" on page 25.

Honor the Earth

conserve
Earth Day
recycle
reduce
reuse

Name _____

_____ is held on April 22 each year. This is a day to remind us to take care of our planet.

1

One way to help the Earth is to _____ the amount of trash we cause. Buy only the things you need and choose products that have less wrapping. Then there will be less trash.

2

Another way to help the Earth is to _____ the things we have. Instead of throwing away old clothes, give them to others who might use them. Repair things that are broken.

3

A third way to help the Earth is to _____. You can do this with things like cans, bottles, and paper.

4

A final way to help the Earth is to _____ our natural resources. This will help make sure that they will be around for years to come!

5

TEC43036

Snowy Day Picture

Add the missing punctuation to the sentences below.
Circle each letter that should be capitalized.
Underline each sentence that has no mistakes.

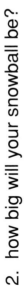

Follow the directions from the sentences you underlined.

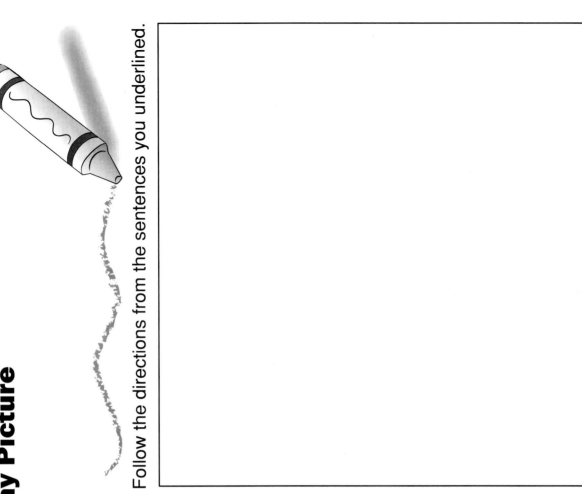

1. Can you draw a snowball

2. how big will your snowball be?

3. Draw a snowman shape in the center of the box.

4. My friend carl likes to draw lots of snowmen.

5. He draws with crayons pencils and chalk.

6. Draw eyes, a nose, and a hat on your snowman.

7. I built a snowman on blizzard drive.

8. Add snowflakes around your snowman.

9. Maybe i will draw a snowpet.

10. Now, color your snowman quickly!

11. do you like your picture?

12. Draw another snowman on the back of this paper.

©The Mailbox® • TEC43034 • Dec./Jan. 2007–8 • Key p. 310

Name _____

Focused on Dr. Martin Luther King Jr.

Choose the best topic sentence for each paragraph.
Write it on the line.

Topic Sentences

School was a big part of Dr. King's life.

How did Dr. King share his message of peace?

The third Monday in January is a U.S. holiday.

1. _____

It is called Martin Luther King Jr. Day. This day was made
a holiday in 1983. It marks the birthday of Martin Luther
King Jr. Most government offices and schools are closed
on this day.

2. _____

He started school at age five. He finished high school when
he was fifteen. Then he went to college. Martin Luther
King Jr. went to school for seven more years after finishing
college. He earned a special degree called a Ph.D.

3. _____

Dr. King wrote five books. He gave speeches. He led
marches and boycotts. Dr. King did these things to show
that all people needed to be treated fairly, but he did them
in a peaceful way.

A Friendly Letter

Write the synonym that completes each sentence.
Color the matching heart.

February 14, 2008

Dear Daisy,

    Did you know that you are a _____ friend? The
                              good

first time I met you, I knew that you were a _____
                                         nice

dog. You shared your _____ bones with me. You
                            tasty

shared your _____ blanket with me. You told me
                      cozy

_____ jokes. You let me see your doghouse, even though
       funny

you said it was _____. I knew that you would be my
                   messy

_____! Maybe someday we could _____
   friend   walk

to the movies and get some _____ ice cream. I am
                                cold

_____ you are my friend!
  happy

Your friend,
Digger

 snug

delicious

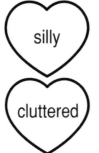 silly

glad

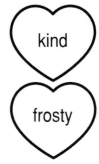 kind

stroll

pal

 cluttered

great

frosty

 ©The Mailbox® • TEC43036 • April/May 2008 • Key p. 310 • Written by Stacie Stone Davis, Livonia Primary School, Livonia, NY

Name_____

Fiesta Time

Subtract.
Help the cactus find the piñata.
Color the sombreros that show regrouping.

A. 436
 − 297

B. 354
 − 148

C. 942
 − 817

D. 437
 − 214

E. 514
 − 226

F. 695
 − 274

G. 849
 − 527

H. 758
 − 636

I. 963
 − 184

J. 725
 − 536

K. 536
 − 231

L. 655
 − 411

M. 372
 − 120

N. 675
 − 179

O. 852
 − 459

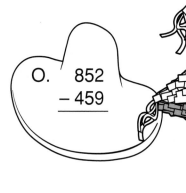

Name _____

Clipping Claws

Read the story to find a homophone for each listed word.
Circle the homophone.
Write the circled homophone next to the listed word.

Kyra works at the salon. Every day she gets to meet new customers and see old friends. As she styles their hair, some customers tell interesting tales. Kyra likes to hear the stories. In fact, Kyra loves her job! Many days, she gets to the salon before anyone else. When they ask her how she does it, she laughs. "It's easy!" she says. "I know all the short cuts."

1. knew _____
2. tails _____
3. here _____
4. sum _____
5. daze _____
6. meat _____
7. sea _____
8. hare _____
9. no _____
10. there _____

©The Mailbox® • TEC43037 • June/July 2008 • Key p. 310 • written by Laura Mihalenko, Holmdel, NJ

CLASSROOM
DISPLAYS

We're Off to a "Paws-itive" Year!

Listen carefully.
Follow directions.
Work quietly.
Use kind words and actions.
Work and play safely.

Tyler · Juan · Mason · Austin · Cam · Jasmine · Kierra · Taylor · Destiny · Paul · Anna · Shelby · Cassidy · Lila · Maria · Colin · Ian

S et the tone for the school year with this display of your classroom rules. Enlarge a copy of a pawprint pattern from page 51 and program it with the class rules. After discussing the rules and expectations, have each child sign a pawprint cutout. Post the pawprints around the posted rules as a reminder to students of their commitment to a positive year.

Tina Bento, Chester Academy, Chester, NH

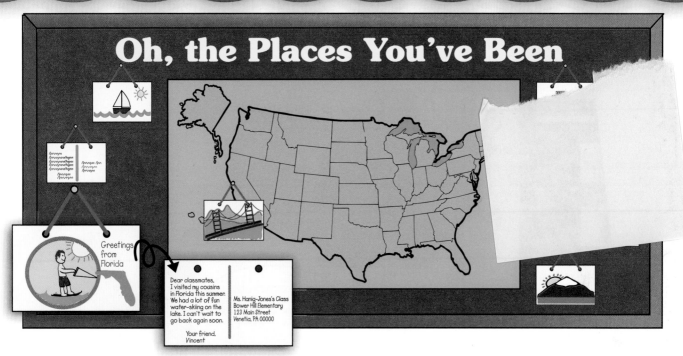

Oh, the Places You've Been

Have each student illustrate on one side of an index card a place he visited or wishes he could have visited over the summer. Then have him write a short postcard message to his new classmates on the other side, telling about his place. Have the child punch two holes in the top of the card, feed a length of yarn through the holes, and tie the ends of the yarn together. Tack the yarn to the board near a laminated U.S. or state map. When a student visits the display, he matches each postcard to the map location it describes and tacks it in place.

Jolene Hanig-Jones, Bower Hill Elementary, Venetia, PA

Students share their goals for the year with this notable display. Have each student cut out a copy of the marker pattern on page 51, write her name on it, and draw a self-portrait. Post each child's cutout on a board covered with black bulletin board paper. Then have her use a gel marker to write a goal for the year underneath her marker.

Julie Snyder, Easton Elementary
Winston-Salem, NC

Classroom Displays

Something to CROW About!

Provide students with an opportunity to share exciting news or accomplishments! Have each child write his name on a copy of the crow pattern on page 52. Then instruct him to color and cut out the pattern. Next, direct each student to write on a speech bubble cutout exciting news he would like to share. Post each speech bubble with its corresponding crow. When a student has more news to crow about, invite him to replace his writing with an updated version.

Mary Ann Gildroy, Roundup, MT

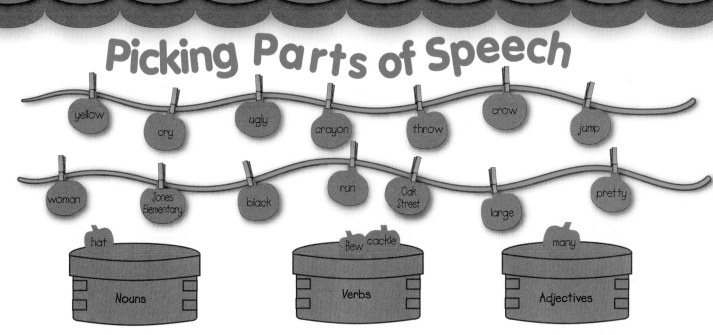

Picking Parts of Speech

When students pick pumpkins at this patch, they sort words by parts of speech! In advance, have each student cut from orange construction paper a pumpkin shape. Collect the pumpkins and write a different word on each, being sure to choose words that represent nouns, verbs, and adjectives. Attach lengths of thick green yarn (vines) to a display and add three basket cutouts labeled as shown. Use clothespins to clip the pumpkins to the vines. A student picks the pumpkins and uses Sticky-Tac to attach each one to the correct basket.

adapted from an idea by Tammy Hille, St. Jean Vianney Elementary School, Baton Rouge, LA

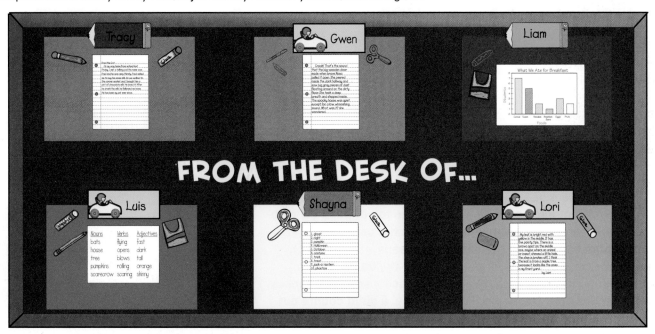

Use your extra desk nameplates to create a long-lasting work display! Have each student write her name on a desk nameplate (or a piece of a sentence strip). Then direct her to glue her nameplate to the top of a horizontally positioned 12" x 18" sheet of construction paper. Next, ask each student to draw several school supplies near the nameplate so that the finished project resembles a desktop. Laminate the student-made desktops and then mount them on a board. Ask each student to choose a sample of her best work and tape it to her desktop. Invite students to periodically change their work samples.

Tracy Reyna, Satilla Marsh Elementary, Brunswick, GA

Classroom Displays

Snacks for Sale

$3.04
$1.95
$4.80
$1.54
$0.86
$2.15
$5.00
$2.62
$3.61

Reinforce money skills with this interactive display. Program each card on a copy of the top of page 53 with a different money amount. Cut out the cards and tape each one to the outside of a separate sandwich-size plastic bag. Open the bags and staple the back of each one, within students' reach, to a board. Place a supply of money manipulatives near the board. For each bag, a child counts out the correct amount of money and places it inside the bag. After counting the money sets again to check his work, he removes the money to prepare the board for another student.

Lisa Kelly, West Bloomfield, MI

Motivate students to exhibit positive behaviors! A student cuts out a copy of the stocking pattern on page 53 and places the stocking's straight edge along the crease of a folded 9" x 12" sheet of construction paper. She traces the stocking and cuts it out, without cutting along the crease, and then decorates the front as desired. Collect the completed stockings and write a different class reward or special privilege on the inside of each. Use pushpins to attach the stockings to a board so the stockings can be opened. When the class displays a positive behavior, invite a child to lift the flap of a stocking and read aloud the reward.

adapted from an idea by Stacey Hosman
Wagner Community School, Wagner, SD

Showcase students' favorite books with a cool display! Have each child first cut out a penguin shape from black construction paper and then cut a white oval to fit on the penguin. On the white oval, ask each child to write the title, the author, and a brief summary of a favorite book. After she glues the book review to the penguin, direct her to add a face, feet, and a personalized hat. Display the completed penguins on paper snow hills and add student-made paper snowflakes.

Lynda Leigh, Sewells Point Elementary, Norfolk, VA

Classroom Displays

GOLDEN MATH

Pot	Coins
2	18 ÷ 9, 14 ÷ 7
5	35 ÷ 7, 25 ÷ 5, 40 ÷ 8
3	24 ÷ 8
8	16 ÷ 2, 32 ÷ 4
6	6 ÷ 1
7	21 ÷ 3, 42 ÷ 6, 14 ÷ 2
4	8 ÷ 2

16 ÷ 4   18 ÷ 3   40 ÷ 5   6 ÷ 2   30 ÷ 5

Reinforce any computation skill with this interactive display. Use the pot-of-gold pattern on page 54 to make several black construction paper pots. Next, use gold glitter glue to write a different sum, difference, product, or quotient on each pot. Then, on each of a supply of yellow paper circles (gold coins), write a different math problem to equal one of the answers. Display the pots, and place the coins, an answer key, and Sticky-Tac nearby. A student solves the problem on each coin and attaches the coin above the corresponding pot. After checking his answers, he removes the coins for the next student.

100 Reasons Why We ♥ Our School

Celebrate the 100th day of school in style! Distribute 100 heart cutouts and then ask each student to write on each heart a different reason why she loves her school. Collect the hearts and then display them on a board to form an extra large 100.

Jodi Zwain, School Street School, Boonton, NJ

This display gives students the opportunity to publish their work after completing a writers' workshop. Have each student personalize and cut out a copy of a pencil pattern from page 54. Then ask him to mount his writing on a sheet of construction paper. Display the papers with the matching pencils on a board. As students complete other writers' workshops, invite them to replace their writing samples as desired.

Jennifer Brokofsky
Confederation Park Community School
Saskatoon, Saskatchewan, Canada

Classroom Displays

Our Class Is Crawling With Super Students!

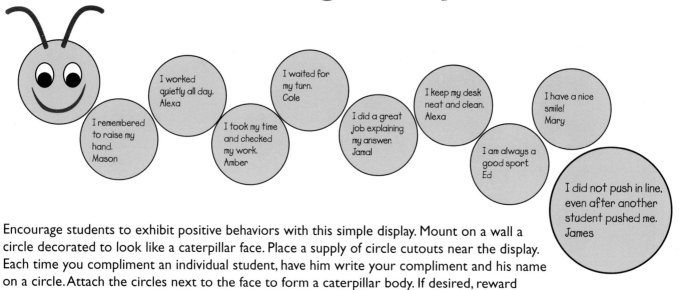

I remembered to raise my hand.
Mason

I worked quietly all day.
Alexa

I took my time and checked my work.
Amber

I waited for my turn.
Cole

I did a great job explaining my answer.
Jamal

I keep my desk neat and clean.
Alexa

I am always a good sport.
Ed

I have a nice smile!
Mary

I did not push in line, even after another student pushed me.
James

Encourage students to exhibit positive behaviors with this simple display. Mount on a wall a circle decorated to look like a caterpillar face. Place a supply of circle cutouts near the display. Each time you compliment an individual student, have him write your compliment and his name on a circle. Attach the circles next to the face to form a caterpillar body. If desired, reward students after a predetermined number of circles have been added to the caterpillar.

adapted from an idea by Nancy Dendrinelis, Hawthorn Elementary, St. Peters, MO

To prepare this work display, post a large beehive cutout with the title shown. Direct each student to write her name on a copy of a bee pattern from page 55; then have her color her bee and cut it out. Post each student's bee around the hive with a sample of her work. Encourage students to periodically choose new work samples to display with their bees.

Kristen McLaughlin
Ambrose Elementary
Winchester, MA

Work to "Bee" Proud Of!

Jenn
Alex
Bryn
Naya
Leo
Rochelle
DeMarcus

Reach Out and Grab a Good Book

Display students' favorite books from the school year! Have each child cut out a construction paper copy of the octopus pattern on page 56. Then instruct him to fold a 5½" x 8" piece of copy paper in half to make a booklet. On the cover of the booklet, have the student write the title and author of a favorite book, draw an illustration, and write his name. Then direct him to open the booklet and write a brief summary of the book. Next, have the student glue the booklet to the octopus body and glue two of the tentacles to the booklet. Mount the completed projects on a board. If desired, add twisted crepe paper seaweed to the display.

Joyce Browning, Challenger 7 Elementary
Cocoa, FL

Classroom Displays

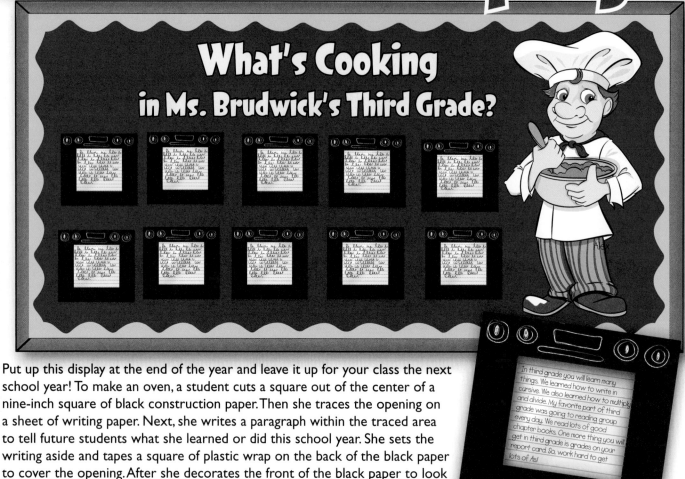

Put up this display at the end of the year and leave it up for your class the next school year! To make an oven, a student cuts a square out of the center of a nine-inch square of black construction paper. Then she traces the opening on a sheet of writing paper. Next, she writes a paragraph within the traced area to tell future students what she learned or did this school year. She sets the writing aside and tapes a square of plastic wrap on the back of the black paper to cover the opening. After she decorates the front of the black paper to look like an oven, she trims around her writing and tapes it behind the plastic wrap. Display the projects on a board. If desired, add a chef character.

adapted from an idea by Rebecca Brudwick, Hoover Elementary, North Mankato, MN

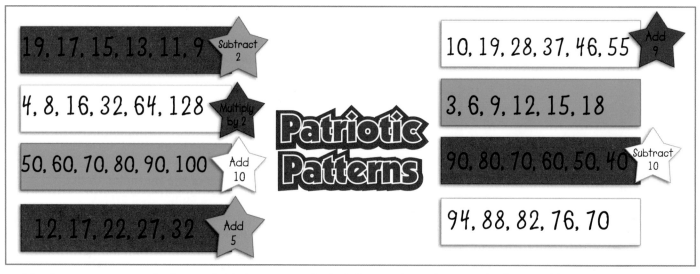

Number patterns are the focus of this interactive display! Give each student a red, white, or blue paper strip and a star cutout. On the paper strip, have her write a number pattern. Then ask her to write the pattern rule on the star. Mount the strips on a display and place the stars nearby. When a student visits the display, she reads the number patterns and uses Sticky-Tac to match each star to its pattern strip.

Pawprint Patterns
Use with "We're Off to a 'Paws-itive' Year!" on page 40.

Marker Pattern
Use with "Make Your Mark in Second Grade" on page 41.

TEC43032

TEC43032

TEC43032

Crow Pattern

Use with "Something to Crow About!" on page 42.

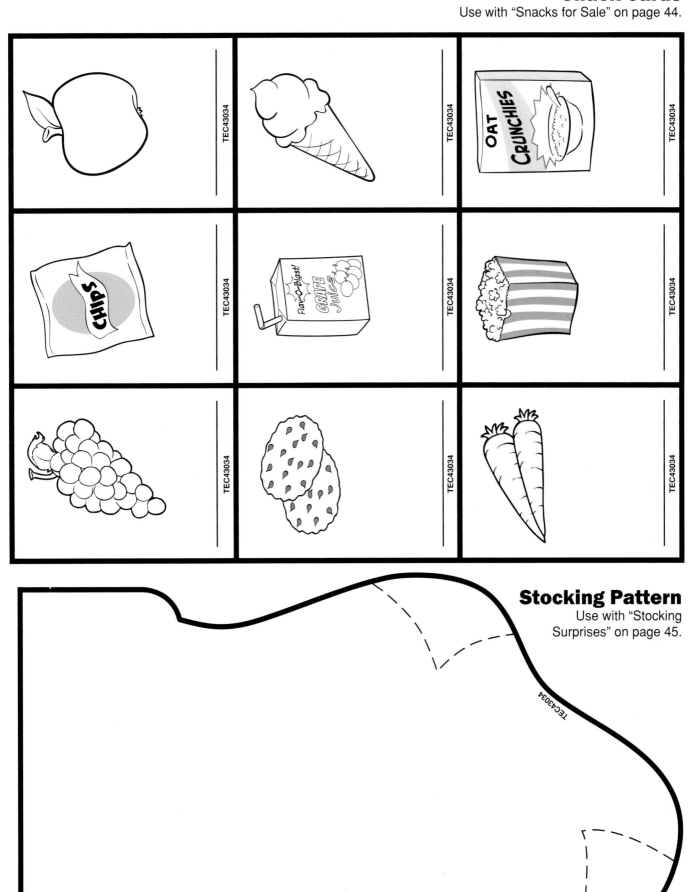

Stocking Pattern
Use with "Stocking Surprises" on page 45.

Pot-of-Gold Pattern

Use with "Golden Math" on page 46.

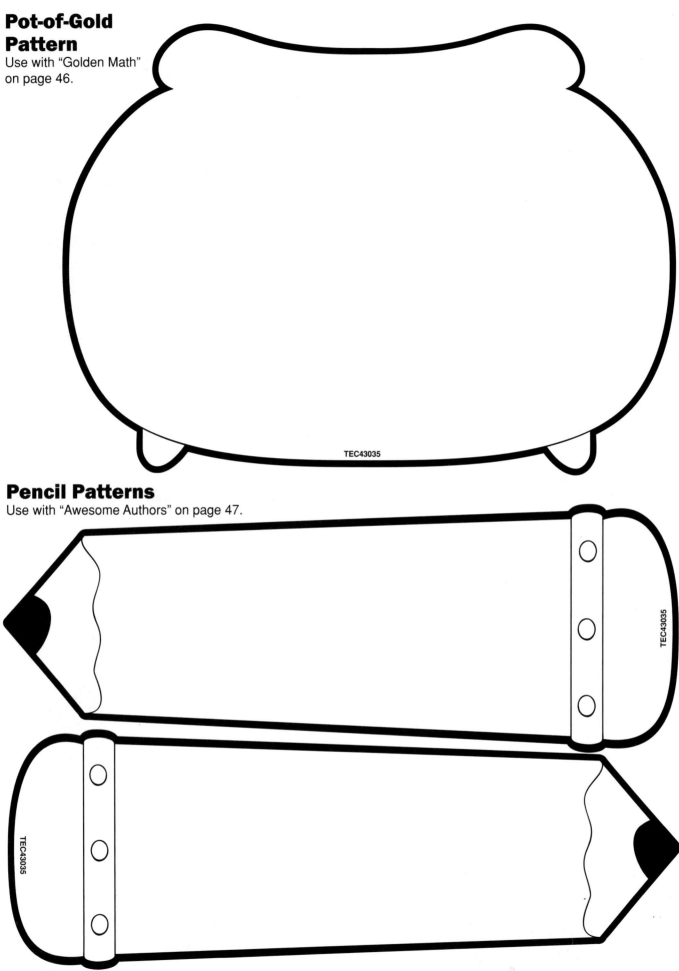

TEC43035

Pencil Patterns

Use with "Awesome Authors" on page 47.

TEC43035

TEC43035

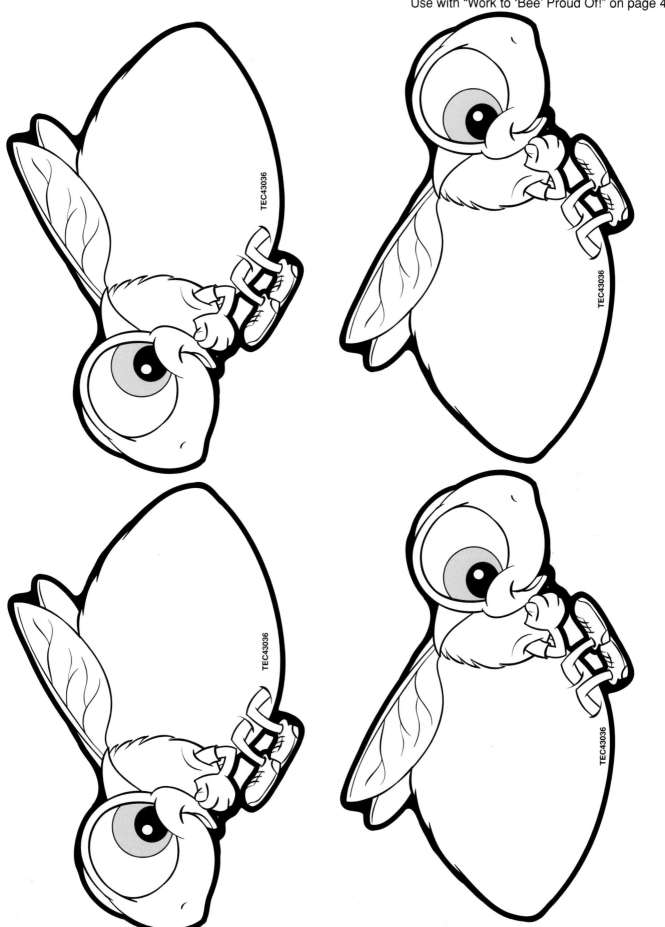

TEC43036

TEC43036

TEC43036

TEC43036

Octopus Pattern
Use with "Reach Out and Grab a Good Book" on page 49.

TEC43037

EXPLORING
SOCIAL STUDIES

Exploring Social Studies

Past and Present Preferences

Time and change, National Grandparents Day

To make a quilt square, each student chooses a topic—such as a favorite food, toy, or book—and writes the topic and his name on a four-inch paper square. On another square, he writes a sentence about that topic from his point of view. Next, he talks with one of his parents and asks her what her feelings on the topic were when she was his age. He writes her response on a third square. Then he talks with a grandparent or another senior and writes her answer to the same question on a fourth square. When he has completed the squares, he adds an illustration to each and then glues the squares to a nine-inch square as shown. Provide time for students to share their projects; then post the projects together so they look like a quilt.

Cindy Barber, St. Cecilia and James Catholic School, Thiensville, WI

Behind the Scenes
Community formation

To help students understand how and why communities form, lead them to think about your school community. First, direct each small group of students to answer the questions shown about either your classroom, the cafeteria, or the office. Next, guide each group to create a skit that shows how people in its setting work together to provide needed services to the school. After each group performs its skit, lead students to think about how people in your community work together to meet citizens' needs.

Laura Wagner, Bais Menachem Hebrew Academy, Austin, TX

What service is provided?
Who provides the service?
Who receives the service?
What are the responsibilities of those who receive the service?

James Madison

We observe Constitution Day on September 17. The Constitution was signed in 1787. It shaped our country's government. It tells who should make laws, who should decide what the laws mean, and who should make sure the laws are followed. There were 39 men from 12 different states who put their names on this important document. We honor their important work on Constitution Day.

Delegates on Display
Constitution Day

Showcase delegates who signed the Constitution with this partner activity. In advance, collect a half-gallon plastic milk jug and an empty can for each student pair. To start the activity, discuss the importance of Constitution Day. Tell students that 39 delegates signed the Constitution and post a list of the delegates' names on the board. Next, provide access to research materials and have each student pair locate a picture of a different delegate.

To make the project, have the duo flip a milk jug upside down and turn it so the handle faces away from them. Have students use construction paper, markers, cotton balls, and other craft items to add facial details so the jug resembles the delegate. Then have students wrap tissue paper and construction paper around a can to fashion the delegate's clothing. To complete the project, have each pair rest its milk jug in its can as shown. Line up the completed projects along a shelf or another flat surface. Then have each pair fold a paper rectangle in half, label it with the delegate's name, and place the resulting tent in front of its project. Finally, write a class paragraph about Constitution Day on chart paper and post it near the completed projects.

Lifka Bennett, Mineral Point Elementary, Mineral Point, WI

Exploring Social Studies

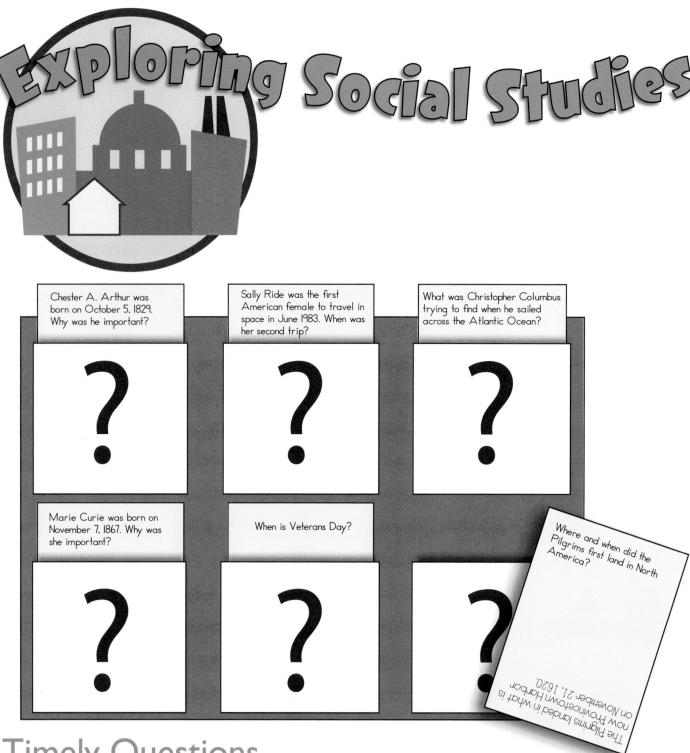

Chester A. Arthur was born on October 5, 1829. Why was he important?

Sally Ride was the first American female to travel in space in June 1983. When was her second trip?

What was Christopher Columbus trying to find when he sailed across the Atlantic Ocean?

Marie Curie was born on November 7, 1867. Why was she important?

When is Veterans Day?

Where and when did the Pilgrims first land in North America?

The Pilgrims landed in what is now Provincetown Harbor on November 21, 1620.

Timely Questions
Cultural celebrations, contributions of historic figures

Research skills merge with seasonal social studies facts in this informational activity. First, write a social studies question on each of a supply of index cards, providing background information when appropriate. Next, cut sealed envelopes in half to make pockets and glue the pockets to a piece of poster board, securing one pocket for each index card. Place the poster board with a supply of research materials near your classroom calendar. When a student has free time, invite him to visit the display, choose an index card, and read the question. He uses the materials to locate the answer and writes it on the bottom of the card. Then he returns the card to the pocket with the answer side up. When all questions have been answered, review the responses with the whole class.

On the Map
Map skills

Help students get the big picture about where they live. Make a copy of page 69 and draw an outline of your state in section 1. Next, give a copy of the page to each child, and have her cut along the bold lines. Then guide each child to label your town or city's location on the state map and circle it with a crayon. Have her use the same crayon to color her state on the U.S. map and then color the United States on the world map. After that, have the child fold the paper as shown, first folding the paper from the bottom backward toward the top, then folding the right side back toward the left, and finally folding from the top to the bottom. When the folding is complete, have each student turn the project so her state is facing her. Then have her use the project to explain where she lives in relation to the map, unfolding the paper as she explains.

Linda McConnelee, Mayfield Elementary, Mayfield, NY

To fold:

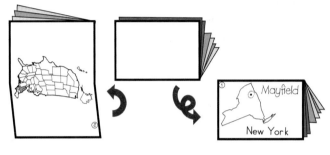

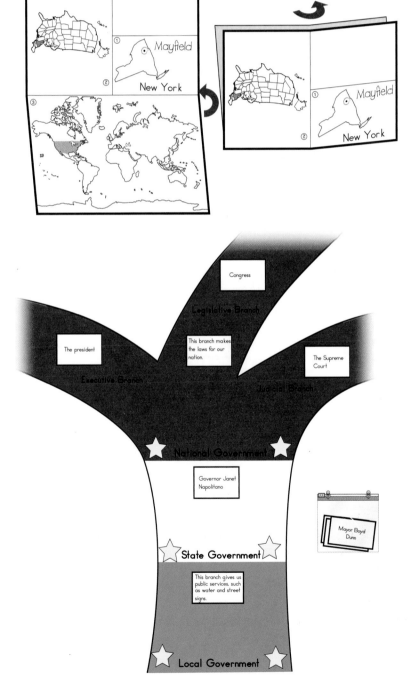

Branching Out
Identifying the levels of government

Government knowledge takes root when this graphic organizer is displayed. To make the tree, use blue paper to make the bottom portion of the tree trunk, continue the tree trunk with white paper, and then use red paper to add three branches for the national government. Label each section as shown; then program each of a supply of index cards with job titles, job descriptions, and current job holders' names for each section. Put the cards in a bag and place the bag near the posted tree. After discussing the different levels of government, select a student to choose a card and attach it to the corresponding section. Continue in this manner, calling on different students to each take a turn, until each card is correctly in place. When the activity is complete, keep the tree posted as a reference.

Carrie Shields, Jane Dee Hull Elementary, Chandler, AZ

Exploring Social Studies

Flip for Facts
Continents

This activity results in a handy reference about the seven continents. Have each student fold a 12" x 18" sheet of construction paper in half lengthwise. Then have him make six evenly spaced cuts through the top flap to the fold, resulting in seven small flaps. Next, direct each student to use reference materials to find and record on a separate flap an interesting fact about each continent. Under each flap, instruct him to draw and label the corresponding continent. Invite students to trade fact flip books with each other to test their knowledge about the continents.

adapted from an idea by Allison Zamparelli
Alexander Elementary, Hamilton, NJ

This is the largest continent.

The Nile River flows through this continent.

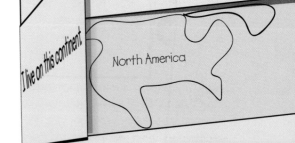

I live on this continent.

North America

Brazil is the largest country in this continent.

This continent is covered with ice.

The world's largest country, Russia, is in this continent.

This continent is also a country.

From Producer to Consumer
Economics

Reinforce economic vocabulary with this simple idea! Divide the class into groups of four. Name a product and then assign each student in each group one of the following terms: *producer, goods, distribution,* or *consumer.* Have each student write her term on one side of a large sheet of paper as shown. Next, have each group member write a brief description of her term and draw a small picture. Provide time for each group to share its resulting poster, with each child holding and reading his part before turning the poster 90° for the next group member.

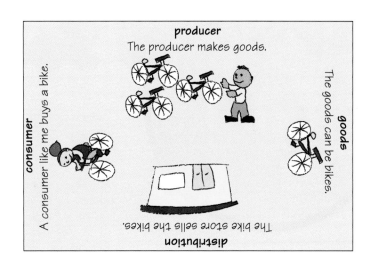

The Continent Song
Naming the continents

Lead students in singing this song to help them remember the names of all seven continents.

(sung to the tune of "The Bear Went Over the Mountain")

Let's name the seven continents.
Let's name the seven continents.
Let's name the seven continents
Before we end this song.

Asia, Europe, and Africa;
North and South America;
Australia and Antarctica;
And now we've named them all!

adapted from an idea by Renee Crawford, Clarendon Elementary
Canton, OH

A Class of Citizens
Local government

To model how citizens play an important part in local government, transform your classroom into its own city or town. To begin, have students name their city and then hold a mock election to select a mayor. Next, write a student-generated list of committees or departments that will work for the class government. Invite student volunteers to join the different groups. Have each group work with the mayor to keep the classroom organized and make decisions. For example, the members of the Sanitation Department may set standards for the cleanliness of the classroom and "charge fines" as needed. Or the Department of Public Records may keep track of daily attendance. Periodically have students switch roles to experience each section of its local government.

Priscilla Carlson, St. Joan of Arc, St. Clair Shores, MI

Carlson City

Health Department

Sanitation Department

Department of Transportation

City Council

School Board

Department of Public Records

Exploring Social Studies

Old Ike
President Wilson had an uncommon pet.
He had a ram named Ike. Ike was one of
many sheep that President Wilson kept at
the White House. He used the sheep to keep
the White House grass neat and tidy.

Name _Payton_

Executive Pets
Presidents' Day, historical figures

Share with students a list of presidential pets, such as the one shown, and provide access to research materials. Next, guide each student to choose a president and his pet to research. Have the child write an informative paragraph about the president and his pet on a copy of page 70; then fold and cut the page to make a pop-up platform as shown. Next, have the student draw the pet on a piece of cardstock, cut it out, and glue it to the platform as shown. Glue students' pages back-to-back to make a pop-up book that's sure to help students connect with our nation's presidents.

adapted from an idea by Melissa Bilyo
St. Joseph School, Fairport, NY

President	Pet(s)
George Washington	horses; almost forty hound dogs
Thomas Jefferson	Dicky, a mockingbird
Franklin Pierce	a tiny dog called a sleeve dog
James Buchanan	Lara, a 170-pound Newfoundland dog
Abraham Lincoln	goats named Nanny and Nanko
Andrew Johnson	mice
Theodore Roosevelt	Skip the terrier
William Taft	Pauline the milk cow
Calvin Coolidge	Rebecca the raccoon
Woodrow Wilson	Old Ike the ram, sheep
John F. Kennedy	Charlie the Welsh terrier
George H. W. Bush	Millie the springer spaniel
William J. Clinton	Socks the cat, Buddy the Labrador
George W. Bush	Barney the Scottish terrier

Term Trio
Identifying landforms

Here's a quick and easy way to build students' knowledge of landforms. Program each of a supply of cards with the name of a different landform. Then write a definition for each term on a second set of cards, and draw an example of each term on a third set of cards. Program the backs of the matching cards with a colored dot. Shuffle each card set and place the sets writing-side up at a center. A child selects a card from one set and locates its matches from the other sets. She places the matching cards to one side and continues in this manner until all matches have been made. Then she flips the cards over to check her work.

Jennifer Cripe
James Bilbray Elementary
Las Vegas, NV

| peninsula |

land surrounded by water on three sides

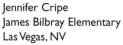

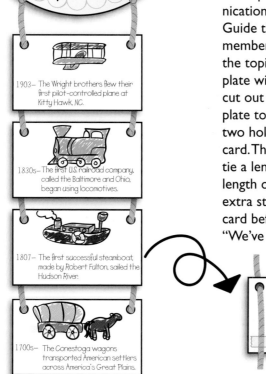

Timeline Ladders
Changes over time

To help students explore the history of transportation, communications, and housing, assign one topic to each small group. Guide the group to research its topic; then have each group member write and illustrate on an index card one fact about the topic's past. Next, have each group label the edge of a paper plate with its topic and the current year. Direct the students to cut out topic-related magazine pictures and glue them to the plate to make a present-day collage. Then have students punch two holes at the bottom of the plate and at the top of each card. They arrange the cards in chronological order and then tie a length of yarn to each plate hole. The students thread each length of yarn through the card holes and secure the ends. For extra stability, the students tape the yarn to the back of each card before adding the completed project to a display titled "We've Come a Long Way!"

Exploring Social Studies

Community

Landforms

Natural Resources

Holidays

USA

Japan

Japan is made of islands. There are also mountains and volcanoes, hills, and coastal plains.

There are many bodies of water, forests, minerals, and good soil.

New Year's Festival
January
Shichi-Go-San
November

Here and There
Comparing communities

This simple project helps students see community characteristics side by side. First, have a child fold a sheet of 12" x 18" paper in half and unfold it. Next, guide him to fold each end in so it stops about two inches from the middle fold; then have him cut four flaps on each resulting flap. He labels the top flaps with the name of each community and writes down the middle of the paper three attributes he will compare. Finally, on each flap he draws a picture to match the corresponding community's attribute and then lifts the flap to write a brief description.

Take My Card
Importance of historic figures

Students use these simple business cards to introduce and learn about important people in history. To make a business card, have each student write on a rectangular piece of cardstock a historic figure's name, one of his or her important job titles, his or her significance, and an image that represents the figure. Next, direct each student to find a partner and pretend to be the figure on his card. Have him hand over his card and give a brief explanation of who he is and why he is important. Then have his partner repeat the process based on her historic figure. Provide time for each student to introduce his historic figure partner to the class and explain her significance.

Jackie Robinson
Brooklyn Dodger
First and Second Baseman

First African American to play major-league baseball

Marie Curie
Scientist
First woman to receive the Nobel Prize

Mastering and Following Directions
Cardinal and intermediate directions

This variation on the Simon Says game will have students on their feet! In advance, post paper strips labeled with cardinal and intermediate directions on corresponding walls around the room. To play, invite students to stand and respond to a command such as, "Simon Says face northeast." Direct any students who react incorrectly to sit down. Continue providing commands until one player remains standing or time is called.

Ann Barkhouse, Fairview Heights Elementary, Halifax, Nova Scotia, Canada

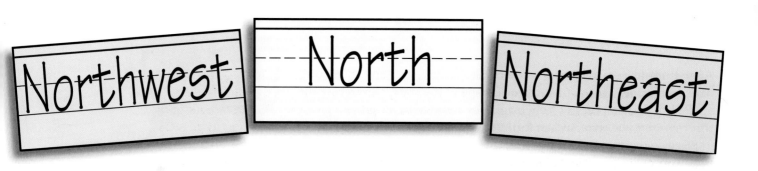

Northwest   North   Northeast

Exploring Social Studies

Ready to Help
How people serve communities

Assign each student a different type of community worker; then guide each student to write a brief paragraph about his community worker. Provide each child with a large sheet of paper and have him draw the worker in uniform from the neck down. At a later time, tape each child's resulting poster to his shoulders and have him read aloud his paragraph.

adapted from an idea by Tricia Sharkey
Immaculate Heart of Mary, Philadelphia, PA

June 2, 2008
Dear Mom and Dad,
Today Grandma took me to an art museum and we rode on a ferryboat. Then we took a taxi uptown to eat at a nice restaurant. After lunch, she and I walked through the park. We sat on a bench and ate ice cream. There are so many people living and working in the city. Maybe someday I will work in one of these skyscrapers!
Love,
Miranda

Greetings from the Big City

Sunsets Across the USA
Types of communities

To begin, a student uses watercolors to paint on a 4" x 6" sheet of tagboard a colorful sunset. After the paint dries, she uses a pencil to draw a silhouette of an urban, suburban, or rural scene along the bottom of the card. Then she uses a black marker to outline and color the silhouette. Finally, the student writes on the back of her resulting postcard a friendly letter to her family describing the sights and sounds of the area.

inspired by an idea from Malinda Pryor, Pine Ridge Elementary
Ellerslie, GA

Our State Is Great!
State community

After students research important facts about their state and its culture, have each student cut out a cardstock shape of the state. Next, guide the student to draw or cut out from magazines and glue to his project pictures that represent the state, such as forms of wildlife, landmarks, and products. Then guide the student to write a paragraph about the state's unique features. Post students' work on a display titled "Celebrating Our Great State!"

Esther Hill, Phoenix Magnet Elementary, Alexandria, LA

Antoine
I love Louisiana. We have a lot of wildlife such as crayfish and egrets. Our state is known for its jazz and tabasco sauce. People come here to eat gumbo and jambalaya.

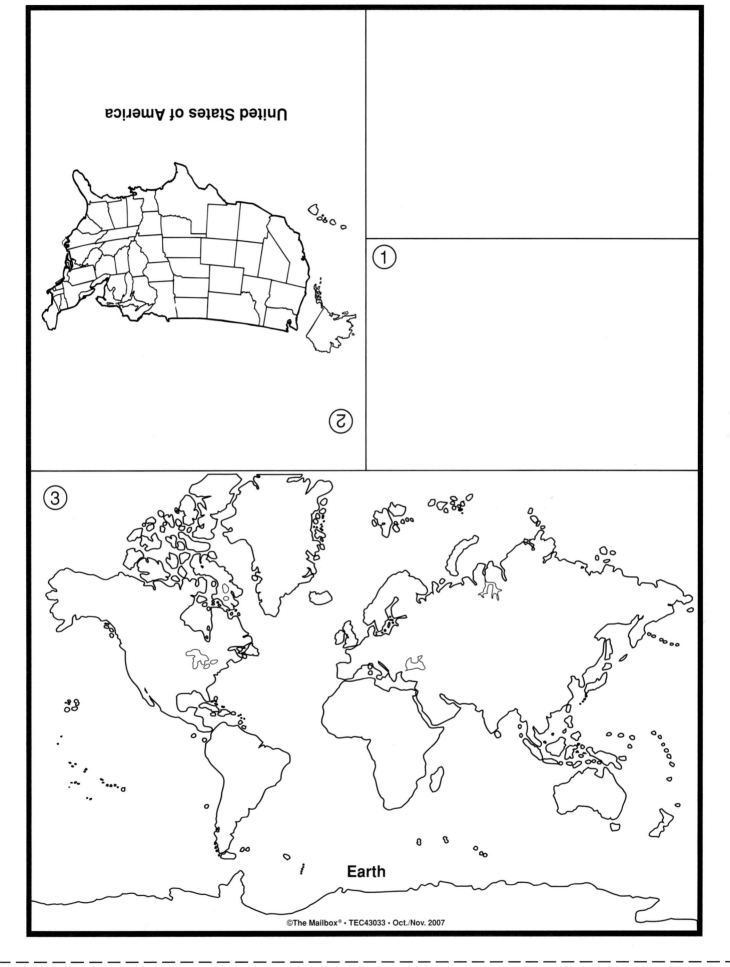

United States of America

① ②

③

Earth

Fold.

Fold.

Fold.

Name _____

Note to the teacher: Use with "Executive Pets" on page 64.

LEARNING CENTERS

Learning Centers

A. Detective Dillon makes a lot of phone calls to get facts. How many phone calls did Dillon make this week? ___ calls
- The ones digit is 1 more than the tens digit.
- The tens digit is the sum of 3 and 2.

Check: Does the sum of the two digits in your answer equal 11?

B. Detective Dora takes pictures to help prove her cases. How many pictures did Dora take for her last case? ___ pictures
- The tens digit is 2 greater than 7.
- The ones digit is the sum of 4 and 4.
- ...the sum of ...s in your c7?

D. Detective Deb writes reports about her cases. The last report was long. How long was Deb's last report? ___
- ... is the largest digit.
- ... digit is 8 less than ...
- ...the sum of 1 and 2.

The Case of the Missing Lunchbox

Calling All Detectives

Determining unknown numbers is the goal of this problem-solving center. Copy the cards on page 82 and then cut them out. Put the cards in a resealable plastic bag and place the bag at a center with a supply of paper. A child chooses a card and writes the corresponding letter on his paper. Then he reads the clues to determine each digit in the missing number. Once he has solved for each digit, he checks that he used the right numbers by answering the last question on the card. If correct, he chooses another card and repeats the process. If incorrect, he reviews his work to determine the correct solution.

inspired by an idea by Joyce Wilson, Trophy Club, TX

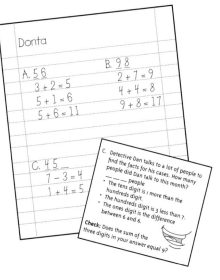

Donta

A. 56   B. 98
3 + 2 = 5   2 + 7 = 9
5 + 1 = 6   4 + 4 = 8
5 + 6 = 11   9 + 8 = 17

C. 45
7 − 3 = 4
1 + 4 = 5

C. Detective Dan talks to a lot of people to find the facts for his cases. How many people did Dan talk to this month? ___ people
- The tens digit is 1 more than the hundreds digit.
- The hundreds digit is 3 less than 7.
- The ones digit is the difference between 6 and 6.

Check: Does the sum of the three digits in your answer equal 9?

Ready to Read

To help student pairs bravely conquer sight words, make several copies of the knight and strip patterns on page 83 and cut them out. Program each section of a strip with a sight word, making strips of different words. If desired, laminate the patterns for durability. Next, cut two slits on each knight's shield and feed a strip through the slits. Glue or tape the ends together and place the completed knights at a center. A child chooses a knight and reads each word to a partner by slowly pulling the back side of the strip. When she correctly reads all ten words, she chooses another knight and repeats the process. After correctly reading two strips, partners trade roles.

Phyllis Steinberg, Wheelock Primary School, Fredonia, NY

Place Value Toss

Students build and compare two-digit numbers at this partner center. To prepare, cut ten three-inch-tall paper tubes and label each with a number from 0 to 9. Glue the tubes together as shown. Place the tubes along with a class supply of the recording sheet on page 84, two plastic dimes, and two plastic pennies at a center. Students in a pair write their names on the top of a recording sheet and place the tubes between the players. Player 1 tosses a penny into a tube to determine the number he writes in the ones place in his column. Then he tosses the dime to determine the number he writes in the tens place. Player 2 repeats the process. After both players have recorded their numbers, a student draws the appropriate symbol between the numbers, and the player with the larger number circles her number. Play continues until all ten rounds have been played or time is called. The player with more circled numbers is the winner. As an alternative, have students build three-digit numbers by tossing a dollar coin for the hundreds place.

Trudy White, Mayflower Elementary, Mayflower, AR

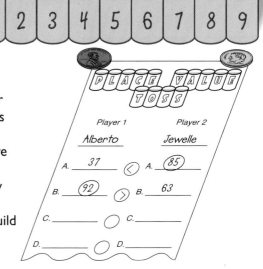

Sorting Out the Rules

This independent center helps students associate words with their capitalization rules. First, use a different-colored marker to label each of a supply of envelopes with a different capitalization rule. Write examples of each rule and then tuck the flap inside the envelope. Next, program a set of index cards with words or phrases that match each rule. To make the cards self-checking, place a like-colored dot on the back of each card. Place the envelopes and cards at a center. A child reads each word or phrase and slides it inside the envelope with the matching rule. When all the cards have been sorted, she removes the cards from an envelope and flips them over to check her work.

Ruthrae Koth, Bear Creek Elementary, St. Petersburg, FL

Monster Mouth

Practicing abc order is anything but scary with this hands-on activity. To prepare, copy the head pattern on page 85 onto a piece of tagboard and cut it out. Next, make several sets of four teeth each by cutting a piece of white paper into one-inch squares. Then program each tooth with a different word. Put each set of four teeth in a resealable plastic bag and place the bags, the head, and a supply of paper at a center. A child chooses a bag, removes the teeth, and places them in alphabetical order on the mouth. Next, he copies the words in order onto his paper. Then he returns the teeth to the bag and chooses another set.

Sue Fleischmann, Sussex, WI

Sorting Sounds

This ready-to-go center is just the thing to help students identify beginning and ending digraphs. First, mount a copy of the mat on page 86 onto construction paper. Also, cut out the cards from a copy of page 87. Place the mat, the cards, and a supply of paper at a center. A child folds a sheet of paper into fourths and labels each section with a different digraph from the mat. She chooses a card, quietly names the picture, and then places the card on the pumpkin with the corresponding sound. When she has sorted all the cards, she uses her best spelling to write each word on her paper, underlining the digraph. For an added challenge, have the child write additional words for each category.

adapted from an idea by Bonnie Gaynor, Franklin, NJ

Flipping for Numbers

Provide extra practice with reading and writing numbers. First, label each of ten sentence strips with a different letter from A through J; then program each strip with a different number written in word form, leaving space at the end of the strip. Fold the end of the strip to the left and write the number in standard form on top of the folded section. Unfold the strips and place them at a center with a supply of paper. A child visiting the center lists the letters A–J on a sheet of paper. Next, he chooses a strip and reads the number on it. He writes the number on his paper in standard form. Then he flips the end section to the left to check his work. The student continues in this manner until he has completed the task for each card.

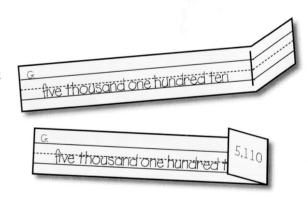

Board Work for Two

Eliminate the need for paper copies while providing practice with any skill. Place an overhead projector in front of your whiteboard. Place a transparency of a skill-based reproducible on the overhead and shine it onto the dry-erase board. Place an answer key nearby. Students work together in pairs to complete the activity, writing their answers with a dry-erase marker on the board. When they finish, the students check their work. Students benefit from working together, and you have fewer papers to check.

Erika Tokarz, Green Acres Elementary, Warren, MI

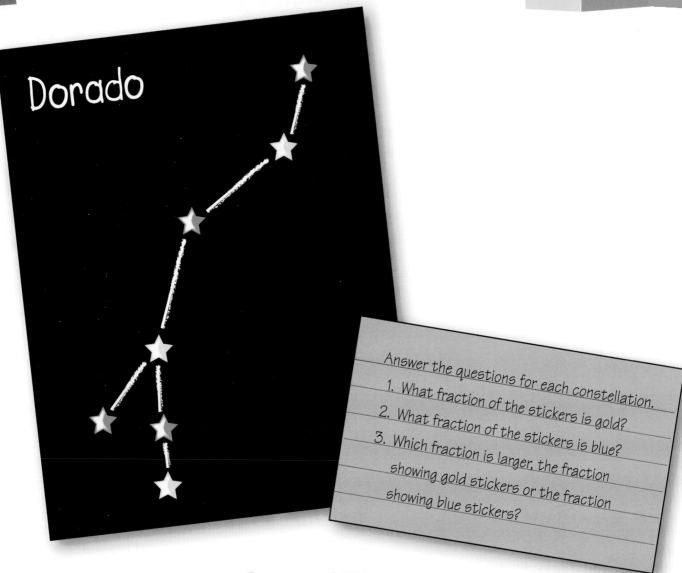

Dorado

Answer the questions for each constellation.
1. What fraction of the stickers is gold?
2. What fraction of the stickers is blue?
3. Which fraction is larger, the fraction showing gold stickers or the fraction showing blue stickers?

Out of This World

Finding fractional amounts is in the stars! Use a white crayon to draw a map of a constellation on black paper. Mark the endpoint of each line with one of two different-colored star stickers. Write the name of the constellation on the map; then repeat the process to make a set of constellations, using the same two sticker colors for each. Also program a large index card with questions like the ones shown. Place the questions, the constellation maps, and a supply of paper at a center. To complete the activity, a child chooses a map and labels his paper with the constellation's name. Then he reads the questions, determines the answers based on the map's stickers, and records the fractional answers on his paper. He repeats the activity with additional constellations as time allows.

Kelly Hanover, Jane Vernon Elementary, Kenosha, WI

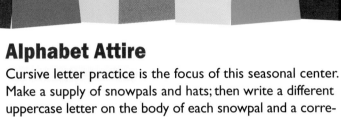

Alphabet Attire

Cursive letter practice is the focus of this seasonal center.
Make a supply of snowpals and hats; then write a different
uppercase letter on the body of each snowpal and a corresponding lowercase letter on each hat. Cut out the
patterns; then place the snowpals, hats, and a cursive
alphabet strip at a center. A child places the lowercase-
letter hat on the snowpal with the matching uppercase
letter. When all matches have been made, she checks
her work with the alphabet strip. For a more challenging
version, laminate the snowpals and have the student
use a wipe-off marker to write the uppercase letter that
matches the hat.

Julie Renee Peria, Delaware Christian School, Delaware, OH

What's Missing?

This hands-on activity gives students practice with showing the
appropriate symbol in a number sentence. To prepare, copy
page 88 on cardstock and cut apart the cards on the thick lines.
Fold each card on the thin line to make a tent; then arrange
the resulting number-sentence tents together in a stack and
the symbol tents in another stack. Place the two stacks and
a supply of scrap paper at a center. A student arranges the
number-sentence tents in alphabetical order. He reviews number
sentence A and, if needed, uses the scratch paper to determine
the missing symbol. Then he places a matching symbol tent atop
the number-sentence tent. After he has added a symbol to each
tent, he turns the completed tents around to check his work.

A.
$$18 \; + \; 16 = 34$$

B.
$$4 \; \times \; 9 = 36$$

Positively Pronouns

To help students identify correct pronouns,
make a front-to-back copy of pages 89 and
90. Cut apart the cards, then punch a hole in
the circle beside each answer choice. Place a
straw with the cards at a center. A child reads
the sentence on card 1. She places the straw
through the hole with the pronoun that best
completes the sentence. She flips the card to
check her work. If she is correct, she places the card to one side. If
the student is incorrect, she rereads the card and uses the correct
pronoun. The student continues in this manner until she has
completed each card correctly.

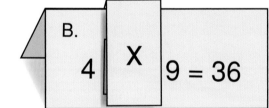

1. Every Monday my classmates and _____ tell about our weekends.

I   ⚪ me

Look again. ⚪   Great!

adapted from an idea by Jennifer Cripe, James Bilbray Elementary, Las Vegas, NV

Learning Centers

What's the "Purr-pose"?

To Inform

A cat's tail helps the cat balance.

To Entertain

Supercat was last seen flying across the city.

A cat uses its claws to climb and to catch its prey.

Once upon a time, there lived a beautiful cat named Katie.

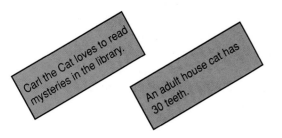

Carl the Cat loves to read mysteries in the library.

An adult house cat has 30 teeth.

What's the "Purr-pose"?

Here's a sorting mat that will help students learn to identify an author's purpose. To prepare, copy page 91; then mount the sorting mat and cards on construction paper. Cut apart the mat and cards, and label the back of each card with its answer for self-checking. Then place the mat and cards at a center. A child reads each card, determines its purpose, and places the card on the corresponding mat section. When all the cards have been sorted, he flips each one over to check his work.

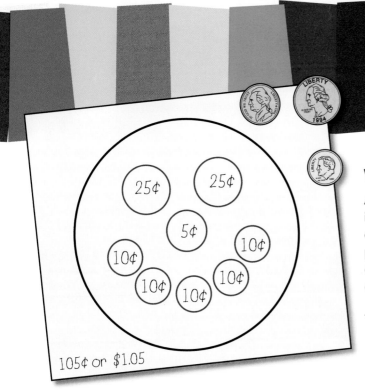

105¢ or $1.05

Value of a Picture

All you need to total coin values at this simple center is a bag of plastic coins and a supply of paper. To complete the activity, a student arranges coins on her paper to make a desired picture. She traces around each coin, writes its value inside its corresponding circle, and then totals the values of all the coins.

Tracy Meabe, Crawford-Rodriguez Elementary, Jackson, NJ

Visual Aids

Help students interpret information from diagrams, charts, and graphs with this independent activity. To prepare, copy and cut out the cards on pages 92 and 93. Place the cards with a supply of paper at a center. A child chooses an information card and its corresponding question card. Then he writes the answers to the questions on a sheet of paper. As an alternative, have the child choose two information cards and create a Venn diagram to compare and contrast the information given on each.

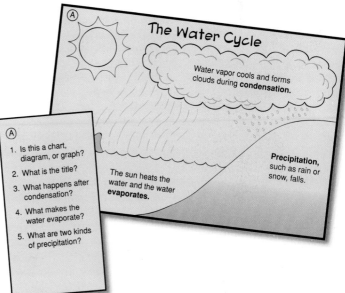

Ⓐ

1. Is this a chart, diagram, or graph?
2. What is the title?
3. What happens after condensation?
4. What makes the water evaporate?
5. What are two kinds of precipitation?

Ⓐ **The Water Cycle**

Water vapor cools and forms clouds during **condensation**.

Precipitation, such as rain or snow, falls.

The sun heats the water and the water **evaporates**.

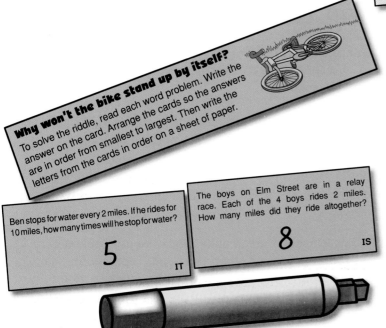

Why won't the bike stand up by itself?
To solve the riddle, read each word problem. Write the answer on the card. Arrange the cards so the answers are in order from smallest to largest. Then write the letters from the cards in order on a sheet of paper.

Ben stops for water every 2 miles. If he rides for 10 miles, how many times will he stop for water?

5   IT

The boys on Elm Street are in a relay race. Each of the 4 boys rides 2 miles. How many miles did they ride altogether?

8   IS

Ready to Ride

Provide extra practice with problem solving and ordering numbers. First, laminate a copy of page 94 and cut apart the cards. Place the cards, a supply of scrap paper, a dry-erase marker, and paper towels at a center; then display the riddle with the materials. A child solves the problems on a sheet of scrap paper and uses the dry-erase marker to record each answer on its corresponding card. She organizes the cards so the answers are in order from smallest to largest. Then she writes the letters from the cards in order on her paper to reveal the answer to the riddle before erasing the cards for the next student.

Learning Centers

Name **Carson**

Tracking the Time

Recording sheet

Number	Start Time	Arrival Time	Length of Trip
1			1 hour 15 minutes
2			
3			
4			
5			
6			

1. The train leaves the station at 8:00 AM. It arrives at the next station at 9:15 AM. How long is the trip?

Tracking the Time

To prepare, cut apart the travel cards from a copy of page 95. Place at a center the cards, student copies of page 96, and a manipulative clock.

To practice recording time, a child first folds back the right-hand column on his recording sheet. He reads the problem on card 1 and manipulates the hands on the clock to represent each time given on the card. Then the student draws on his recording sheet the hands representing each time. He continues in this manner with each remaining card.

To practice finding elapsed time, a child reads the problem on card 1 and then draws on his recording sheet the hands representing each time given on the card. He uses the manipulative clock to determine the length of the trip and records it in the corresponding column. The student continues in this manner with each remaining card.

Jean Erickson, Grace Christian Academy, West Allis, WI

Sticking to the Rules

To provide editing practice, copy page 97; then mount the top of the page on tagboard and cut out the sticks. Place the sticks in a resealable plastic bag and place the bag at a center. After a child completes a writing assignment, she selects a stick and reads the rule written on it. She places the stick under each line of her assignment, checking that she followed the stated rule. She marks any needed corrections on her paper and then chooses another stick and repeats the process. As an alternative, the student uses the sticks to guide her as she edits a copy of the passage from the bottom of page 97.

Jean Raetz-Topetzes, Holt Elementary, Lawrenceville, GA

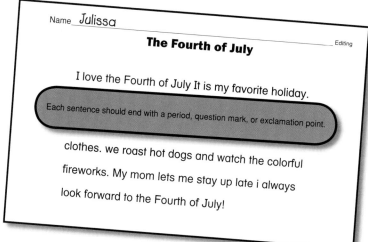

Name _Julissa_

The Fourth of July   Editing

I love the Fourth of July It is my favorite holiday.

Each sentence should end with a period, question mark, or exclamation point.

clothes. we roast hot dogs and watch the colorful fireworks. My mom lets me stay up late i always look forward to the Fourth of July!

A Perfect Fit

Everything falls into place with this number pattern activity. To prepare, cut apart the cards from a copy of page 98 and put them in an envelope. Place the envelope with a supply of paper at a center. A student chooses a number pattern card and determines the rule. He finds the card with the matching rule and places it on the number pattern card to complete the pattern. Then he writes the rule and pattern on a sheet of paper. The student continues in this manner until he has completed each pattern.

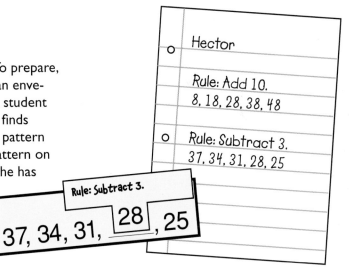

Hector

Rule: Add 10.
8, 18, 28, 38, 48

Rule: Subtract 3.
37, 34, 31, 28, 25

Rule: Subtract 3.
37, 34, 31, 28 , 25

Shopping for Examples

This easy-to-prepare center helps students recognize plural and possessive nouns. Collect a variety of food labels and place them in a paper bag. Place the bag at a center with a supply of blank paper and cards labeled like the ones shown. A child reads the parts of speech on the card and then draws two shopping cart shapes on her paper. She places a card on each cart; then she refers to the products' names as she sorts each label onto the corresponding cart. If a label does not match one of the parts of speech, she sets it aside. After she's sorted the labels, the student writes the product names in a two-column chart on another sheet of paper.

Renee Green, Hooper Bay School, Hooper Bay, AK

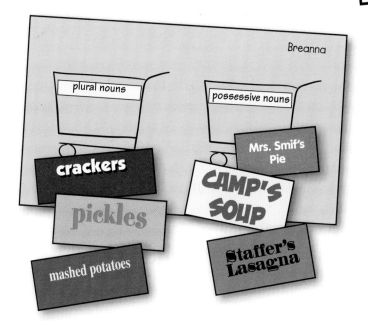

Breanna

plural nouns

possessive nouns

crackers

pickles

mashed potatoes

Mrs. Smif's Pie

CAMP'S SOUP

Staffer's Lasagna

Clue Cards

Use with "Calling All Detectives" on page 72.

A. Detective Dillon makes a lot of phone calls to get facts. How many phone calls did Dillon make this week? __ __ calls
- The ones digit is 1 more than the tens digit.
- The tens digit is the sum of 3 and 2.

Check: Does the sum of the two digits in your answer equal 11?

TEC43032

B. Detective Dora takes pictures to help prove her cases. How many pictures did Dora take for her last case? __ __ pictures
- The tens digit is 2 greater than 7.
- The ones digit is the sum of 4 and 4.

Check: Does the sum of the two digits in your answer equal 17?

TEC43032

C. Detective Dan talks to a lot of people to find the facts for his cases. How many people did Dan talk to this month? __ __ __ people
- The tens digit is 1 more than the hundreds digit.
- The hundreds digit is 3 less than 7.
- The ones digit is the difference between 6 and 6.

Check: Does the sum of the three digits in your answer equal 9?

TEC43032

D. Detective Deb writes reports about her cases. The last report was long. How long was Deb's last report? __ __ __ pages
- The ones digit is the largest digit.
- The hundreds digit is 8 less than the ones digit.
- The tens digit is the sum of 1 and 2.

Check: Does the sum of the digits in your answer equal 13?

The Case of the Missing Lunchbox

TEC43032

E. Detective Dave travels many miles to track his clues. How many miles did Dave travel last year? __, __ __ __ miles
- The thousands digit is 6 less than 8.
- The hundreds digit is 5 more than the thousands digit.
- The ones digit is the same as the thousands digit.
- The tens digit is 2 more than 5.

Check: Does the sum of the digits in your answer equal 18?

TEC43032

F. Detective Dawn is very good at her job. She has solved a lot of cases. How many cases has she solved? __, __ __ __ cases
- The ones digit is 1 more than 7.
- The tens digit is 8 less than the ones digit.
- The thousands digit is 5 less than the ones digit.
- The hundreds digit is 1 less than 6.

Check: Does the sum of the digits in your answer equal 16?

TEC43032

©The Mailbox® • TEC43032 • Aug./Sept. 2007 • Key p. 310

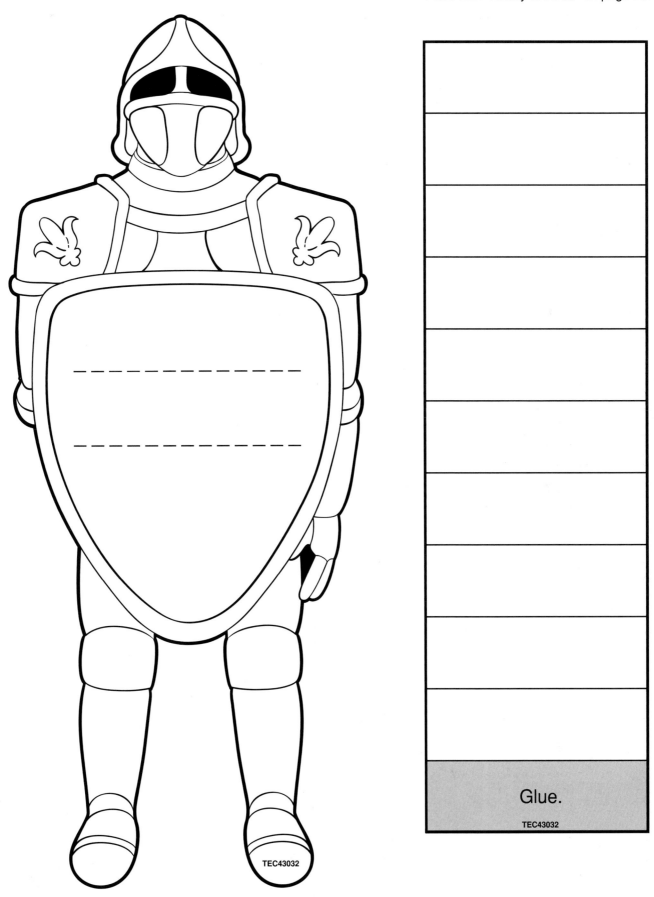

Glue.

TEC43032

Recording Sheets

Use with "Place Value Toss" on page 73.

PLACE VALUE TOSS

Player 1		Player 2
_____		_____
A. _____	◯	A. _____
B. _____	◯	B. _____
C. _____	◯	C. _____
D. _____	◯	D. _____
E. _____	◯	E. _____
F. _____	◯	F. _____
G. _____	◯	G. _____
H. _____	◯	H. _____
I. _____	◯	I. _____
J. _____	◯	J. _____

TEC43032

PLACE VALUE TOSS

Player 1		Player 2
_____		_____
A. _____	◯	A. _____
B. _____	◯	B. _____
C. _____	◯	C. _____
D. _____	◯	D. _____
E. _____	◯	E. _____
F. _____	◯	F. _____
G. _____	◯	G. _____
H. _____	◯	H. _____
I. _____	◯	I. _____
J. _____	◯	J. _____

TEC43032

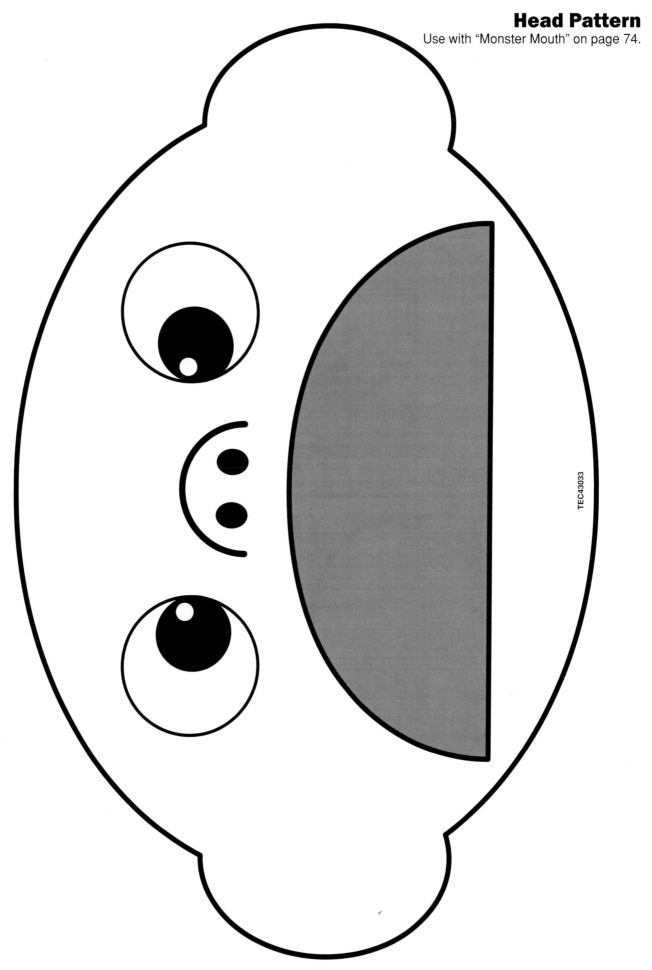

TEC43033

ch

sh

th

wh

Note to the teacher: Use with "Sorting Sounds" on page 75.

Use with “Sorting Sounds” on page 75.

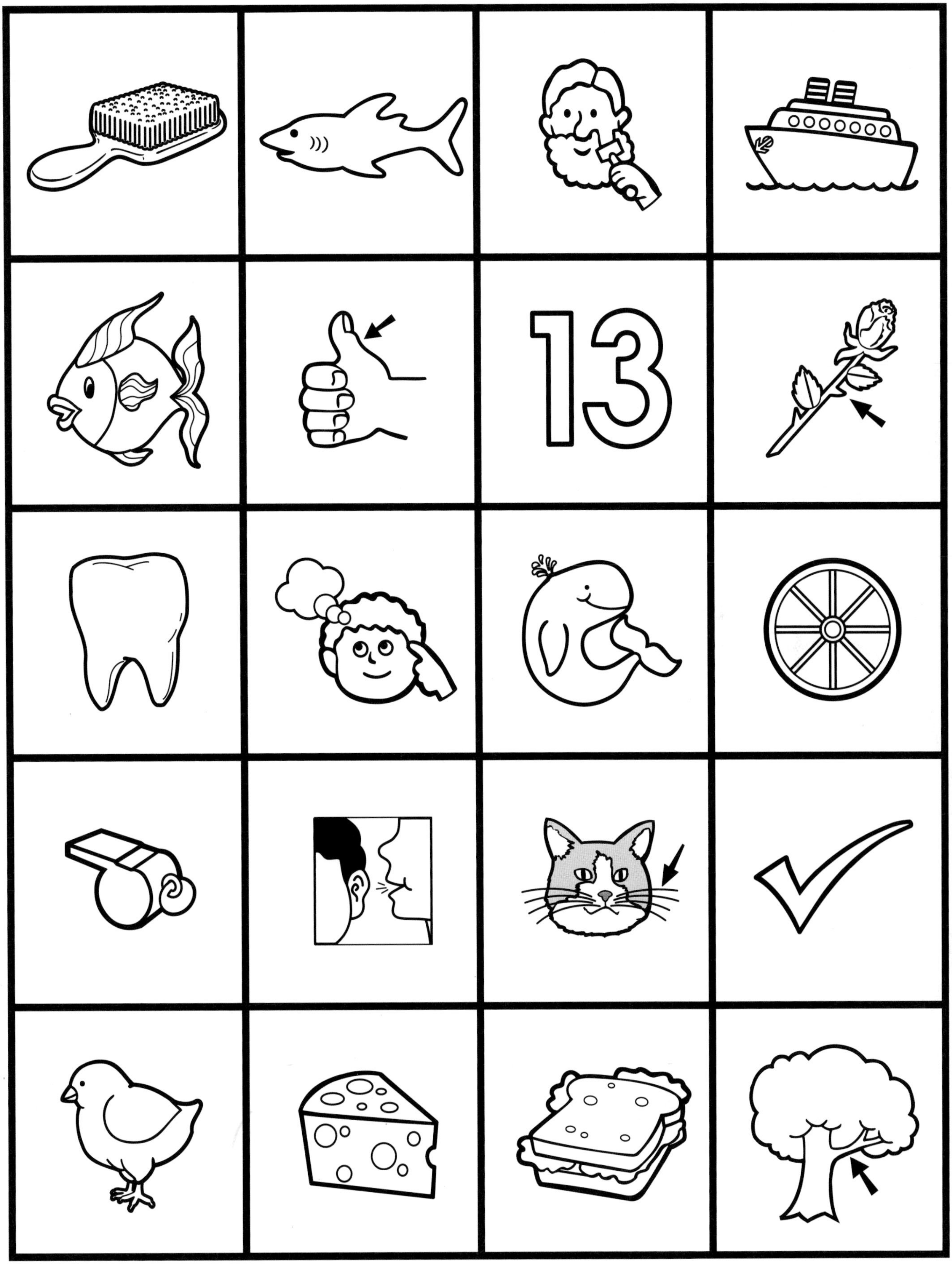

Number Sentence and Symbol Cards

Use with "What's Missing?" on page 77.

A. 18 ☐ 16 = 34 TEC43034	B. 4 ☐ 9 = 36 TEC43034	C. 30 ☐ 5 = 6 TEC43034
D. 100 ☐ 27 = 73 TEC43034	E. 7 ☐ 3 = 21 TEC43034	F. 94 ☐ 49 TEC43034
G. 2 x 4 ☐ 3 x 3 TEC43034	H. 9 + 8 ☐ 10 + 7 TEC43034	I. 30 – 20 ☐ 40 ÷ 4 TEC43034

A.	D.	B. or E.	B. or E.	C.	F.	G.	H. or I.	H. or I.
+	−	X	X	÷	>	<	=	=
TEC43034	TEC43034	TEC43034	TEC43034	TEC43034	TEC43034	TEC43034	TEC43034	TEC43034

Use with "Positively Pronouns" on page 77.

1. Every Monday my classmates and ______ tell about our weekends. ○ I ○ me	2. ______ call it "The Weekend News Report." ○ Our ○ We
3. First, ______ teacher tells her news. ○ our ○ we	4. Then each student tells a partner what ______ did. ○ she ○ me
5. Cara said that ______ went fishing. ○ her ○ she	6. Miguel and his family had a party. ______ had fun. ○ They ○ It
7. ______ told my partner how I went out for dinner on Saturday. ○ She ○ I	8. Would ______ believe that I ate five tacos? ○ us ○ you
9. My partner said ______ has never eaten that many tacos. ○ they ○ he	10. I think ______ was a great weekend for everyone! ○ we ○ it

Terrific!

There's a
better choice.

Look again.

Great!

TEC43034

TEC43034

Look again.

Good for you!

Look again.

That's it!

TEC43034

TEC43034

That's not
the one.

Right on!

Super!

Look again.

TEC43034

TEC43034

Great!

Look again.

Good job!

There's a
better choice.

TEC43034

TEC43034

Well done!

Look again.

Terrific!

That's not
the one.

TEC43034

TEC43034

What's the "Purr-pose"?

To Inform

To Entertain

©The Mailbox® • TEC43036 • April/May 2008

A house cat can weigh between 6 and 15 pounds.	A cat's tail helps the cat balance.	An adult house cat has 30 teeth.
TEC43036	TEC43036	TEC43036
A female cat is called a queen.	A cat uses its claws to climb and to catch its prey.	A cat can help keep a farm or home free of mice and snakes.
TEC43036	TEC43036	TEC43036
Carl the Cat loves to read mysteries in the library.	Supercat was last seen flying across the city.	Once upon a time, there lived a beautiful cat named Katie.
TEC43036	TEC43036	TEC43036
The dogs couldn't believe their eyes when they saw Robocat coming their way!	Did you know that there is a pizza-making alley cat in New York?	The kittens like to help their mom cook, clean, and shop for food.
TEC43036	TEC43036	TEC43036

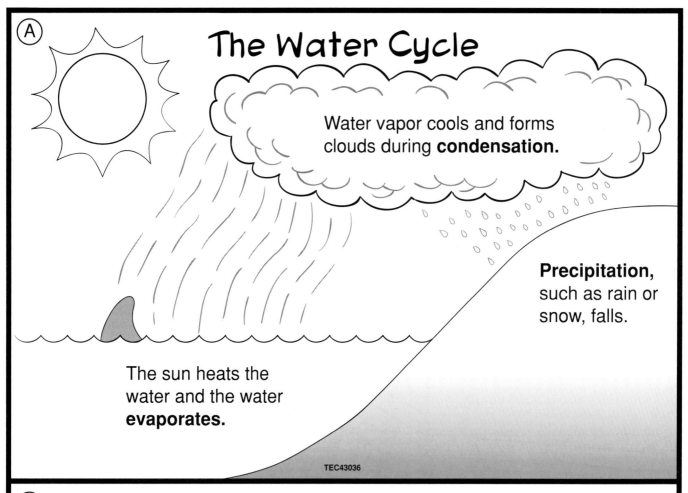

Ⓐ

The Water Cycle

Water vapor cools and forms clouds during **condensation.**

Precipitation, such as rain or snow, falls.

The sun heats the water and the water **evaporates.**

TEC43036

Ⓑ

This Week's Weather

Day	Weather
Sunday	sunny and hot
Monday	sunny
Tuesday	sunny but windy
Wednesday	rainy
Thursday	cloudy
Friday	sunny but cool
Saturday	sunny but cool

TEC43036

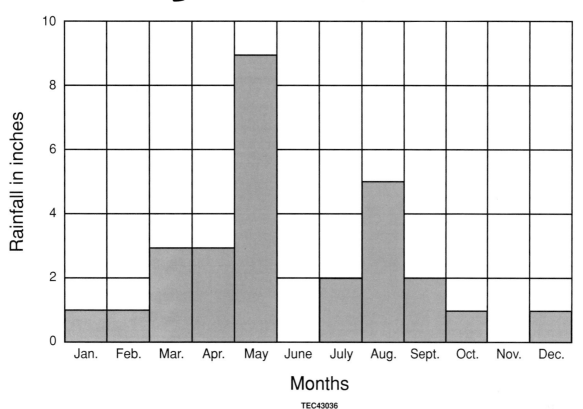

Monthly Rainfall at Green Lake

Rainfall in inches

Months

TEC43036

A

1. Is this a chart, diagram, or graph?

2. What is the title?

3. What happens after condensation?

4. What makes the water evaporate?

5. What are two kinds of precipitation?

TEC43036

B

1. Is this a chart, diagram, or graph?

2. What is the title?

3. What was the weather like on Tuesday?

4. How many days were rainy that week?

5. Were there more sunny days or more cloudy days?

TEC43036

C

1. Is this a chart, diagram, or graph?

2. What is the title?

3. Was the rain measured in inches or feet? How do you know?

4. When did the most rain fall?

5. How much rain fell during April?

TEC43036

Riddle and Word Problem Cards

Use with "Ready to Ride" on page 79.

Why won't the bike stand up by itself?

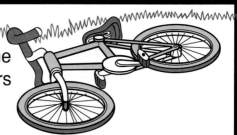

To solve the riddle, read each word problem. Write the answer on the card. Arrange the cards so the answers are in order from smallest to largest. Then write the letters from the cards in order on a sheet of paper.

There are 80 children ready to ride in a bike parade. Then 6 bikes get flat tires. How many children ride in the bike parade? TEC43036 **E**	Ben stops for water every 2 miles. If he rides for 10 miles, how many times will he stop for water? TEC43036 **IT**
There are 14 girls and 17 boys riding bikes at the dirt track. How many children are riding bikes? TEC43036 **O"**	The boys on Elm Street are in a relay race. Each of the 4 boys rides 2 miles. How many miles did they ride altogether? TEC43036 **IS**
There are 4 tricycles on the playground. How many wheels are there? TEC43036 **W**	Mr. Wilson rode 26 miles on his bike last week. This week he rode 28 miles. How many miles did he ride in all? TEC43036 **I**
There are 5 bicycles in the bike rack. How many wheels are there? TEC43036 **"T**	The 10 girls on Oak Street have a bike wash. Each girl washes 4 bikes. How many bikes did they wash altogether? TEC43036 **T**
There are 97 bike riders at the park. Then 19 of them go home. How many bike riders are left at the park? TEC43036 **D**	Brooke counts the houses she passes while she rides her bike. On Monday she counts 15 houses. On Tuesday she counts 24 houses. On Wednesday she counts 31 houses. How many houses does she count in all? TEC43036 **R**

(1) The train leaves the station at 8:00 AM. It arrives at the next station at 9:15 AM. How long is the trip?

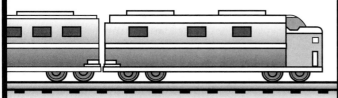

TEC43037

(2) The family gets in the car at 4:30 PM to go to the soccer game. They arrive at the soccer field at 4:50 PM. How long is the trip?

TEC43037

(3) The truck leaves the farm at 10:10 AM. It arrives at the grocery store at 2:05 PM. How long is the trip?

TEC43037

(4) A woman hops on her motorcycle at 1:45 PM. She rides her motorcycle until 6:20 PM. How long was her trip?

TEC43037

(5) The bus leaves for the field trip site at 7:30 AM. The bus arrives at the field trip site at 8:55 AM. How long is the bus trip?

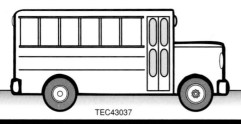

TEC43037

(6) The boat leaves the dock at 3:35 PM. It sails until 5:25 PM. How long is the trip?

TEC43037

(7) The boy starts his bike ride at 12:30 PM. He rides until 1:40 PM. How long is his trip?

TEC43037

(8) The helicopter takes off at 11:15 AM. It flies over the countryside until noon. How long is the trip?

TEC43037

Tracking the Time

Number	Start Time	Arrival Time	Length of Trip
1	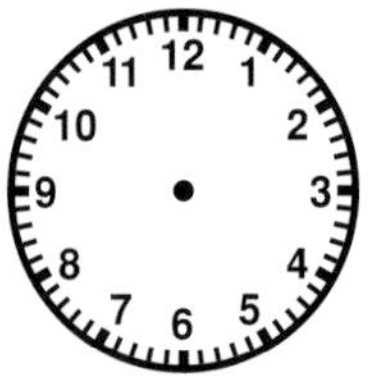	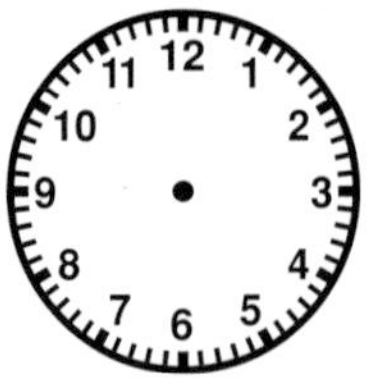	
2	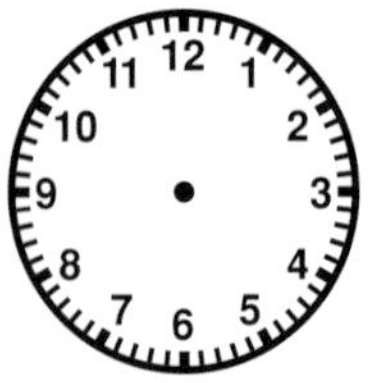	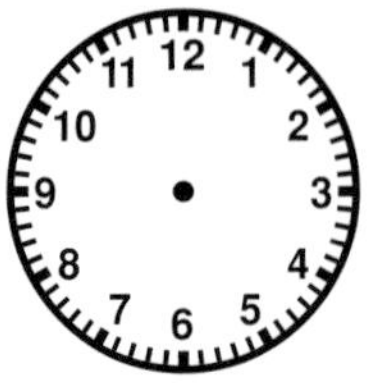	
3	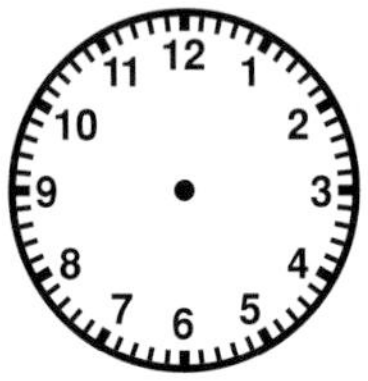	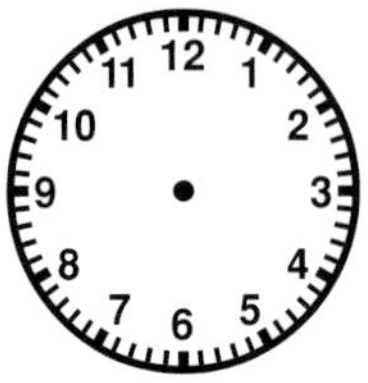	
4	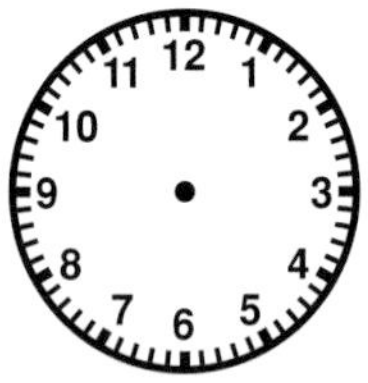	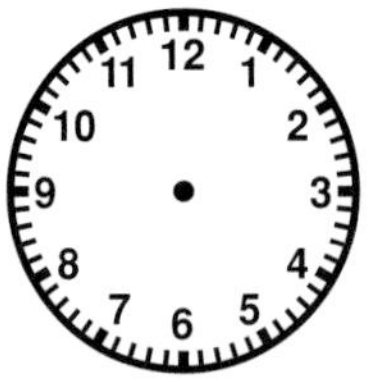	
5	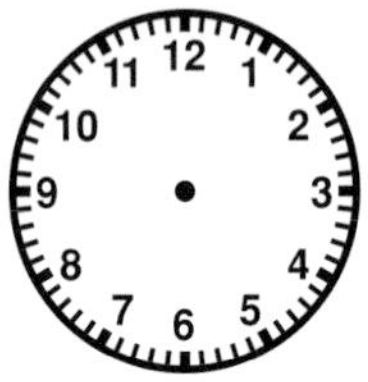	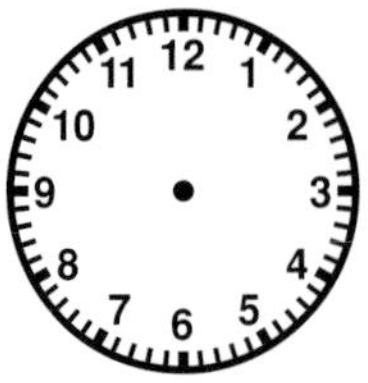	
6	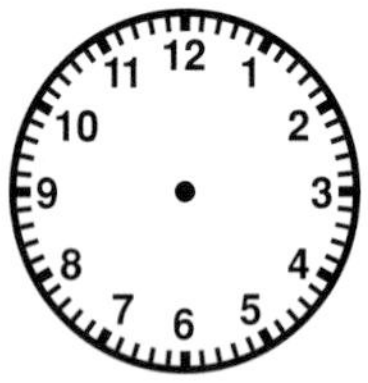	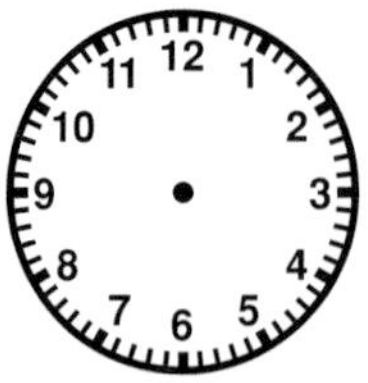	
7	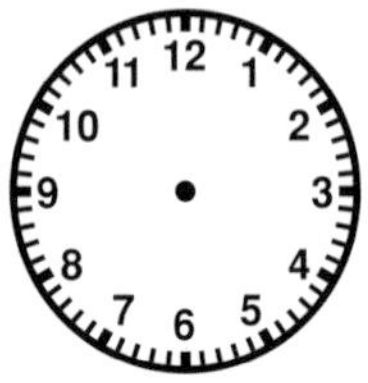	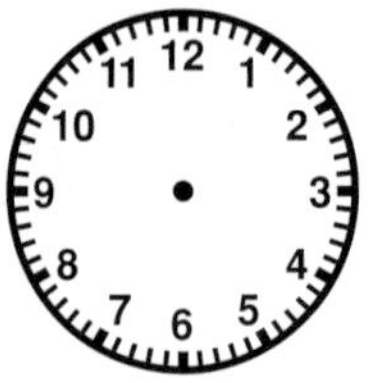	
8	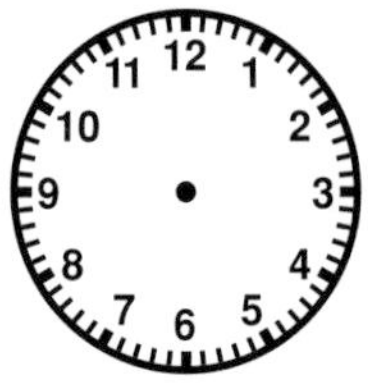	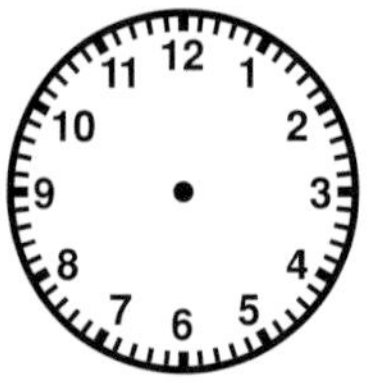	

Each sentence should start with a capital letter.

TEC43037

Each sentence should have a subject and a verb.

TEC43037

Each sentence should include important details.

TEC43037

Each sentence should end with a period, question mark, or exclamation point.

TEC43037

Name _____ Editing

The Fourth of July

I love the Fourth of July It is my favorite holiday. My family spends this holiday at the beach, and I love the beach. Like to dress in red, white, and blue clothes. we roast hot dogs and watch the colorful fireworks. My mom lets me stay up late i always look forward to the Fourth of July!

Number Pattern and Rule Cards

Use with "A Perfect Fit" on page 81.

7, 10, 13, 16, _____	**Rule: Add 3.** Cut out · 19 · Cut out TEC43037
29, 25, _____, 17, 13	**Rule: Add 4.** Cut out · 16 · Cut out TEC43037
60, 55, 50, _____, 40	**Rule: Add 5.** Cut out · 42 · Cut out TEC43037
8, _____, 28, 38, 48	**Rule: Add 10.** Cut out · 18 · Cut out TEC43037
22, 27, 32, 37, _____	**Rule: Subtract 3.** Cut out · 28 · Cut out TEC43037
4, 8, 12, _____, 20	**Rule: Subtract 4.** Cut out · 21 · Cut out TEC43037
37, 34, 31, _____, 25	**Rule: Subtract 5.** Cut out · 45 · Cut out TEC43037
53, 43, 33, 23, _____	**Rule: Subtract 10.** Cut out · 13 · Cut out TEC43037

©The Mailbox® · TEC43037 · June/July 2008 · Key p. 311

Management Tips & Timesavers

Management Tips & Timesavers

Brennen #16

Arianna #20

Multipurpose Magnets

Keep track of students with this versatile idea. Make a magnet by imprinting each child's photo, name, and student number on a business card magnet (available at office supply stores). Keep the magnets posted on an easy-to-see magnetic board. Have each child move his magnet to a designated spot on the board to indicate his lunch choice, to sign up for a restroom break or library visit, or to record his personal data on a class graph. Best of all, visiting teachers will know who's who with a glance at the board.

**Merry Lenz, Columbiaville Elementary
Columbiaville, MI**

Clothespin Checkout

An organized class library is the result of this easy-to-implement idea. First, put your books into plastic tubs based on genre, theme, or author. Then label each of a supply of clothespins with a child's name or student number. Clip the clothespins to a sentence strip and mount the strip near your class library. When a child chooses a book, she attaches her clothespin to the corresponding tub. Then, when she's ready to return the book, she knows just where to place it!

**Kristi Zimmerman, Lillian Black Elementary, Spring Lake, NC, and Jaime Arbogast
Fairgrounds Elementary, Nashua, NH**

Poetry

Stuff Friday folders.

Make 22 copies of page 15.

Cut 22 green circles on die-cut machine.

For My Valuable Volunteers

Ready-to-Go Help

To keep materials for parent volunteers organized, place a plastic crate in an easily accessible part of the room. Label the crate so the volunteers can find it. Then place a list of tasks and the materials needed to complete them inside the crate.

June Conley, Abel Elementary, Sarasota, FL

Weatherproof Nametags

Here's an easy way to label student cubbies, coat hooks, or lockers. Carefully cut a pocket from a corner of a nine-pocket sports card page. (One page makes up to four pockets.) Trim a piece of construction paper to fit inside the pocket, write a child's name on the paper, and add any desired decorative touches. Slide the paper into the pocket and attach it to the wall near the cubby, hook, or locker. Repeat the process for each child. Reuse the pockets year after year by simply changing the nametags inside.

Marian Yovorsky, St. John Bosco Catholic School, Toronto, Ontario

Max

c o m p l i m e n _ _ _

Sing Their Praises

Encourage good manners and teamwork! Whenever you catch your students following classroom rules or showing good effort, give them a compliment. Follow the verbal praise by writing a letter from the word *compliments* on the board. Add a letter when a parent or another teacher praises the class and add two letters if the class earns a compliment from an administrator. Once the word *compliments* has been spelled out, reward students with a fun class activity such as an outdoor picnic or extra recess time.

Christine Taylor, Augusta Preparatory Day School, Martinez, GA

Positive Problem Solving

This idea promotes active problem solving for students facing problems at school. First, label a spiral notebook as shown and place it near your desk. When a child has a problem, have her write it in the notebook and include a possible solution. Once a week, review recent entries during a class meeting and have students brainstorm possible solutions for each problem discussed. Later, privately check in with the students who encountered the problems to see how the situations turned out for them. Not only does this help you stay on top of class happenings, but it also gives all your students strategies for solving future problems.

Kim Metzger, Thorne Primary School, Dearborn Heights, MI

The Tell-Something Book

Management Tips & Timesavers

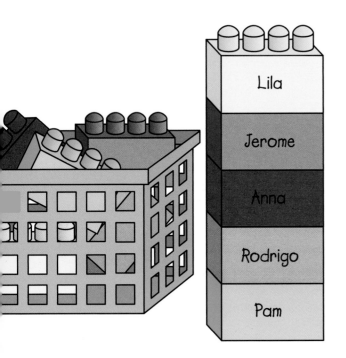

One-on-One

Here's a simple way for students to request an individual meeting with you! Use a permanent marker to write each student's name on a large interlocking block. Store the blocks in a bin and place the bin in an easily accessible location. When a student needs your assistance during independent work, or needs you to edit his written work during a writer's workshop, he stacks his block next to the bin. As time allows, remove the block from the bottom of the stack and meet with the named student. Not only can a student easily see when his turn will be, but he can also count on your undivided attention when his name is called!

adapted from an idea by Pamela Anastasio
Waterman School, Skaneateles, NY

Take It Home!

To help students organize take-home papers, use a FISH (For Information Sent Home) folder. For each student, label one of the inside pockets of a two-pocket folder "Keep at Home" and the other pocket "Read and Return." Prepare a folder cover like the one shown with a fish and air bubbles. Then copy the paper to make a class supply. Have each student write her name on the fish and staple the paper to the front of a prepared folder. Each day, a student places her papers in the appropriate sections of her folder and takes it home. A parent or guardian reviews the contents and then initials and dates one of the air bubbles. After all the air bubbles have been used, attach a new sheet to the front of the folder.

Rachel Aupied, Florida Avenue Elementary, Slidell, LA

Good Behavior Counts

Encourage students to work toward a class goal! Present a large, blank hundred chart to students and explain that for each positive behavior they show, a space will be colored. Attach a sticker at each increment of 25 and tell students that each time the coloring reaches a sticker, they will receive a predetermined reward or privilege. When the class exhibits a positive behavior, invite a student to color in the next available square on the chart. Reward students at each marker and once the chart is full, congratulate the class for completing 100 positive behaviors!

Vicki Simpson, Hayes Grade Center, Ada, OK

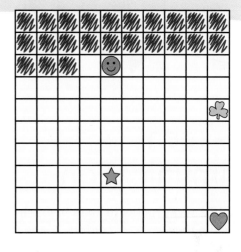

Quick Collecting

Use file folders to avoid collecting papers after students complete each assignment! Have each student personalize and decorate a file folder and store it in her desk. Ask her to place all work to be collected in the folder. At the end of the day, have each child remove her papers from her folder, staple them together, and place them in a designated location. Then have the child return the folder to her desk.

Dee Teaqtke, Nebraska Unified Schools, Verdigre, NE

Homework at a Glance

To make sure students take home all the necessary materials to complete their homework, try this picture-perfect tip! Take a close-up photograph of each textbook, journal, or notebook commonly needed for homework assignments. Glue each photo to a sheet of tagboard and then laminate it for durability. Attach a piece of magnetic tape to the back of each picture. Title an area of the board "What to Bring Home." Each day, place the appropriate pictures on the board. With a quick glance at the board, students are sure to be prepared to complete their homework!

Anna Parrish, Joseph Keels Elementary, Columbia, SC
Dana Johansen, Greenwich Academy, Greenwich, CT

Computer Time

Ensure that all students get equal opportunity to use a classroom computer. Attach a library pocket to one side of each computer. Write each student's name on a separate craft stick and store the craft sticks name-side down in a cup. Prior to students' arrival, place a craft stick in each library pocket to assign a student to that computer. After a student's turn is over, place his craft stick name-side up in the cup to signify that he has had a turn. Simply flip the sticks over to begin a new rotation.

Anne Wiszowaty, North Shore Community School, Duluth, MN

Management Tips & Timesavers

High-Tech Communication

Use two-way radios to keep in touch with students while they work on centers. Place a walkie-talkie in each center area, set each one to a different channel, and keep one with you. When you need to speak to a child, simply turn your radio to the corresponding channel and talk. What a great way to reduce whole class disruptions while you work in other parts of the room.

C. Gray
Sims Elementary
Conyers, GA

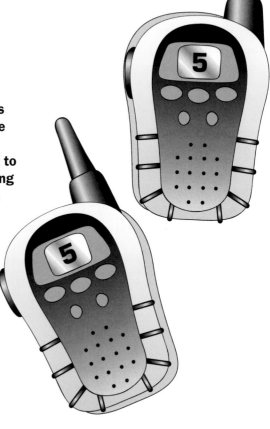

Reward Coordinates

Encourage on-time homework completion with this multipurpose reward grid. Prepare a 10 x 10 grid on a large sheet of tagboard. Label the columns with numbers and the rows with letters; then prepare lettered and numbered craft sticks to match. Laminate the board for reuse. When a student turns in a homework assignment on time, he uses a dry-erase marker to initial a square of his choice. At the end of the week, choose one craft stick from each set to determine the coordinates. If there are no initials in that square, draw again until a winner is selected. Reward the winning student with a predetermined prize!

Mel Fox, Charles Quentin Elementary, Palatine, IL

Extra Shelf

Get more out of your shelf space with a handy undershelf organizer! These inexpensive baskets, available at housewares stores, attach easily by sliding over any shelf and provide an extra space for papers or books.

Dawn Unger, Arnett C. Lines Elementary, Barrington, IL

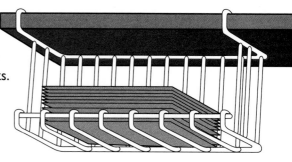

Paper Pans

To organize student papers, purchase inexpensive rectangular cake pans. Label each one with a subject area and decorate with paint. Assign each student a number and attach corresponding numbered magnets to one side of each metal pan. When a child finishes her work, she places it in the appropriate pan and then moves her numbered magnet to another side of the pan. The pans are just the right size for notebook paper and make it easy to see who hasn't yet turned in their work.

Tina Alvarado, Houston Elementary, Mineral Wells, TX

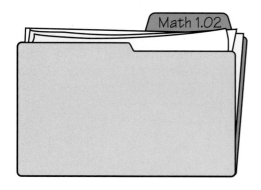

Blooming Behavior

This idea promotes teamwork as well as good behavior! Divide students into teams by tables or groupings of desks. Reward tally marks to teams throughout the week as you observe them exhibiting positive behaviors or following class rules. At the end of each day, have a student total the tally marks. On Friday, award the team with the most tally marks a vase of flowers for their table.

Megan Mathers, Chevy Chase Elementary, Chevy Chase, MD

Organized Objectives

This tip helps me organize ideas I find in *The Mailbox*® magazines by curriculum objectives. As I browse through a magazine, I keep a copy of my objectives nearby. When I locate an idea I plan to use, I write the objective number at the top of the page. Then I copy the numbered pages and file them in folders labeled according to objective. Now all those great ideas are right where I can find them!

Stacey Allen, Chickasaw Elementary, Olive Branch, MS

Management Tips & Timesavers

"Catch-up" Work

Here's a clever visual aid to remind students of work that needs to be completed. Fill a clean plastic ketchup bottle with red tissue paper strips so the bottle appears full. Put a strip of magnetic tape on the back of the bottle, and attach it to the board. Write "'Catch-up' Work" below the bottle and list any assignments students may need to complete. With a quick glance at the board, students see which assignments need to be finished.

Suzanne Stankoskey, Erickson Elementary, Bloomingdale, IL

Prompt Planning

Save time planning morning work with this simple routine.
- **Math Mania Monday:** Write a problem of the day on the board for students to solve and then check with a partner.
- **Take Two Tuesday:** Write several scrambled spelling or vocabulary words on the board. Direct each student to choose two words to unscramble and write in a sentence.
- **Wacky Writing Wednesday:** Display sentences for students to copy, edit, and rewrite.
- **Think It Through Thursday:** Give students a puzzle page or a following-directions activity to complete.
- **Fun Friday:** Provide students with time to read, draw, play games, or talk quietly with a friend.

What a great way to schedule your students' morning activities!

Leigh Ann Self, Whitefield Academy, Louisville, KY

Classroom Rewards

Motivate students to work as a team with this eye-catching reward system. On poster board, draw a gameboard like the one shown. Program some spaces with decorative school-related symbols and other spaces with rewards. Place a sticky note (game piece) at "Start" and display the gameboard in an easy-to-see location. When the class follows the rules or receives a compliment, select a student to roll a die and move the game piece the corresponding number of spaces. If the game piece lands on a reward, determine a time for students to enjoy it. Continue in this manner until the game piece reaches the "Finish" space; then start over again.

adapted from an idea by Rebecca Boehler, Devaney Elementary, Terre Haute, IN

Time for a Change

Use this positive reinforcement idea to manage student behavior. Have each student draw and label on a half sheet of 11" x 18" paper the stages of metamorphosis of a butterfly or a frog. Then give each student a paper clip to slide onto the paper by the first stage of metamorphosis and have him tape the paper to a side of his desk. Explain that for each positive behavior a student shows, he will be asked to slide his paper clip to the next stage. Once a student reaches the last stage, he earns a small reward and resets his paper clip to the first stage.

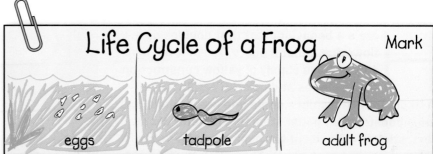

Brooke Beverly, Dudley Elementary, Dudley, MA

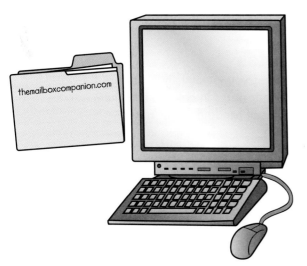

Web Files

Save time searching for your favorite Web sites with this useful tip. After printing ideas or activities from a Web site, place the copies inside a file folder. Then label the outside of the folder with the Web address for future reference.

Jodi Strack, White Oaks Elementary, Virginia Beach, VA

Project Parades

This easy idea ensures that students have time to share their work! Give each student a loop of masking tape or a wad of Sticky-Tac. On your signal, direct the students to post their work along the perimeter of the room and wait for your next cue. Then have the students walk around the room to read and view each other's work.

Heather Wynne, Tobyhanna Elementary, Pocono Pines, PA

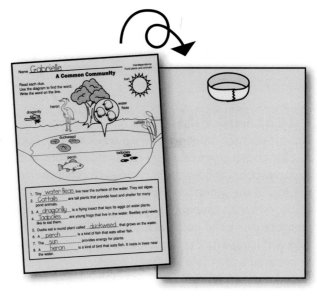

Management Tips & Timesavers

Blooming Behavior

Here's a behavior chart that doubles as a flowering bulletin board. To set it up, laminate a class supply of yellow construction paper circles and colorful petals. Label each circle with a child's name and staple the circle and a construction paper stem to a bulletin board. Next, stick five pieces of the hook side of a Velcro fastener around each circle. Then stick the loop side of a piece of a Velcro fastener to the back of each petal. When a student has a good day, direct him to choose a petal and stick it on his flower. When a child earns five petals, provide a small reward; then remove his petals to begin again.

Laurie Ginsberg, Milbrook Elementary, Baltimore, MD

Noticeable Notes

To quickly spot the notes you jot on handouts during a workshop or conference, write your notes in colored ink. Then, when you glance through a packet of handouts, your notes will stand out.

Anna Parrish, Joseph Keels Elementary, Columbia, SC

Paper Clip Postings

Make it easy for students to keep track of their cooperative group roles. Post a color-coded chart of group roles and responsibilities and obtain paper clips in corresponding colors. Then, for each group, write the students' names across the top of the group's work folder and place a colored paper clip on each child's name. When it's time for the group to work, have each member check the color of his paper clip, identify his role, and review its description. Rearrange the paper clips as necessary to rotate students' roles.

Janine Firmender, Stony Brook Elementary, Rockaway, NJ

Cooperative Group Roles
Manager: makes sure your group completes its task
Time keeper: helps your group finish on time
Recorder: writes things down for your group
Reporter: presents your group's work to the class

Math Mailbag

Math Mailbag

Do you like P.E. or Art?

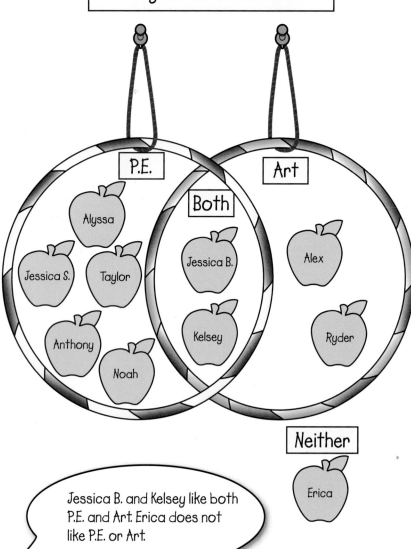

P.E.

Art

Both

Alyssa

Jessica S.   Taylor

Anthony

Noah

Jessica B.

Kelsey

Alex

Ryder

Neither

Erica

Jessica B. and Kelsey like both P.E. and Art. Erica does not like P.E. or Art.

Rounding Up Answers

Organizing and displaying data

To start, tie a length of yarn to each of two plastic hoops. Use the yarn to hang each hoop on a low display board, making sure that the hoops overlap as shown. Next, provide each student with a simple paper cutout and have him record his name on it. Pose a question to the class, such as "Do you like P.E. or Art?" Then discuss with students ways that they might collect and display the class results. Draw students' attention to the plastic hoops and explain that the hoops form a Venn diagram. Show the students how to label the Venn diagram so it corresponds to your question. Then have each student pin or tape his cutout in the appropriate spot on the diagram. Lead the class in a discussion of the results. Repeat the process throughout the year with new questions, and as students' proficiency increases, add another hoop for more answer options.

Kari Mart, LaMoure Elementary, Lamoure, ND, and Carrie Mihojevich, Arundel Elementary, San Carlos, CA

On the Ball
Basic facts

Review basic computation skills with this hands-on activity. Use a permanent marker to label each of ten tennis balls with a different number from 0 to 9. Place the balls in a basket and have students sit in a circle. Invite one student to select a ball and roll it to another student. The student who receives the ball announces the number and the child who rolled the ball rolls another to the same recipient. She announces the second number and then uses the numbers to announce an addition problem. Her classmates respond with the sum. Then she announces a related subtraction problem, and her classmates name the difference. The basket is then passed to a new student, who starts the process again with new balls and a new recipient. As an alternative, have students name multiplication facts and related division facts instead.

Bonnie Gaynor, Franklin, NJ

○	4, 8, 12, 16, 20, 24, 28	7 points
	3, 6, 9, 12, 15, 18, 21, 24, 27	9 points
○		

Moving Toward Multiplication
Skip-counting

Give each small group a sheet of paper. Shuffle eight playing cards, numbers two through nine, and place them facedown along a ledge. Reveal one card and have a student in each group write the card's number on a sheet of paper. He passes the paper to another group member, who writes the next number in the skip-counting pattern. The paper gets passed around the group until time is called. Award one point for each correct number in the pattern. Play another round by revealing a new card and repeating the process.

Laura Wagner, Bais Menachem Hebrew Academy, Austin, TX

Tackling Scores
Computation, problem solving

Kick off the football season with this idea for realistic math practice. First, have each student choose a high school, college, or professional football team to follow for the season. One day each week, have her bring in a sports article from the Internet or a newspaper that reports the team's game results. Have her glue the article onto a piece of paper and then use the final score to answer questions such as

- If your team won, by how many points did it win?
- If your team lost, how many more points would it have needed to tie?
- How might your team have scored its points this week? Show as many ways as you can.
- How many points has your team scored so far this season?

If desired, provide time for students to share their answers with a small group.

Katy Hoh, W. C. K. Walls Elementary, Pitman, NJ

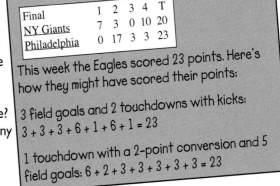

Math Mailbag

Dear Class,
    Help! We have a problem. We need your help, and we need the answer today by 4:00.
    We have money from 35 students for a field trip. We need to collect money from 82 students in all. How many more students need to turn in their money?

        Thank you for helping us!
        The Office Staff

①

47 more students need to turn in their field trip money.
Excellent work, class!

Mission: Math Mystery

Problem solving

To give problem solving a motivating twist, cut apart the notes on a copy of page 120 and place each note inside an envelope addressed to your class. Then, once a week, ask an office staff member to deliver an envelope to you. During math time, open the envelope, take out the note, and read it aloud. Next, guide each small group of students to solve the problem and share its work with the class. Then put students' completed work in an envelope and send it to the office. Before students arrive the next morning, tape the note to the board and write the correct answer along with a note of congratulations for students' hard work.

adapted from an idea by Brenda Wilke
Davison Elementary, Detroit, MI

On the March
Multiplication concepts

For this idea, have each student line up beside a partner. Next, announce, "One group of two students marches." As the first two students begin marching, guide students to repeat, "One group of two equals two." Then announce, "Two groups of two students march," have two more students join the march, and lead students to repeat, "Two groups of two equal four." Repeat with the remaining students, adding one pair of marchers at a time and leading students to state each matching multiplication sentence. For a memorable follow up, guide each child to make a booklet in which she illustrates each set of marchers and writes the matching multiplication sentences. Then, at a later time, repeat the process but have students line up in groups of three or four.

Debbie Berris, Poinciana Day School, West Palm Beach, FL

$$3 \times 2 = 6$$

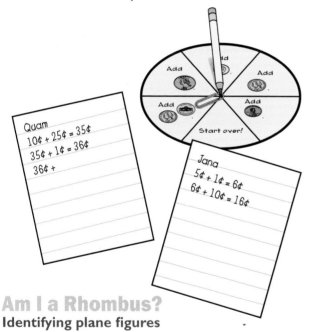

Race to a Dollar
Identifying and adding coins to one dollar

To prepare for this partner game, cut out the spinner from a copy of page 121 and place it at a center with a pencil, a paper clip, and a supply of lined paper. To play, Partner 1 uses the pencil and paper clip to spin the spinner. When the spinner stops, Partner 1 reads and follows the directions, recording his work on his paper. Then Partner 2 takes a turn in a like manner. On subsequent turns, each partner spins the spinner and adjusts his total as guided by the directions. The partner who reaches one dollar first wins the game. Have students play again as time allows.

adapted from an idea by Katherine Boldt, McKinley Elementary, Appleton, WI

Am I a Rhombus?
Identifying plane figures

Here's an idea that gives students practice naming plane figures. In advance, trim construction paper sheets to make plane figures such as triangles, squares, rectangles, rhombuses, parallelograms, trapezoids, pentagons, hexagons, and octagons. To make sure you have a shape for every two students, make extra shapes of various sizes. Then make a matching label for each shape. Next, tape one paper shape or label to each student's back. Guide the child to ask questions about the shape's sides and angles to a student standing behind him. When the child has used the clues to determine his shape, have him find another student with a matching piece. Once each student finds his match, the pair adds the shape and label to a bulletin board titled "Do You Know These Plane Figures?"

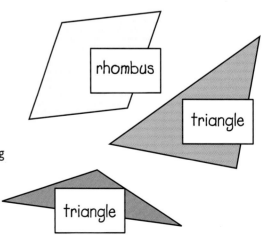

Laura Godwin, SS. Peter and Paul School, Saginaw, MI

Math Mailbag

Name Brendan

Recording sheet

Animal Weights

Animal	Approximate Weight	Number of Unifix Cubes	Number of Fish-shaped Crackers	Number of Craft Sticks
canary	$\frac{1}{2}$ ounce	4	14	7
goldfish	1 ounce	8	44	15
gerbil	3 ounces	24	134	46
hamster	4 ounces	32	171	60
small ferret	$\frac{3}{4}$ pound	96	more than 214	165
guinea pig	2 pounds	256	more than 214	more than 250

Weighing In
Using nonstandard units to measure weight

Make a class supply of the recording sheets on page 122 and place the copies at a center with a balance scale and Unifix cubes. Also set out a variety of sets of objects, such as fish-shaped crackers, beans, craft sticks, or base-ten cubes. To complete the activity, a child refers to the table and places Unifix cubes in one bucket to equal the first animal's weight. Next, the student chooses a set of objects to compare with the animal's weight. He adds the objects to the other bucket until the scale balances. Then the child counts the objects, writes the number on his paper, and repeats the process for each of the remaining animals. As time allows, have the student complete another column on his chart and compare the animals' weights using a different set of objects.

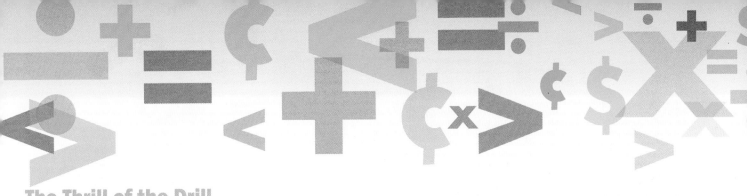

The Thrill of the Drill
Basic facts, computation

For this fast-paced review, have each student turn a page of computation practice facedown on her desk. On the count of three, have the child flip her paper, solve any two problems on the page, and flip her paper back over. Then, on your signal, each student stands, pushes in her chair, and walks around the room. On your next signal, the child sits down at the nearest desk, flips the practice page on that desk, solves two problems, and flips the paper back over. Repeat several more times and then have each student return to her desk, where she completes the unsolved problems and corrects any mistakes on the page.

Kristin Riley, Helen Mae Sauter Elementary, Gardner, MA

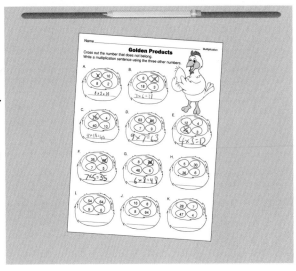

Ready With a Rubric
Problem solving

Help students focus on successful problem solving by guiding them to create a class rubric. Review with students the traits of effective problem solving and write the traits on a sheet of chart paper. Next, guide students to determine a scale to use with each trait. Post the completed rubric and have each child make a copy to keep as a handy reminder.

Monica Cavender, Winsted, CT

Let's Divide!
Dividing two-digit numbers by one digit

Give each twosome a copy of the gameboard on page 123, two game markers, and a paper clip for the game's spinner. To play, both players put their markers on Start. Player 1 spins the spinner and moves his marker. Both players read the problem on the space and calculate the answer. If both players get the same answer, Player 2 takes her turn. If both players do not get the same answer, they check the answer on a calculator. If Player 1 has the correct answer, he leaves his marker on the space and Player 2 takes her turn. If Player 1 has the wrong answer, he moves his marker back one space and Player 2 takes her turn. The first player to reach Finish wins the game.

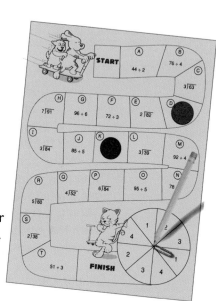

Top Banana

Place value

Here's a game for three that reinforces reading and writing numbers up to the hundred thousands place. To prepare, cut apart the game cards from three copies of page 124. Place the cards in a resealable bag with three dice and, if desired, tape a direction card to the bag. To play, one student shuffles the cards and places the deck in the center of the group. Then Player 1 rolls a die and selects the corresponding number of cards from the deck. The other players take turns in a similar manner and play continues for two more rounds. At the end of the third round, each player arranges his cards to form the largest number possible and writes the number on a dry-erase board. Then the students place the boards in numerical order from least to greatest. The player with the greatest number wins and claims the title "Top Banana." Students erase the boards, return the cards to the center, and play again.

adapted from an idea by Stephanie Turner, Atlanta, GA

"Turn Around" Facts
Fact families

Students will step up to recite related math facts with this whole-group activity. Prepare a set of flash cards so there is a multiplication card and a division card from the same fact family for each pair of students. Distribute a card to each student; then have the class stand and form a circle. Select a student to step into the circle, read aloud his math fact, and provide the answer. Then have him turn around to show his card to the rest of the group. The student with the related fact card steps forward and repeats the process. The students step back in line and the activity continues until all the facts have been matched.

adapted from an idea by Colleen Fitzgerald, Sylvania, OH

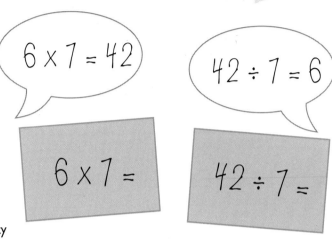

Guesswork
Estimation

At the beginning of each week, count a quantity of similar items and place them in a clear container. Then provide time for students to write on a slip of paper their names and estimates of how many items are in the container. Collect the papers, record the estimates and the actual number of items on chart paper, and display the results near the container. Later in the week, have students solve a story problem that uses the displayed results. For additional challenges, ask students to create their own story problems or make graphs about the estimates.

Stella Sorbo, Two Harbors, MN

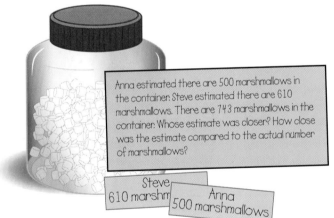

Anna estimated there are 500 marshmallows in the container. Steve estimated there are 610 marshmallows. There are 743 marshmallows in the container. Whose estimate was closer? How close was the estimate compared to the actual number of marshmallows?

Steve 610 marshm

Anna 500 marshmallows

It's a Breeze
Fractional parts

To prepare this partner game, divide a large poster board into 13 sections and label each section as shown. Give each student three medium pom-poms of the same color, a drinking straw, and a copy of the recording sheet (page 125). To begin, Player 1 places her pom-pom in the section marked "Start" and uses her straw to blow one of her pom-poms across the gameboard. Player 2 takes her turn in the same manner. The players alternate play until all six pom-poms are on the board. Then each player colors the corresponding fractional parts on her recording sheet, collects her pom-poms, and resumes playing until all six circles on the recording sheet are completely colored.

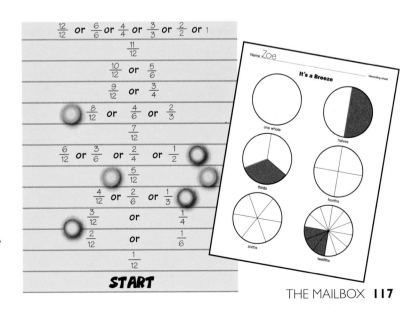

Math Mailbag

Name _Gabriel_

Toss the Dough Around

Problem solving

Pizza Toppings	Tomato sauce (color red)	Cheese	Pepperoni	Sausage	Green Peppers	Mushrooms
Price	$ 1.75	$ 1.50	$ 1.25	$ 1.25	$ 0.85	$ 0.85

Pizza Toppings	Olives	Onions
Price	$ 0.80	$ 0.75

Pizza sizes:

	small	medium	large	extra large
		$2.00	$2.50	$3.00	$3.50

Budget $ 15.00
Price of pizza crust $ 3.00

Toppings:

tomato sauce	$	1.75
cheese	$	1.50
pepperoni	$	1.25
sausage	$	1.25
green peppers	$	0.85
mushrooms	$	0.85
olives	$	0.80
onions	$	0.75

How much would it cost to make your pizza? _$12.00_

How much money would be left in your budget? _$3.00_

How did you figure out which size pizza crust to choose? _I added the prices of all the toppings to get a total. Then I subtracted that number from my budget to figure out the crust size I could afford._

Pricing Pizzas

Problem solving with money

n advance, program a copy of page 126 with prices for the toppings and pizza sizes; then make a copy for each student. Also cut out four different-size pizza-crust templates. To begin, announce a budget of ten to 15 dollars and guide each student to use his copy of page 126 to plan a pizza that stays within the budget. After the student completes his plan and answers the questions, have him trace the corresponding pizza-crust template onto a piece of tagboard. Then have him cut out the tracing and draw the pizza toppings he selected. Display students' pizzas and recording sheets on a board titled "We've Got the Dough."

adapted from an idea by Hope Nolte, Elizabeth Waters Elementary, Fond du Lac, WI

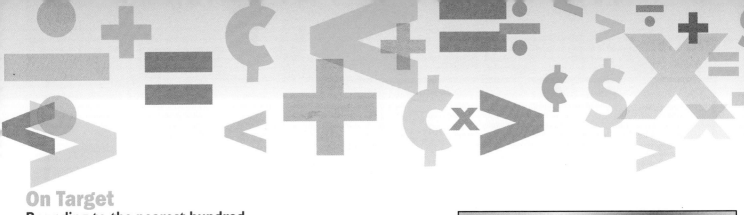

On Target
Rounding to the nearest hundred

To begin this whole-class game, draw across the length of the board a number line with two endpoints and a midpoint. Write one of two consecutive hundreds by each endpoint and then label the midpoint with the number that falls halfway between the two. Select a volunteer to choose one of the hundreds as the target number, write his choice on a piece of scrap paper, and then turn over the paper. Next, have each remaining student, in turn, write a number on the board that falls on the number line, initialing by her number. After each student has recorded a number, direct the volunteer to reveal the target number. Guide every student whose number rounds to the target number to form a line at the board; then erase the numbers on the board. Write three new numbers at the points and repeat the process with only the students in line writing on the board. Play continues in this manner until one student remains. Then he leads the next game.

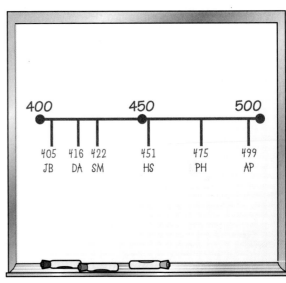

The Treat Shack
Plane and solid figures

Have partners brainstorm a list of snacks found at an amusement park or movie theater concession stand. Next, direct the pair to divide a sheet of paper into three columns and label them with the headings shown. Then, in the corresponding columns, have the duo write the name of a snack item, draw and label the plane figure(s) that symbolizes the snack item, and write the name(s) of the solid figure that resembles the snack. Encourage the students to record other snack foods on the chart in a similar manner.

adapted from an idea by Michael D. Foster, Summerfield Elementary, Summerfield, KS

Cool Combinations
Problem solving: possible outcomes

To prepare, cut three circles (ice cream scoops) in each of four different colors and tape the scoops to the board. Guide students to choose a different flavor for each color to represent. Next, draw eight to ten ice cream cones on the board. Have a student select two different-colored scoops and stack the scoops on top of a cone. Then have the student write on the board the flavor combination represented. Continue in this manner until all possible ice cream scoop color combinations are formed and a list of flavor combinations is written.

adapted from an idea by Heather Colbert, Wytheville, VA

Problem-Solving Notes

Use with "Mission: Math Mystery" on page 112.

Dear Class,
 Help! We have a problem. We need your help, and we need the answer today by 4:00.
 We have money from 35 students for a field trip. We need to collect money from 82 students in all. How many more students need to turn in their money?

 Thank you for helping us!
 The Office Staff
(1)

Dear Class,
 Help! We have a problem. We need your help, and we need the answer today by 4:00.
 There is a new bus. It has nine rows. If four students sit in each row, how many students can ride the bus?

 Thank you for helping us!
 The Office Staff
(2)

Dear Class,
 Help! We have a problem. We need your help, and we need the answer today by 4:00.
 There are three bike racks. Each bike rack holds seven bikes. How many students can park their bikes in the racks?

 Thank you for helping us!
 The Office Staff
(3)

Dear Class,
 Help! We have a problem. We need your help, and we need the answer today by 4:00.
 Students from eight classes sign up for the spelling bee. Five students from each class sign up. How many students sign up for the spelling bee in all?

 Thank you for helping us!
 The Office Staff
(4)

Dear Class,
 Help! We have a problem. We need your help, and we need the answer today by 4:00.
 Two classes will each get two new students. Another class will get three new students. How many new students will there be in all?

 Thank you for helping us!
 The Office Staff
(5)

Dear Class,
 Help! We have a problem. We need your help, and we need the answer today by 4:00.
 One class needs 17 cartons of milk. Another class needs 23 cartons of milk. Another class needs 19 cartons of milk. We have 75 cartons of milk. Do we have enough milk? Is there any extra milk?

 Thank you for helping us!
 The Office Staff
(6)

Dear Class,
 Help! We have a problem. We need your help, and we need the answer today by 4:00.
 There are children on the swings. They swing from 10:00 until 10:25. How long do the children swing?

 Thank you for helping us!
 The Office Staff
(7)

Dear Class,
 Help! We have a problem. We need your help, and we need the answer today by 4:00.
 There will be 42 parents at the meeting after school. How would you arrange 42 chairs? How many rows will there be? How many chairs will be in each row?

 Thank you for helping us!
 The Office Staff
(8)

©The Mailbox® • TEC43034 • Dec./Jan. 2007–8 • Key p. 311

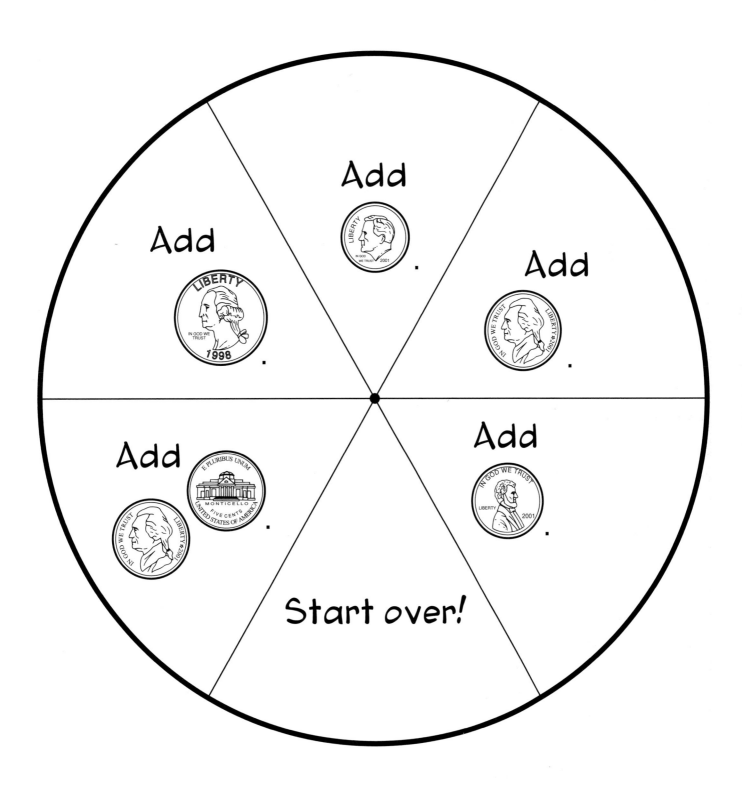

Animal Weights

Animal	Approximate Weight	Number of Unifix Cubes	Number of _____	Number of _____
canary	$\frac{1}{2}$ ounce	4		
goldfish	1 ounce	8		
gerbil	3 ounces	24		
hamster	4 ounces	32		
small ferret	$\frac{3}{4}$ pound	96		
guinea pig	2 pounds	256		

©The Mailbox® • TEC43035 • Feb./Mar. 2008

Name_____ Recording sheet

Animal Weights

Animal	Approximate Weight	Number of Unifix Cubes	Number of _____	Number of _____
canary	$\frac{1}{2}$ ounce	4		
goldfish	1 ounce	8		
gerbil	3 ounces	24		
hamster	4 ounces	32		
small ferret	$\frac{3}{4}$ pound	96		
guinea pig	2 pounds	256		

©The Mailbox® • TEC43035 • Feb./Mar. 2008

Note to the teacher: Use with "Weighing In" on page 114.

START

A — $44 \div 2$

B — $76 \div 4$

C — $3 \overline{)63}$

D — $75 \div 5$

E — $2 \overline{)82}$

F — $72 \div 3$

G — $96 \div 6$

H — $7 \overline{)91}$

I — $3 \overline{)84}$

J — $85 \div 5$

K — $5 \overline{)90}$

L — $3 \overline{)39}$

M — $92 \div 4$

N — $78 \div 2$

O — $95 \div 5$

P — $6 \overline{)84}$

Q — $4 \overline{)52}$

R — $5 \overline{)80}$

S — $2 \overline{)38}$

T — $51 \div 3$

FINISH

1 2 3 4 2 1 3 4

©The Mailbox® · TEC43035 · Feb./Mar. 2008 · Key p. 311

Note to the teacher: Use with "Let's Divide!" on page 115.

Place-Value Game Cards

Use with "Top Banana" on page 116.

How to Play
1. Each child rolls a die and selects that many cards from the deck.
2. Repeat Step 1 two more times.
3. Each child uses his cards to write the largest number he can make.
4. The child with the largest number wins and is named "Top Banana."
5. Play again.

TEC43036

	one TEC43036	one TEC43036
one TEC43036	ten TEC43036	ten TEC43036	ten TEC43036
hundred TEC43036	hundred TEC43036	hundred TEC43036	thousand TEC43036
thousand TEC43036	thousand TEC43036	ten thousand TEC43036	ten thousand TEC43036
ten thousand TEC43036	hundred thousand TEC43036	hundred thousand TEC43036	hundred thousand TEC43036

It's a Breeze

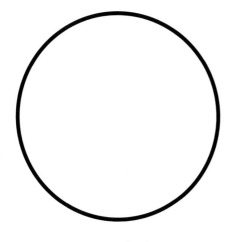

one whole

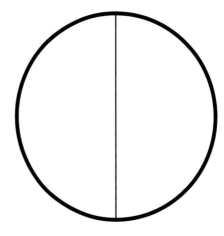

halves

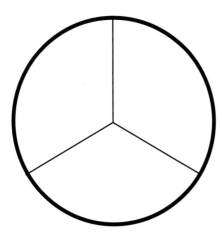

thirds

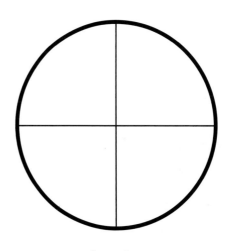

fourths

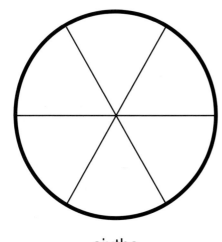

sixths

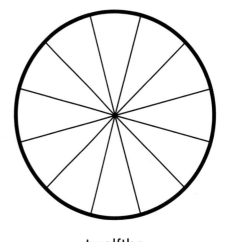

twelfths

Toss the Dough Around

Pizza Toppings	Tomato sauce (color	Cheese	Pepperoni	Sausage	Green Peppers	Mushrooms
Price	$____ . ____	$____ . ____	$____ . ____	$____ . ____	$____ . ____	$____ . ____

Pizza Toppings	Olives	Onions	Pizza sizes:			
Price	$____ . ____	$____ . ____	small $____ . ____	medium $____ . ____	large $____ . ____	extra large $____ . ____

Budget $ _____ . ____

Price of pizza crust $ _____ . ____

Toppings: _____ $ _____

_____ $ _____

_____ $ _____

_____ $ _____

_____ $ _____

_____ $ _____

_____ $ _____

_____ $ _____

_____ $ _____

How much would it cost to make your pizza? _____

How much money would be left in your budget? _____

How did you figure out which size pizza crust to choose? _____

_____

_____

Note to the teacher: Use with "Pricing Pizzas" on page 118.

Students' Selections

Read the Venn diagram.

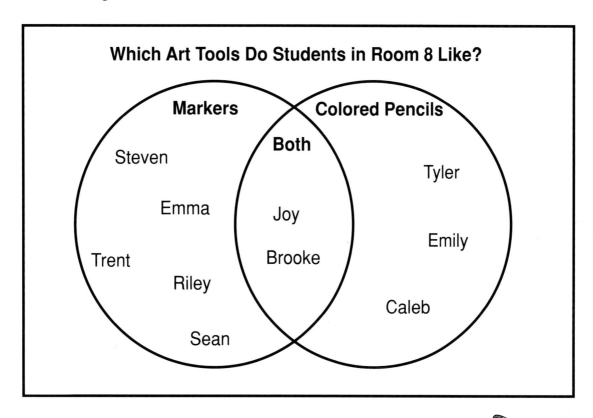

Which Art Tools Do Students in Room 8 Like?

Markers   **Colored Pencils**

Both

Steven

Emma   Joy

Trent   Brooke

Riley

Sean

Tyler

Emily

Caleb

Answer the questions.

1. How many students like markers only? _____

2. How many students like colored pencils only? _____

3. How many students like both markers and colored pencils?

   _____

4. How many total students like markers? _____

5. What does Emma like? _____

6. How many total students like colored pencils? _____

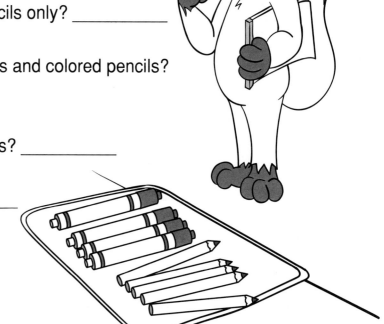

Name _____

Welcome!

Cut out the puzzle pieces on the left.
Glue each piece on the space with its matching expanded form.

The Friendliest State

200 + 30 + 9	600 + 4	300 + 70 + 2
500 + 40 + 1	100 + 90 + 5	400 + 10
700 + 50 + 3	300 + 20 + 7	800 + 80 + 6
900 + 60 + 8	400 + 1	500 + 10 + 4
600 + 40	200 + 90 + 3	900 + 80 + 6
800 + 60 + 8	100 + 50 + 9	700 + 30 + 5

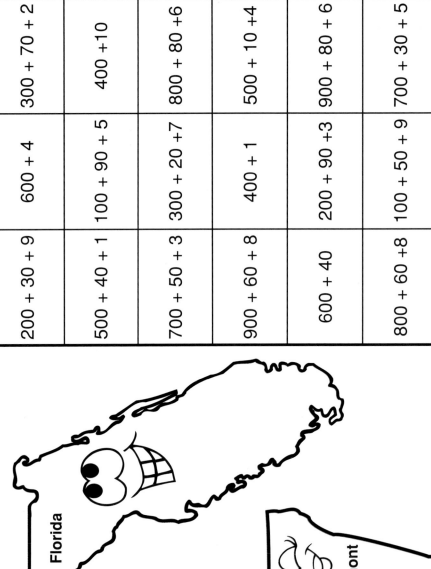

Florida

Vermont

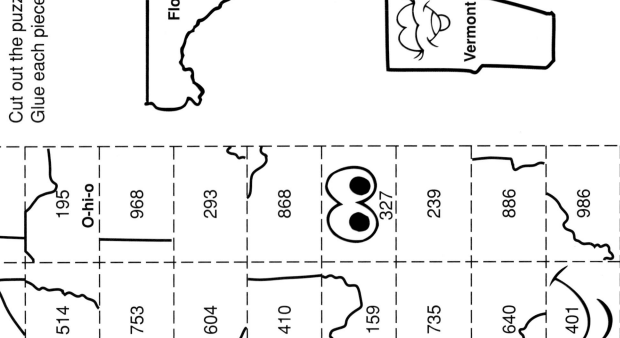

372	541
514	195
	O-hi-o
753	968
604	293
410	868
159	327
735	239
640	886
401	986

©The Mailbox® • TEC43033 • Oct./Nov. 2007 • Key p. 311

Silly School

Subtract.

Q. 258 − 197	C. 324 − 127	E. 855 − 673	R. 229 − 153	K. 422 − 375	A. 641 − 337
I. 183 − 115	R. 467 − 391	S. 921 − 792	C. 615 − 418	W. 703 − 493	E. 554 − 372
U. 721 − 335	A. 502 − 198			I. 333 − 265	W. 409 − 199

Why are the ducklings always laughing?
To solve the riddle, write each letter from above on its matching numbered line below.

Their classmate is a real

" ___ ___ ___ ___ - ___ ___ ___ ___ ___ ___ ___ "!
210 68 129 182   61 386 304 197 47 182 76

Spring Cleaning

Find the area of each window.
Write the area on the line.

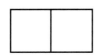

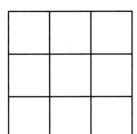

1. _____ square units

2. _____ square units   3. _____ square units

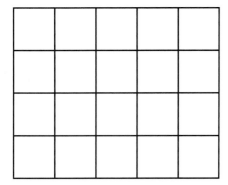

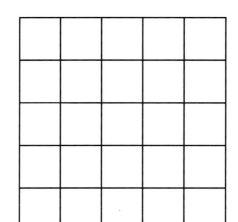

4. _____ square units

5. _____ square units

6. _____ square units

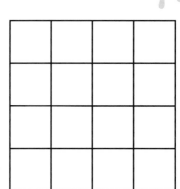

7. _____ square units

8. _____ square units

©The Mailbox® • TEC43035 • Feb./Mar. 2008 • Key p. 311

Name_____

Capacity
Customary units

Quench Your Thirst

Fill in each blank to show equal amounts.
Color the sports drink bottles by the code.

A. 1 gallon = 16 _____

B. 8 pints = 1 _____

C. 4 pints = 2 _____

D. 8 cups = 4 _____

E. 4 cups = 2 _____

F. 2 pints = 1 _____

G. 8 quarts = 2 _____

H. 6 pints = 12 _____

I. 4 quarts = 8 _____

J. 2 gallons = 8 _____

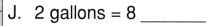

Color Code
cups = orange
pints = yellow
quarts = red
gallons = purple

What Am I?

Use the coordinate pairs to mark the dots on the grid.
Draw a blue line to connect the dots.

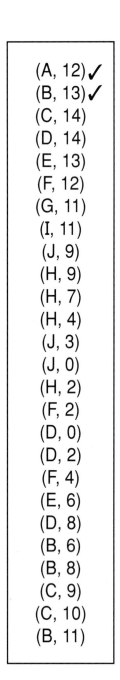

(A, 12) ✓
(B, 13) ✓
(C, 14)
(D, 14)
(E, 13)
(F, 12)
(G, 11)
(I, 11)
(J, 9)
(H, 9)
(H, 7)
(H, 4)
(J, 3)
(J, 0)
(H, 2)
(F, 2)
(D, 0)
(D, 2)
(F, 4)
(E, 6)
(D, 8)
(B, 6)
(B, 8)
(C, 9)
(C, 10)
(B, 11)

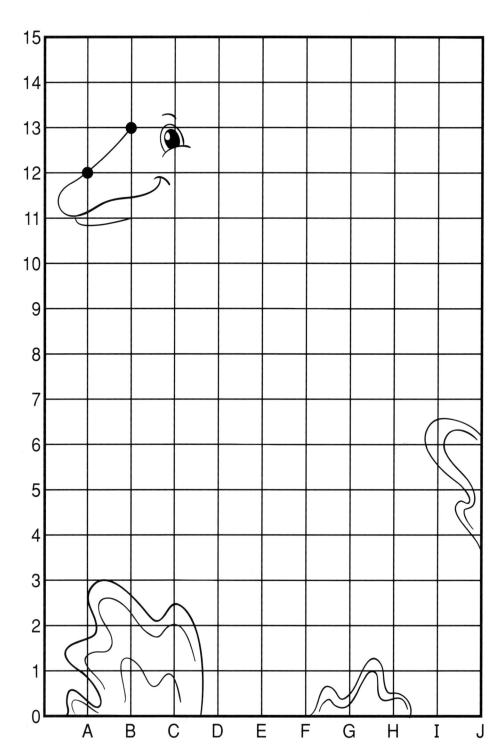

I am not a fish, but I live in water. I am warm-blooded. My skin is smooth, and it feels like

rubber. I am a very smart animal. What am I? _____

©The Mailbox® • TEC43037 • June/July 2008 • Key p. 311

OUR READERS WRITE

Our Readers Write

Ready Photo Reference

I keep a disposable camera at school to take pictures of my classroom displays. When I develop the prints, I make duplicate copies. I place one copy in my professional portfolio and keep the rest for sharing with colleagues and student teachers.

Kathy Kephart, West Boulevard Elementary, Columbia, MO

Erase With Ease

I've found a way to make cleaning my whiteboard a snap. I simply slide my hand into an oven mitt and wipe away. It's a great way to keep marker dust off my hands and clothes.

Kristy Dennison, Warsaw Elementary, Warsaw, NC

Stress-Free Open House

I create a successful open house by making my students classroom tour guides. First, I model for students how to guide parents around the room. Then I brainstorm with students locations in the classroom that we would like the parents to see. I use their ideas to type a master list of locations, and I add a comment section to the bottom before making a copy for each student. Each student clips the list to a clipboard and uses it to guide his parents around the room during open house. While they are doing this, I mingle and meet the adults. At the end of the tour, parents record their comments, and I go home stress free!

Cheryl P. Chartrand
Glenfield Elementary
Glenfield, NY

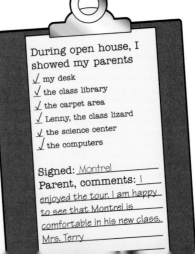

During open house, I showed my parents
√ my desk
√ the class library
√ the carpet area
√ Lenny, the class lizard
√ the science center
√ the computers

Signed: _Montrel_
Parent, comments: _I enjoyed the tour. I am happy to see that Montrel is comfortable in his new class. Mrs. Terry_

Birthday Goody Bags

Before the start of each school year, I prepare birthday goody bags for my students. I fill a decorative paper bag for each student with a signed birthday card, a themed pencil, stickers, and a homework pass. Then I store the bags until needed. On the morning of a student's birthday (or half-birthday if he was born in the summer), I place a bag on his desk. Students enjoy the surprise, and I love the convenience of having these birthday treats already made!

Wendy Barber, Omega School, Omega, GA

New-Teacher Shower

Celebrate additions to your staff with a new-teacher shower. Have each veteran teacher write a favorite idea or tip on decorative paper. Collect the papers and bind them in a book. Or have staff members chip in for a gift

certificate to a teacher supply store. Present the gift to the new teacher at an afterschool party filled with light snacks and getting-to-know-you games. What a fun way to welcome new teachers to your school!

Beth Vos
St. Bonaventure School
Columbus, NE

Professional Pick-Me-Ups

Each week, I like to show my appreciation for my colleagues' hard work with a special note. I write notes that include encouraging words, a fun fact, or information about a little-known holiday celebrated at that time of year. Then I copy the notes and put them in staff mailboxes. Teachers often share these facts and holidays with their students, or the information becomes a lunchtime conversation topic. Either way, it's an easy way to bring smiles to the teachers at my school.

Janelle Jones, Meadowcreek Elementary, Fort Worth, TX

Magical Math Wand

This idea engages my students in review activities using our classroom number line. First, I cover an old yardstick with glitter glue to make a wand. Then I wave the wand toward a well-behaved student and have her use it to demonstrate a math skill, such as skip-counting on our class number line. The wand is big enough for her classmates to follow. Plus students pay attention to their behavior so they can be chosen to use the wand. It works great on a hundred chart too.

Leanne Baur, Our Lady of Mount Carmel School, Baltimore, MD

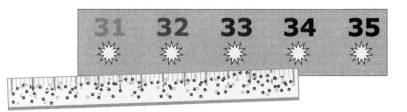

Kiosk Displays

If display space is at a minimum in your room, here's a solution! Stack two or three sturdy cardboard boxes on top of one another. Tape them together and then cover the resulting form with fabric or paper. Staple on student work or other important paperwork, and your new display is ready.

Debbie Berris, Poinciana Day School, West Palm Beach, FL

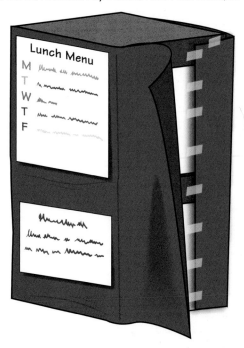

Stately Management

I integrate a positive behavior system with social studies standards. Here's how. I purchase an inexpensive United States puzzle. Each day I introduce a state by showing my students what the piece looks like and telling about the state's capital, resources, and tourist attractions. When the class meets my behavior goals for the day, we add the piece to the puzzle. Then, when we've completed the puzzle, we celebrate with a United States–themed party, complete with a related video and red, white, and blue treats.

Megan Hobaugh, Central Elementary
Beech Grove, IN

Our Readers Write

candy
costume
ghost
jack-o'-lantern
leaves
October
orange
pumpkin
scarecrow
squirrel

Seasonal Shapes

Use seasonal shapes as a **fun way to practice alphabetical order.** I have each student use large sheets of construction paper and other craft materials to create a fall or Halloween shape such as a pumpkin, ghost, or scarecrow. Using a fun font, I create a list of ten seasonal words. I give a copy of the list to each student and have her cut the words out, arrange them in alphabetical order, and glue them on her shape. When completed, I display the autumn-inspired shapes around the room for an eye-catching reminder of alphabetical order.

Kathy Folz, North Elementary, Franklin Park, IL

Super Storage

Inexpensive plastic soap boxes are perfect for organizing small classroom items. I use them to store decks of playing cards, flash cards, sets of crayons, small game pieces, and manipulatives. I add a label to the lid of each box and store them within students' reach. Students no longer misplace small items, and cleanup is a breeze!

Paige Foltz, Pleasant Elementary, Norwalk, OH

where

game pieces

Reading Cursive

To give my students practice reading cursive writing, I type short dictations in a cursive font. For each student, I print out his dictation and have him read it aloud to a partner or small group. Students are motivated to read in cursive because the words are their own!

Rhonda Chiles, South Park Elementary, Shawnee Mission, KS

This weekend I went to my grandparents' house. I helped my grandmother make a pumpkin pie. I watched my grandfather work on his truck. We went to a fall festival together. It was a great weekend!

Easy Gluing

When a student is working on an art project that requires a lot of gluing, I give him spring-loaded clothespins to hold objects together while the glue dries. It couldn't be simpler, and it frees up his fingers for other artistic endeavors!

Julie Reinders, Emmetsburg Catholic School, Emmetsburg, IA

Preconference Letter

To prepare parents for what to expect during our first parent-teacher conference, I send an information letter home prior to our meeting. In this letter, I include information that will help the conference run more smoothly, such as where to park, the location of the meeting, the time and length of the conference, and the purpose of the conference. I also give parents suggestions for questions they might want to bring to the meeting. I find that now when parents arrive they are much more prepared and eager to participate.

Karin-Leigh Spicer, Centerville, OH

No-Mess Tape

Looking for an all-purpose tape that doesn't leave a sticky mess? Try painter's tape. I use it on the floor to mark off areas of the classroom, to demonstrate area and perimeter, and to create floor graphs. It sticks to carpet and cabinets and even clothing, but it comes off easily without leaving a mess! Plus, it comes in a variety of colors!

Danika Ripley, Frank M. Sokolowski Elementary, Chelsea, MA

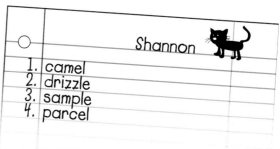

No-Name Papers

Here's a simple solution for papers with no names. My students love to draw, so before they turn in a class assignment I ask them to draw a mini illustration beside their names. If a student has forgotten to write her name, she is sure to remember once she starts drawing.

Shannon Sanford, Nannie Berry Elementary, Hendersonville, TN

The Name Game

To get my students motivated and moving in the morning, we play a name game. As soon as each student completes his morning work, he writes his name in a designated area of the board. Since the children enjoy writing on the board, this is a perfect way to get our day started quickly!

Justina Sivacek, North Shore Christian School
Port Jefferson Station, NY

Field Trip File

This tip helps me organize everything I need for a field trip. I prepare a large mailing envelope by stapling a class roster on one side and a copy of the field trip parent information letter on the other. As I receive permission slips and money, I can easily check off student names and place everything inside. If I need to send home another copy of the original information sheet, it's right there for me to copy!

Rachel Emans, Prairie Lincoln Elementary, Columbus, OH

Our Reader's Write

Quotation marks
show a speaker's exact words.

"What is a mouse's favorite game?" Missy asked.

Martin said, "Hide and squeak."

Easy-to-Use Posters

I found the perfect way to display my poster collection from *The Mailbox®* magazine. I sequence the posters by when I use them, laminate them for durability, and then bind them to create a flipchart. Then I place the flipchart on an easel or my chalk tray and reveal the desired skill. Students enjoy the colorful art, and I love the convenience of having such helpful visual aids on display.

Brooke Boyd
Shedeck Elementary
Yukon, OK

Instant Nametags

Here is an easy way to keep student nametags handy. I simply give each child a sheet of personalized labels and have him place the sheet in his desk for safekeeping. Whenever there is a substitute teacher or we go on a field trip, students easily peel off and stick on a nametag for the day!

Rachel Patterson
Austin Elementary
Abilene, TX

Directional Names

I reinforce cardinal and intermediate directions on a daily basis. Before students hand in papers, I direct them to write their names at a specific location. For example, I might ask them to write their names in the southeast corner of their papers or due north. Now we have no more nameless papers and practicing directions is fun!

Deb Brun
Orlo Avenue Elementary
East Providence, RI

Word Skills Challenge

My students' vocabularies really grow with this friendly competition! My class pairs with another class and a category—such as synonyms, adjectives, or action verbs—is announced. Both groups are challenged to list as many words that fall into that category as they can. We begin the list during group time, and then I post it so students can add more words throughout the day. At the end of the day, each class totals its words, a winner is announced, and the winning class displays a silly trophy until the next challenge!

Tara Hartline
Allatoona Elementary
Acworth, GA

Emily's Reading Bookmark

2/4/08 Where the Wild Things Are by Maurice Sendak

2/11/08 Nate the Great by Marjorie Weinman Sharmat

2/12/08 Cloudy With a Chance of Meatballs by Judi Barrett

Ready Reading Logs

To help students keep track of their **independent reading**, I have them make bookmarks! First, I give each student a construction paper strip to personalize and decorate. I have him use the resulting bookmark in the book he is reading. After finishing the book, he writes the date and the book's title and author on his bookmark. He continues adding entries to his bookmark on the front and then on the back. When he has run out of writing room, he makes another bookmark. I save the completed bookmarks and return them to students at the end of the school year. Students are always very surprised to see how many books they read throughout the year!

Emily Dearstyne, Howe School, Schenectady, NY

Place Value Practice

Instead of naming a page number for students to turn to in a textbook, I use a variety of place value concepts as clues! For example, when I want students to turn to page 125, I ask them to turn to the page numbered with a one in the hundreds place, a two in the tens place, and a five in the ones place. Or I may direct them to turn to the page that is 100 less than 225. This is a great way to work in quick practice with math skills throughout the day!

Deb Brun, Orlo Avenue School, East Providence, RI

Simple Storage

I ask parents and colleagues to save empty plastic baby-food containers. I clean the containers and their lids and use them to store a variety of classroom materials, such as counters, incentive tickets, coins, and even paint.

Jackie Barr, Baden Elementary, St. Louis, MO

Reading Buddies

When I have an ELL student who is a beginning reader, I enlist the help of my English-proficient students. On a rotating basis, each English reader pairs up with an ELL student to take turns reading for a predetermined amount of time. Both students benefit from this shared learning experience.

Brenda Candia-Lara, Moroni Elementary, Moroni, UT

Our Readers Write

Sheet Protector Displays

To display students' work, I tape a clear plastic sheet protector on each student's locker and slide one of his best work samples inside it. After some time, I have my students change their displays with other assignments of their choice.

Veronica Abii, Vivian Elementary, Vivian, LA

Fluent Phone Calls

When a student is successful with reading fluency, she calls home. I have the student read a page to a family member or, if no one is home, to the answering machine. Either way the student shares her great accomplishment with her family.

Christine Kirley, Lincoln School, Hartford, WI

Teacher Manual Organizer

Here's an inexpensive way to keep your teacher manuals accessible and orderly. I store them in a slotted wire dish rack. Then I place the rack on a desk or shelf for easy access.

Kathy Deneault, Mater Dei Catholic School, Topeka, KS

Shaking Things Up

To manage dice during center games and math activities, I keep them in this handy shaker. First, I place a pair of dice inside a clean clear gelatin cup. Then I hot-glue another gelatin cup on top. Now my dice stay in one place!

Laurel Schwartz
C. V. Bush Elementary
Jamestown, NY

Literature Folders

Organizing materials for my literature units is a breeze with this idea! I glue a copy of a book cover to the front of a two-pocket folder. Inside the left pocket, I insert the book. Inside the right pocket, I place copies of any reproducibles or quizzes that accompany the book. On the back of the folder, I glue a list of questions for before, during, and after reading. Everything I need is right at my fingertips!

Rebecca Baxter, Cameron Park Elementary, Hillsborough, NC

Whiteboard Wipe Off

To make working with individual whiteboards quick and easy, I put a wipe-off marker in a clean sock for each student. When it's time to use whiteboards, students take their markers out of the socks. When it's time to erase, they wipe their boards off with the socks. Markers do not get lost and cleanup is simple!

Jeanne Barrett, Valle Verde Elementary, Bakersfield, CA

Paint Pumps

Disposable hand-soap dispensers are perfect for dispensing paint. I leave a few drops of soap in the dispenser (for easier cleaning) and then add paint. My students can easily access the paint they need with less mess!

Amy Finn, John Allen Elementary
Soddy-Daisy, TN

Treats After Testing

After a day of standardized testing, my students deserve a treat! I ask parents to donate small treats, such as pencils, stickers, erasers, or pretzels. I label a paper bag for each testing day and fill it with a class supply of a donated item. At the end of a testing session, I invite a student volunteer to open a bag and reveal the day's surprise.

Lori Flynn, Biddeford Primary, Biddeford, ME

100 Pennies

My students and I love to celebrate the 100th day of school with activities that involve 100 pennies! For each small group of students, I place 100 pennies in a bag. Here are some activities that groups can do with the pennies:

- Stack the pennies and measure the height of the stack in inches and centimeters.
- Line up the pennies and measure the length of the line in feet or yards.
- Make a tally chart showing the different years on the pennies and how many pennies were made in each year.
- Make arrays and write the corresponding multiplication number sentences.

Heather Schumacher, Coronado Village Elementary
Universal City, TX

Our Reader's Write

Bright Idea

To help my students search their text for answers to comprehension questions, I give each child a small penlight to use. During guided reading lessons or small-group time, I have each student use the small, inexpensive light to indicate the location of a question's answer. This bright idea certainly helps students stay focused on their reading!

Jean Raetz-Topetzes
Holt Elementary, Lawrenceville, GA

Refreshing Reward

This cool idea is just the trick to inspire my students to learn their vocabulary words! After introducing a new list of vocabulary words, I give each child a craft stick to keep at her desk. When she masters a word's meaning, I initial the stick. Once she has accumulated ten initials, she earns a frozen treat as her sweet reward!

Christine Ames, Sweetwater Elementary, Port Orange, FL

Photo Finish

For a unique and special gift at the end of the year, I give each child a card with a personalized note and a class photo. First, I take a class photo. Then I have the photo printed on thank-you cards. I write a special note to each student on his card and send the cards home on the last day of school. What a nice keepsake to help remember a wonderful year!

Joanne Harnish, Immaculate Conception
Prince George, British Columbia, Canada

High Five!

To motivate my students to work hard and be on their best behavior, I reward them with a big high five! I stuff an oversize glove with pillow batting. Then I use yarn to secure the glove to a wooden dowel with a base. Whenever I catch an individual or small group of students doing a great job, I give a high five by placing the hand nearby.

Margaret Ritland
Pineview Elementary
Iowa Falls, IA

In the Spotlight

This idea motivates and inspires my students to read and write! I designed a spotlight to shine on my students as they read aloud from their journals. First, I cut a three-inch circle in the center of a large sheet of construction paper and place it atop a light-colored transparency sheet. Then I put the sheets on the overhead and project the light toward a student sitting on a stool. This simple idea makes my students feel like stars.

Sandra Anderson
Meadowbrook Elementary
Corpus Christi, TX

What an Exhibit!

To add more bulletin boards to my classroom, I bought ceiling tiles from a home improvement store. I hang the tiles on a wall with liquid nails and cover the tiles with decorative cutouts and trim. I use the additional space to display a variety of papers and projects!

Kelli Higgins, P. L. Bolin Elementary, East Peoria, IL

Magnetic Pencil Holders

Here's a simple solution for having sharpened pencils available during instructional time. I purchase inexpensive magnetic locker organizers. I attach them to the sides of my students' desks and fill the organizers with a supply of sharpened pencils. Now a student can borrow an extra pencil without leaving her seat!

Michelle Kessler
Wendell Gifted and Talented Magnet School
Wendell, NC

Friendly Letter Chant

I use this body-movement rhyme to reinforce the parts of a friendly letter.

Paula McVay, Tobey Elementary, Scotts, MI

A friendly letter has five parts.
Hold up five fingers.

The date on the right is where it starts.
Raise right arm and keep it extended.

On your left, you say, "Hello."
Raise left arm, wave hand, and keep your arm extended.

Fill in the body right below.
Sway hands and body down to floor and then stand.

Back to the right for closing the letter.
Kick right foot out.

Add your signature. It couldn't be better!
Kick right foot out again.

A Handy Apron

To keep students in their seats during a test, I walk around the classroom wearing an apron filled with sharpened pencils, tissues, and a notepad. I use the notepad to keep track of the time, and when a student needs a supply, I'm ready to provide it!

Tyna Wynne, Hamilton Accelerated Elementary, Hamilton, MO

Wandering Word Wall

If you find yourself changing rooms from year to year, this idea makes moving your word wall a snap! The teachers at my school each attach a piece of the hook side of a Velcro fastener to each letter of our alphabet charts. We also attach pieces of the loop side of a Velcro fastener to three-foot lengths of grosgrain ribbon and hang a ribbon from each letter. To post words on the word wall, each word is written on a card and each card is stapled to the ribbon under its corresponding letter. At the end of the year, we simply take down the ribbons and store them in resealable plastic bags. The following year, the strips are quickly reattached no matter what room each of us is in!

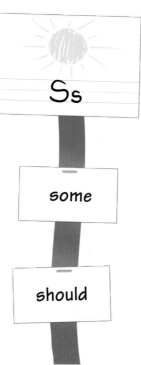

Bridget Cole, Soaring Hawk Elementary, Castle Rock, CO

Goodbye Books

At the end of the year, I give my students a keepsake of their writing. First, I take apart all my student-made class books from the year. I compile for each student a book containing the pages she contributed to the class books. Then I make a cover, bind her book, and write a personalized message on the inside cover. Students love to see the progress they've made throughout the year!

Molly Lynch, Arundel School, San Carlos, CA

Card Cleaners

Removing sticky residue from classroom desks can be a tricky task. Here's a safe way to let students pitch in so the job gets done in a flash! I give each child a plastic card, such as a grocery store savings cards or an expired gift card, to use as a scraper. With a few scrapes and a little elbow grease, my classroom gets spic and span!

Carolyn Lewis, Amelia County Elementary, Amelia Court House, VA

Friday Fun!

As a reward for having turned in their homework for the week, students receive a game hour on Friday afternoon. Students play educational file-folder games, board games, and even computer games. What a fun way to end the week!

Jean Goins, Brookville Elementary, Brookville, IN

T-Shirt Togetherness

To create a fun, reflective, and unifying end to the school year, I have my students decorate T-shirts. After the shirts are decorated, I have each child write a paragraph reflecting on her favorite memory of the year. On the last day of school, we all wear our shirts and share our memories of an awesome year!

Anne Barsness, Orangewood Elementary, Phoenix, AZ

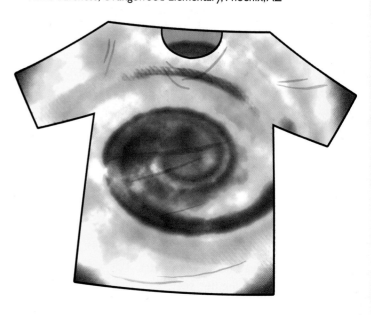

READING

READING

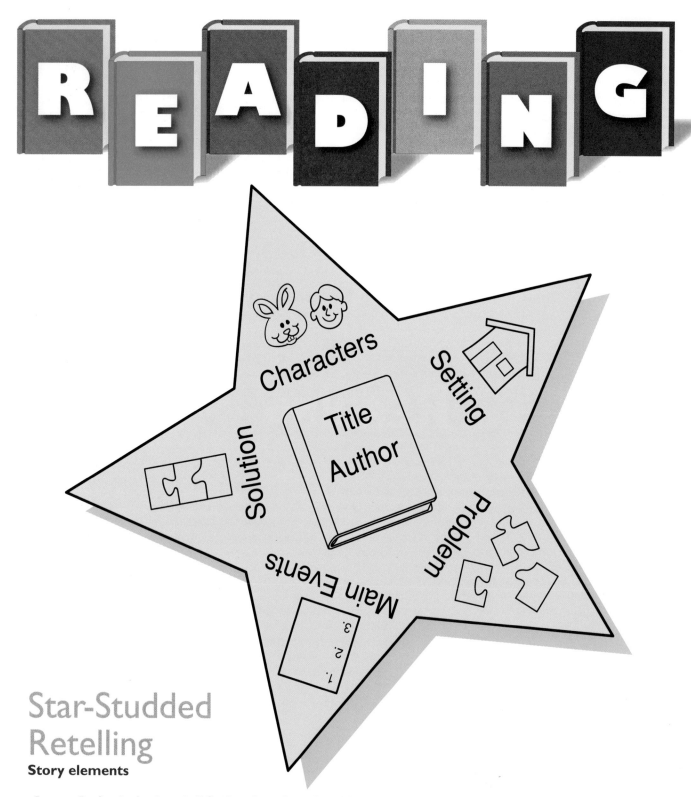

Star-Studded Retelling
Story elements

Help students retell fictional stories with this handy manipulative. First, have each student cut out a tagboard copy of the star on page 157. After reading, have a student use the reminder in the center of the star to name the story's title and its author. Next, he moves to the "Characters" point and then names and describes the important characters. He rotates the star counterclockwise to each point and uses complete sentences to retell each story part referenced. He continues in this manner until each point has been read and his retelling is complete. Then he stores his manipulative in a safe place to reuse for future retellings.

Dayle Timmons, Chets Creek Elementary, Jacksonville, FL

Listen and Learn
Fluency, predicting, skill review

Involve students in a teacher-led reading review with this independent listening center. Read aloud a classroom book or basal story while recording it on a cassette tape. Stop at appropriate points in the story and ask students to make predictions about upcoming story events, locate rhyming words, or name words with designated blends. Then place the tape at a center along with a tape player, headphones, and a copy of the book. As a student reads along with your recorded version of the story, have her silently respond to your directions. If desired, have each student write her responses on a sheet of paper. What a great way to work with a student, even when you can't be there!

April Lewis, Warsaw Elementary, Warsaw, NC

In the Bag
Vocabulary

Make connections to new words with this simple idea. Post desired vocabulary words and fill a gift bag with items that represent some of those words. For example, place a party hat in the bag for the word *celebration,* a piece of mail for the word *delivery,* or a picture of a ballerina for the word *graceful.* Invite different students to pull items from the bag and ask each child to name words he associates with his item. Then challenge the student to link the item with a word from the list. This is a great way to help students make connections with vocabulary and to provide background knowledge for upcoming reading activities.

April Lewis

Rewarding Extra Efforts
Reading incentive

To encourage weekend reading, give each student a simple reading recording sheet and challenge her to spend time each Saturday or Sunday reading. The student records her time in minutes on the recording sheet, has a parent sign it, and turns in her form each Monday. When the class earns a total of 1,440 minutes of weekend reading time—equal to the minutes in a day—invite students to a before-school treat. Have students wear comfortable clothes and bring pillows. Serve breakfast foods and show videos based on students' favorite book characters.

Courtney Heigele, Nottingham Elementary, Eudora, KS

Name __Raquel__

Date	Minutes Read	Parent Signature
Sept. 8	35	Mrs. Smith
Sept. 15	45	Mrs. Smith
Sept. 22	60	Mrs. Smith
Sept. 29	40	Mrs. Smith

READING

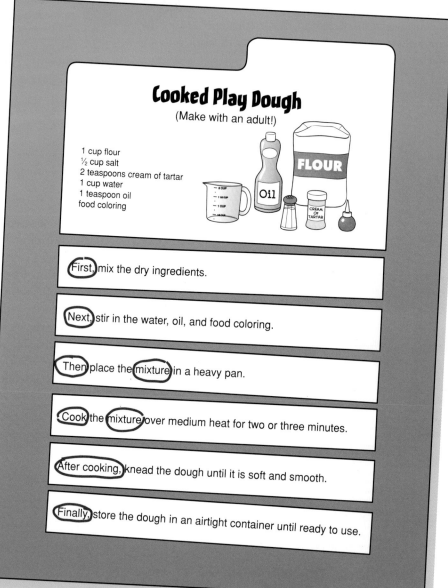

Cooked Play Dough
(Make with an adult!)

1 cup flour
½ cup salt
2 teaspoons cream of tartar
1 cup water
1 teaspoon oil
food coloring

First, mix the dry ingredients.

Next, stir in the water, oil, and food coloring.

Then place the mixture in a heavy pan.

Cook the mixture over medium heat for two or three minutes.

After cooking, knead the dough until it is soft and smooth.

Finally, store the dough in an airtight container until ready to use.

Recipe Jumble
Sequencing directions

To provide extra practice with putting directions in order, give each child a copy of page 158 and have him cut apart the sections. Direct him to place the section with the recipe's name and ingredients at the top of a sheet of paper. Then have him refer to the sequence words and other context clues to arrange the directions in order. After the student reviews his work, have him glue the cutouts in place on his paper. If desired, also have the student circle each word that provides a clue about the section's placement.

adapted from an idea by Sarah DiMarco, J. Houston Elementary, Austin, TX

Word Wall Spotlight
Recognizing high-frequency words

Boost interest in word wall activities with this bright idea! Dim the lights and select a student to shine a flashlight toward a word on the word wall. Have another student hold a pointer and lead the class in reading the word aloud. After practicing a few words, choose two new helpers to lead the activity.

Toni Walker, Southern Elementary, Lexington, KY

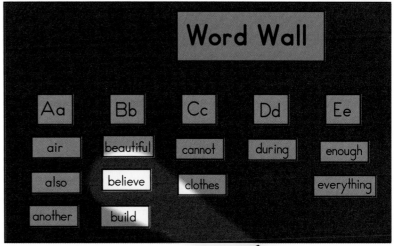

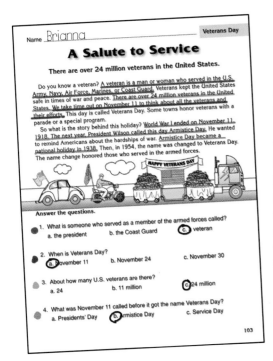

Color-Coded Questions
Using text to support answers

Guide students to use this simple strategy when completing reproducibles with nonfiction text. First, have a student read the passage. Next, have her read the first question that follows the text and put a colored dot next to it. She locates the answer in the text and underlines it with the corresponding color before recording her answer in pencil. If the answer cannot be found in or inferred from the text, she writes "MO" next to the dot for "my opinion" and records her thoughts. She continues the process with the remaining questions, using a different color for each.

Kelli Jones, East Clayton Elementary, Clayton, NC

Mystery Reader
Motivating students to read with fluency

At the beginning of each week, choose one student to serve as the mystery reader. Place a book at the child's reading level in a large envelope and discreetly pass it to the child. Remind the child to practice reading the book each night, or for stronger readers, have the student practice reading the first chapter. On Friday, designate a time to provide clues about the mystery reader and have the rest of the class guess his identity. Then invite the mystery reader to read his book or chapter aloud to the class. Not only does the student practice fluency and reading for a group, but his classmates get exposed to new stories as well.

Ashley Lovette, Warsaw Elementary, Warsaw, NC

READING

The Critics Are Talking!

Critic: __James__
name

Date: __March 10, 2008__

Book Title: __Sojourner Truth: Path to Glory__

Author: __Peter Merchant__

This book is really __interesting__! In this book,
you will learn all about the life of Sojourner Truth. She spent
summary
the first part of her life as a slave. Then she was freed and
traveled as a preacher. Later in life Sojourner Truth also spoke
out for women's rights. It's a good book to read to learn all
about this well-known African American woman.

Critics' Corner

Summarizing, book sharing

To provide summarizing practice and boost interest in reading, glue a photo of each student to the top right corner of a sheet of colored tagboard. Place the prepared tagboard sheets and copies of the recommendation form from page 159 near your reading area. Each time a student finishes a book, have him complete a recommendation form and cut it out. Then have him paper-clip the form to his paper and place it in the reading area. Encourage students to refer to the recommendations to make informed choices about their next reading selections. For added motivation and exposure to well-written summaries, ask teachers and support staff to recommend books as well.

Amy McAllister, Grassy Waters Elementary, West Palm Beach, FL

In Fine Form
Suffixes

To prepare this whole-class activity, program a supply of index cards with a few suffixes. Then program another set of index cards with words that will form new words when added to at least one of the chosen suffixes. Place each set of cards in a bag and place the bags with a roll of tape near the board. Choose a pair of students to draw a card from each bag and hold the two cards together. The duo reads the resulting word aloud; then the class indicates if a real word was made by giving a thumbs-up or thumbs-down signal. If the cards make a word, the students tape them together on the board. If they do not make a word, the cards are returned to the corresponding bags. Continue in this manner, choosing two new students to select two cards and repeat the process. For an added challenge, write on the board the meaning of each suffix and have students write their created word under the corresponding definition.

Jean Erickson, Grace Christian Academy, West Allis, WI

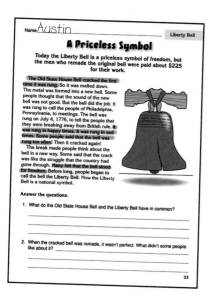

Yellow, Blue, and Then Green
Comprehension

Draw attention to reading skills with this self-checking activity. Provide each student with a copy of a reading passage and two highlighters (yellow and blue). Direct the student to locate an example of a particular skill, such as the cause statements in the passage, and mark them with the yellow highlighter. Then display a transparency of the passage. Mark the correct answers with a blue pen while each student uses the blue highlighter to mark the same answers on his paper. When the two marker colors blend, both you and the student will easily recognize the correct responses.

Debra McIntosh, North Elementary, Morgantown, WV

Fired Up for Reading
Reading environment

Encourage students to snuggle up with a good book by building a classroom fireplace! Simply cover the back and sides of a bookcase with red or brown (brick-colored) bulletin board paper. Next, glue a black paper rectangle to the bottom of the covered bookcase to look like a firebox. Attach to the black rectangle brown paper logs and tissue paper flames. Place a few comfortable pillows and a basket filled with seasonal favorites nearby. For a decorative fireplace, cover the bookcase with marbled Contact covering instead.

RoseAnn Cahill, Union Avenue School, Margate, NJ

READING

It can climb trees.

It hunts mostly at night.

The tiger is one cool cat!

Every tiger has its own unique stripe pattern.

Pocketful of Information

Identifying main idea and details

To create this decorative project, a student writes the main idea of a reading passage across the bottom half of a paper plate. Next, he cuts the plate in half and glues its edges to the edges of a whole plate to make a pocket. The student adds construction paper details to the plate to reflect the main idea. Then he writes a different supporting detail on each card in a supply of index cards and places the cards inside the pocket. Finally, he puts his completed project at a reading center for others to review.

Sue Fleischmann, Catholic East Elementary, Milwaukee, WI

"I Wonder" Wheel
Generating questions for expository texts

Before reading a nonfiction passage or book, have each student draw a large circle on a sheet of blank paper. Then have her draw a smaller circle in the middle of the larger one. Direct the student to write the topic of the book in the small circle; then have her draw five lines (spokes) from the circle as shown. After previewing the text, guide the child to write a question in each wheel section, starting each question with the words "I wonder." Have the child read the assigned text and then record the answers she found or inferred from the text in the corresponding spaces. If she is unable to answer a question, direct her to write "not found" in the space.

Jennifer Kohnke, St. Charles, IL

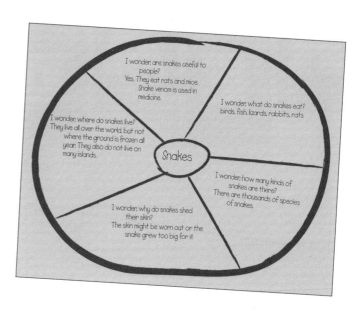

Chain of Events
Cause and effect

Give each small group a cause statement, such as "I left my lunch at home" or "I found ten dollars in my pocket." Guide the students to discuss and list on a sheet of paper a chain of effects that could occur as a result of the event. Next, have students use a different-colored crayon or marker to box in each cause-and-effect pair, overlapping colors as needed. Then have a member of each group read aloud the cause-and-effect statements while the rest of her group acts out each one. Lead students to understand that the effect of one event can actually cause another event to occur, thus creating a story.

Amy Barsanti, Pines Elementary, Plymouth, NC

Moving Along
Word skills review

This variation on the Around the World game helps students review word skills. In advance, program a word or word part on each of a supply of index cards. To play, have one student stand near another student, then flash a card. The first of the two students to correctly read the word or word part advances, moving to stand near the next child on her right. Continue play in this manner as time allows.

Cora Boyer, Hunters Creek Elementary, Jacksonville, NC

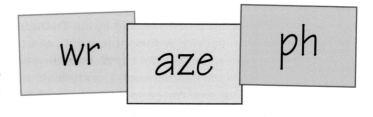

READING

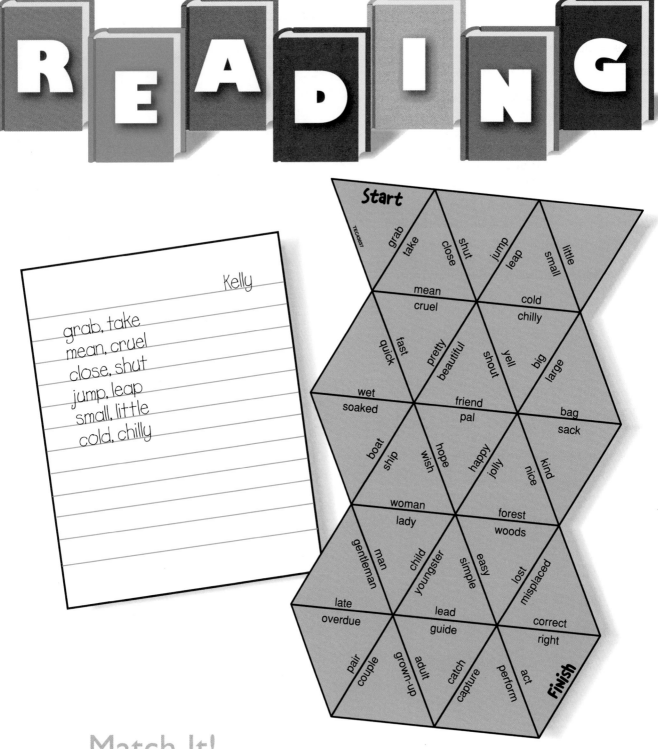

Kelly

grab, take
mean, cruel
close, shut
jump, leap
small, little
cold, chilly

Match It!

Synonyms

This puzzle inspired by the Tri-Ominos game makes for a perfect partner activity! A student pair cuts apart a copy of the game cards on page 160 and mixes the cards. Then the students find the Start and Finish cards and set them out. The students work together to complete the puzzle by matching synonym pairs. After the puzzle is complete, each student writes the synonym pairs on a sheet of paper.

Cindy Barber, Fredonia, WI

Thinking Ahead
Making predictions, setting a purpose for reading

Before reading, provide students with the title of the story they will read and a list of five to ten key words from the story. Have students work in pairs to create a short story that reflects the title and uses as many of the key words as they can. Provide time for each pair to share its resulting story; then encourage students to locate similarities between their stories and the assigned story as they read.

Ellen Malkiewicz, Hillview Elementary, Lancaster, NY

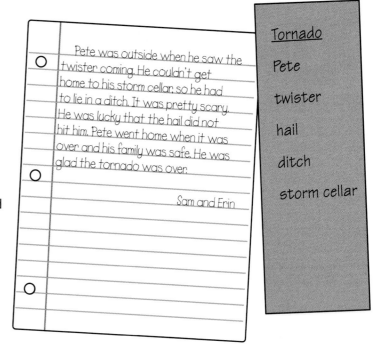

Pete was outside when he saw the twister coming. He couldn't get home to his storm cellar, so he had to lie in a ditch. It was pretty scary. He was lucky that the hail did not hit him. Pete went home when it was over and his family was safe. He was glad the tornado was over.

Sam and Erin

Tornado

Pete

twister

hail

ditch

storm cellar

Today I finished reading chapter 3 of Ramona the Pest. In this chapter Ramona learned all about seatwork. One thing she had to do was practice writing her name. She made the Q in her last name look like a cat! She also tried to help Davy make a better D. Miss Binney didn't think Ramona was much help.

It seems like Ramona is having a hard time in kindergarten. Did she get in trouble with Miss Binney?

Summary Swap
Responding to literature

Designate a few minutes after independent reading time for each student to write about what she read. Direct her to exchange her paper or journal with a classmate, read what her partner wrote, and then write a response back to her partner. Repeat the process daily, encouraging students to exchange papers with a different partner each time. Before long, each child will have a personal record of what she's read and her classmates will be exposed to new stories.

Laura Smith, Toliver Elementary, Danville, KY

#1

Outstanding Reader
First Place
Ms. Webb's Class

Award-Winning Reader
Reading motivation

To encourage students' best reading, label a paper rectangle like the one shown and tape it to the base of an old or toy trophy. When a student reads with fluency, provides an outstanding response during a reading group, or makes an impressive observation about a story, present the trophy to the student. Allow the student to display the trophy at his desk until another child exhibits an award-winning reading behavior; then pass the trophy on.

adapted from an idea by Jane Webb, McClelland Elementary, Indianapolis, IN

READING

Royal Reading Chair
Silent reading

Motivate students to make the most of their silent reading time! Decorate a chair to resemble a throne by covering it with a royal blue or purple blanket. Add other royal touches such as gold ribbon or sequins. Place the chair in a designated classroom location. During silent reading time each day, invite a student who is on task and reading independently to sit in the chair. If desired, allow time for the student to share the book he is reading with his classmates.

Mary Davis, Keokuk Christian Academy, Keokuk, IA

Sweet Reading
Developing fluency

Follow up a small-group reading lesson with fun fluency practice. On each piece in a supply of wrapped candies, write a different number that signifies how many sentences or pages (depending on the level of the book) you would like for a child to read aloud. Store the candies in a lunch bag. After your reading lesson, have a student remove a candy and announce the number. Then ask the student to read aloud, with fluency, the corresponding number of sentences or pages. Continue in the same manner for each student. Then reward students by inviting them to eat their sweet treats.

Alesia Richards, Redbud Run Elementary, Winchester, VA

Hidden Message
Reading directions

To make sure students carefully read and follow written directions, occasionally add attention grabbers to directions on the board or on teacher-made reproducibles. Students are sure to read directions carefully to look for any hidden messages.

Kristin Glunt, Bower Hill Elementary, Venetia, PA

> Take out your spelling books and turn to page 89. Write each spelling word in a sentence. Stand up, pat your head, and then sit back down. Then choose five spelling words and use them in a story.

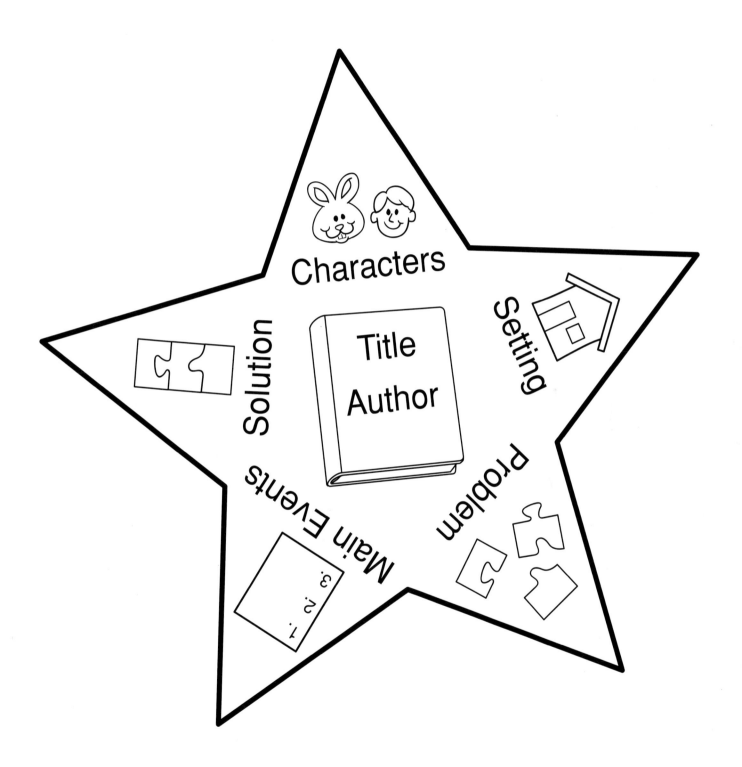

Cooked Play Dough
(Make with an adult!)

1 cup flour
½ cup salt
2 teaspoons cream of tartar
1 cup water
1 teaspoon oil
food coloring

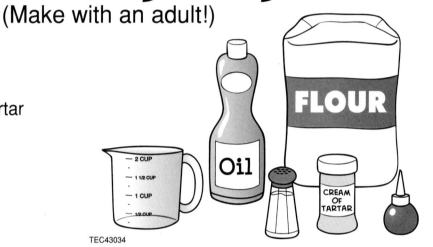

TEC43034

Cook the mixture over medium heat for two or three minutes.

Finally, store the dough in an airtight container until ready to use.

First, mix the dry ingredients.

After cooking, knead the dough until it is soft and smooth.

Next, stir in the water, oil, and food coloring.

Then place the mixture in a heavy pan.

The Critics Are Talking!

Critic _____
name

Date _____

Book Title: _____

Author: _____

This book is really _____! In this book,

_____
summary

_____

_____

_____

_____

_____

_____

_____

_____

TEC43035

Note to the teacher: Use with "Critics' Corner" on page 150.

Game Cards

Use with "Match It!" on page 154.

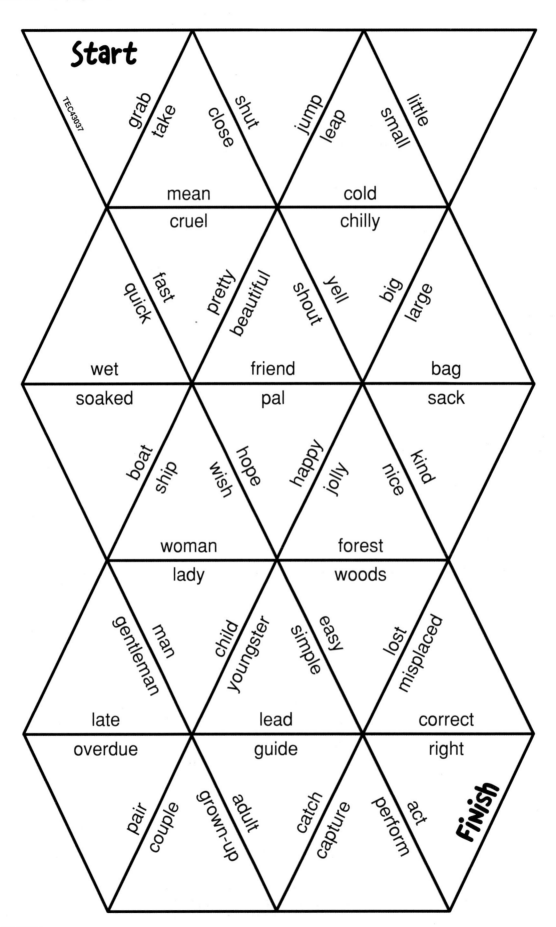

Hanging on Every Word

Read.

---

bat • hibernate

bat ('bat) An animal with a furry body and wings. A bat is a mammal, not a bird. (pp. 3–23)

echolocation (ˌe-kō-lō-'kā-shən) A way to find objects using sounds. Bats use echolocation to find food at night. (pp. 15–16)

flying fox ('flī-ŋ 'fäks) The largest kind of bat. (p. 5)

hibernate ('hī-bər-ˌnāt) To sleep through the winter. (p. 7)

24 Glossary

mammal • roost

mammal ('ma-məl) Warm-blooded animals that have fur, give birth to live young, and feed milk to their babies. People and bats are mammals. (p. 3)

migrate ('mī-ˌgrāt) To move from one place to another. Some bats migrate in winter to find food or to find a better place to hibernate. (p. 10)

nursery colony ('nərs-rē 'kä-lə-nē) A place where bat mothers give birth and raise their young. (pp.18–20)

roost ('rüst) A place where flying animals, such as bats, rest. (p. 17)

Glossary 25

Answer the questions.

1. On which glossary page is *migrate* found? _____

2. On which glossary page could *brown bat* be added? _____

3. Where in the book could you find out more about a *nursery colony*? _____

4. What is a *flying fox?* _____

5. What do you think is the topic of this book? _____

Bonus Box: Circle the words that could be added to glossary page 25.   cave   prey   wings   nocturnal

Ready to Roll

Write a word that begins with *mis-*, *pre-*, or *re-* to match each clue.

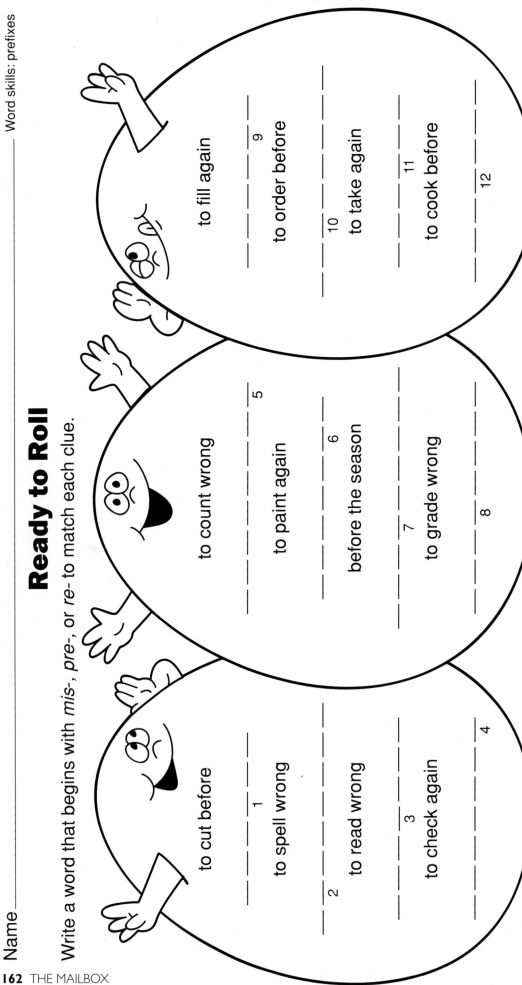

to cut before
_____ _____ _____ _____
1

to spell wrong
_____ _____ _____
2

to read wrong
_____ _____ _____
3

to check again
_____ _____ _____ _____
4

to count wrong
_____ _____ _____ _____
5

to paint again
_____ _____ _____
6

before the season
_____ _____ _____
7

to grade wrong
_____ _____ _____ _____
8

to fill again
_____ _____ _____
9

to order before
_____ _____ _____ _____
10

to take again
_____ _____ _____
11

to cook before
_____ _____ _____
12

What did one egg say to the other eggs?

To solve the riddle, write each letter from above on its matching numbered line or lines below.

" _____ _____ _____ , _____ _____ _____ _____ _____
  9   10   7   5   1   3   11   12   4

_____ _____ _____ _____ _____ _____ _____ !"
 2   6   8   10   5   1   3   11   12   4   2   6   8

SIMPLY SCIENCE

Simply Science

Scientist

Gavin   September 5, 2007

Scientist

Gavin   December 14, 2007

Scientists All Around

Understanding science as a human endeavor

This simple idea helps students recognize that people of all ages and backgrounds make contributions to science. First, have each student illustrate his vision of a scientist; then provide time for him to share his completed drawing with the rest of the class. Use the drawings to lead the class in a discussion of the many different kinds of scientists. Guide students to understand that scientists are all around us and include people such as a parent who cooks dinner or fixes a broken appliance, a doctor who examines a patient, and a farmer who grows crops as examples. Introduce some of the science topics that will be covered during the year and share with students the kinds of scientists who work in those fields. Repeat the activity at a later date to assess students' understanding of people's roles in science.

Dawn Maucieri, Signal Hill Elementary, Dix Hills, NY

Looking For Life
Living and nonliving things

To prepare, give each student pair a clipboard, a paper plate, and a piece of yarn equal in length to the plate's circumference. Have students bring their supplies and pencils to an outdoor space. Next, have one student in each pair lightly toss the plate; then have his partner mark the area by placing the yarn around the plate before removing it. On the center of the paper plate, have the partners work together to draw and label a detailed diagram of what they see inside the yarn circle. After returning to the room, have each student pair color the edge of the plate and glue a construction paper rectangle to the back so it resembles a magnifying glass. If desired, also have each student pair color its diagram. Lead the class in a discussion of the findings and write the results on two pieces of chart paper: one labeled "Living Things" and the other labeled "Nonliving Things." Post the charts and the magnifying glasses together as an easy reference.

Julie Hamilton, Renaissance Academy, Colorado Springs, CO

What a Machine!
Simple machines

After introducing the six kinds of simple machines, assign each small group a different machine. Have the students brainstorm and list examples of their machine and how it is used. Next, have the group label the top of a large sheet of construction paper as shown. Then have the students illustrate and label examples of their assigned machine on the page. Also have students tell how each example uses the assigned machine. Finally, bind the completed pages in a class book and place it at a science or reference center.

Julie Hamilton

Simply Science

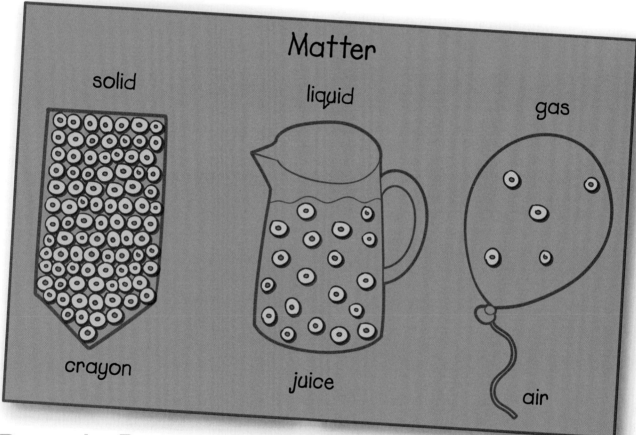

Matter

solid

liquid

gas

crayon

juice

air

Particle Pictures

States of matter

After discussing the main states of matter and their characteristics, give each student a large sheet of construction paper and have him label it with the states of matter as shown. Next, direct him to draw the outline of a picture to represent each state of matter. Then have him glue O-shaped cereal in each outline, placing the cereal pieces in the solid shape close together, in the liquid a little farther apart, and in the gas very far apart. Provide time for each student to share his examples; then post the completed projects around the room.

Debbie Ann Troha, Wrights Mill Road Elementary, Auburn, AL, and Theresa Bales, Kimball Elementary, Kimball, WV

Planets Without Pluto
Objects in space

Try this mnemonic device to help students remember the order of the eight planets!

Renee Parker, Selinsgrove Area Intermediate School, Selinsgrove, PA

My (Mercury)
Very (Venus)
Eager (Earth)
Mother (Mars)
Just (Jupiter)
Served (Saturn)
Us (Uranus)
Nachos (Neptune)

Matter in Action
States of matter

Get students moving toward a better understanding of the states of matter. After reviewing how the particles in different states of matter interact with each other, take students to a large open space, such as a multipurpose room. Divide the students into two groups and quietly share an example of a state of matter, such as the gas in a balloon, with one group. Have those students move around the space as though they are particles in that state while the other group watches. On your signal, have the students freeze; then call on a student in the other group to name the state of matter demonstrated. If desired, have him support his thinking by referencing the actions of the group. When the state has been correctly named, switch groups. Continue in this manner until each group has acted out each state of matter.

Brooke Beverly, Dudley Elementary, Dudley, MA

Sightseeing
Observing moon phases

Help students track the phases of the moon with this portable project. To make one, cut a sheet of 11" x 18" paper in half horizontally. Fold each resulting half into fourths. Apply glue to the first section of one of the strips and place the last section of the other strip on top of the glued area. Accordion-fold the sections to make a stack. Next, select a student to take the stack home and observe the moon for one week. As she observes the moon from the same position each night, she draws a picture of what she sees and records other important data as shown. At the end of the week she shares her findings with the class. Post the project as shown. Then, as each child completes a project of his own, add it to the display and use the resulting timeline of lunar events to jump-start a class discussion of the moon.

adapted from an idea by
Kathie Laug
Van Cortlandtville
   Elementary
Mohegan Lake, NY

Simply Science

Dolphin Diner

Jessica

COYOTE CAFÉ

Ty

Bear's Bistro

Forest Features

Ants on a Log $2.95

Gooey Grubs $3.25

Mouthwatering Mice $4.00

Local Stream Specialties

Fresh Fish $5.00

What Bears Eat
mice
fish
ants eggs, grubs
acorns, berries, nuts

May I Take Your Order?
Animal needs

For this simple project, have each student choose an animal and research its diet. Next, guide the child to invent a restaurant for the animal and brainstorm dishes that would meet the animal's needs. Then have the student create a menu for the restaurant that includes an appetizing listing of dishes the animal would surely order. Have each student share his work and then add it to a display titled "On the Menu: What Animals Eat."

Stephanie Fisher, Woodland Hills Elementary, Kingwood, TX

Learning the Terms
Properties of light

To help students understand that light passes differently through transparent, translucent, and opaque objects, give each pair of students a small square of each of the following: plastic wrap, waxed paper, and foil. Next, guide the partners to fold a sheet of paper in thirds, unfold it, and sign their names at the top of each section. Then have the pair glue one square over each set of signatures. Lead partners to describe their observations using the terms *transparent, translucent,* and *opaque* and then list examples from around the classroom. Invite each pair to share its list as you create a class chart.

Bernadette Todaro, Kadimah School
Amherst, NY

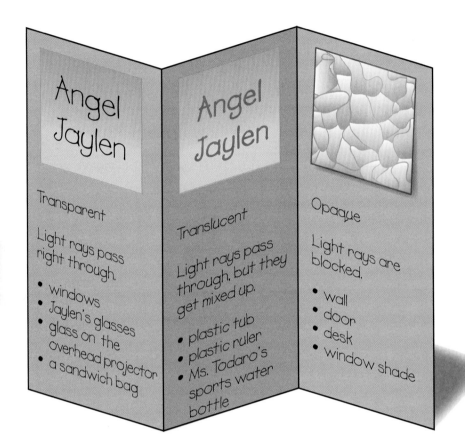

Angel
Jaylen

Transparent

Light rays pass
right through.
- windows
- Jaylen's glasses
- glass on the overhead projector
- a sandwich bag

Angel
Jaylen

Translucent

Light rays pass through, but they get mixed up.
- plastic tub
- plastic ruler
- Ms. Todaro's sports water bottle

Opaque

Light rays are blocked.
- wall
- door
- desk
- window shade

Hunters, Grazers, and Gatherers
Animal adaptations

Prepare for this instructional role-playing activity by putting a class supply of yellow, green, and brown construction paper squares in a bag. Next, take students outside or to the school gym and have each student draw a square from the bag. Explain that students with green squares will pretend to eat grass as grazers, students with brown squares will be gatherers pretending to gather nuts and take them to their dens, and students with yellow squares will portray hunters by sneaking up and trying to tap the grazers and gatherers. After several minutes, have students switch roles and repeat until each student has played every role. To follow up, guide each child to respond to the questions shown.

Bonnie Phillips, Olive Branch Elementary
Portsmouth, VA

What dangers do grazing and gathering animals face? *(A hunter might sneak up and catch them.)*

How can a grazing animal stay safe? *(It has to be watchful. It can freeze and try to blend in. It can try to run away.)*

How can an animal gathering its food stay safe? *(It has to be watchful. It can freeze and try to blend in. It can run back to its den.)*

What must a hunter do to catch its food? *(It has to be watchful. It has to sneak up on other animals. It has to be strong and move fast.)*

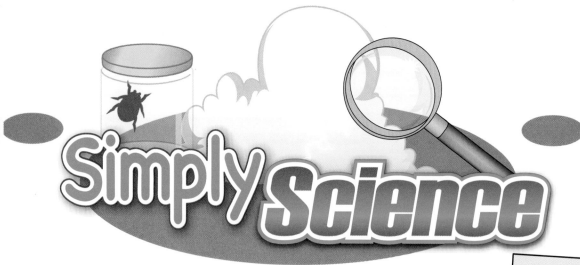

Simply Science

All About Seeds
Observing and describing seeds

To prepare, obtain two types of seeds and place several of each in a separate labeled bag. Place the bags and a supply of paper at a center. A student divides a sheet of paper into four sections. Then he illustrates and labels a seed in the first section of his paper. Next, he observes the seed and writes his observations in the second section. In the third section, he draws the plant the seed will grow into. In the last section, he records uses for the seed or plant. If time permits, have the student complete the activity with the other seed to make comparisons.

Carolyn Burant, St. John Vianney School, Brookfield, WI

corn seed	It is yellow. It is about 1 cm long. It is smooth. It is shaped like a raindrop.
Corn	We eat corn. Some animals eat corn seeds.

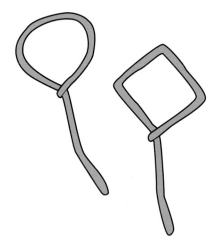

Bubbles, Bubbles!
Testing a hypothesis

For this simple experiment, use pipe cleaners to make two bubble wands: one round and one rectangular. Show students the wands and ask them to write a prediction about what shape the bubbles will be if each wand is used to blow bubbles. Next, have each student use pipe cleaners to make two bubble wands: one round and one another shape. Take students outside, provide bubble solution, and invite students to test their predictions. After the experiment, ask students to draw and write about the results and compare them to their predictions.

Kelli Higgins, P. L. Bolin Elementary School, East Peoria, IL

Be a Scientist
Writing about a science investigation

After completing an investigation, tell students to imagine that they are mad scientists who need to tell someone who is not in the class about an experiment they have completed. Have each student write to explain the purpose of the experiment, the materials used, the steps, and the results. Invite each student, in turn, to read aloud his completed work in his best mad scientist voice.

Joy West, Cross Creek Elementary, Thomasville, GA

> Jay
> The purpose of the investigation was to observe and describe different types of dirt. We used potting soil, soil from the playground, sand, a magnifying glass, and a recording sheet. First, we used the magnifying glass to observe each soil sample. Then we drew a picture of each type of soil. Then we compared the color and texture of each one. We concluded

What Are We Made Of?
Body systems

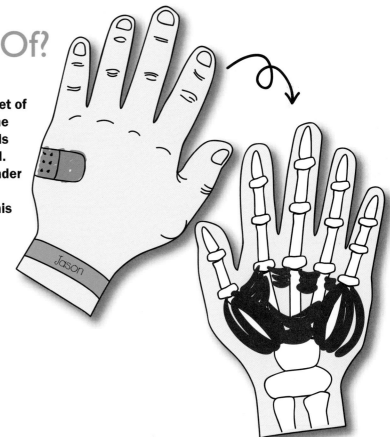

Have each child trace his hand on a sheet of construction paper and then cut out the tracing. Next, have the child add details to make the drawing look like his hand. Review with students that bones and muscles under their skin give their fingers shape and help them move. Then lead each child to feel the bones in his hand and fingers, flip his drawing, and draw his hand's skeleton. After that, guide each child to flex and relax his fingers, feel the muscles as they change, and then draw muscles where he feels them.

Kristin Priola, Hickory Day School, Hickory, NC

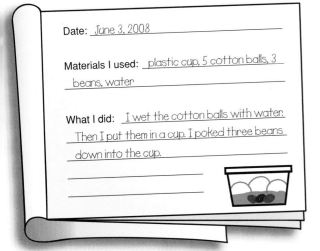

Watch Them Grow!
Plant life cycle

For this exploration, a child puts several wet cotton balls in a clear plastic cup and then pushes three beans down around the edges. Next, she cuts apart a copy of page 175. She stacks the materials page over the observation pages and then staples the pages behind the cover. After she personalizes the cover, she lists her materials and draws a picture of her cup and seeds on the first page. Each time the child observes her plant after that, she moistens the cotton balls if needed. Then she completes a new journal page by writing the date and her observations and drawing a picture. If she needs booklet pages for more entries, provide her with additional copies of the observation pages.

Kelli Higgins, P. L. Bolin Elementary, East Peoria, IL

How Warm Is It?

Make a Hypothesis

You will hold the candy inside a glove or mitten.
Which will you use? (circle one)

a glove   a mitten

What do you think will happen to the candy?

_____

_____

Test Your Hypothesis

1. Put on your glove or mitten.
2. Put the bag of candy inside your glove or mitten.
3. Hold the candy for 15 minutes.

Record Your Results

Describe the candy.

_____

_____

Make an X on the line to show how much the candy melted.

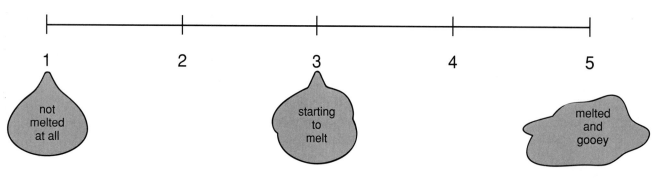

Draw a Conclusion

Why do you think the investigation turned out this way?

_____

_____

_____'s

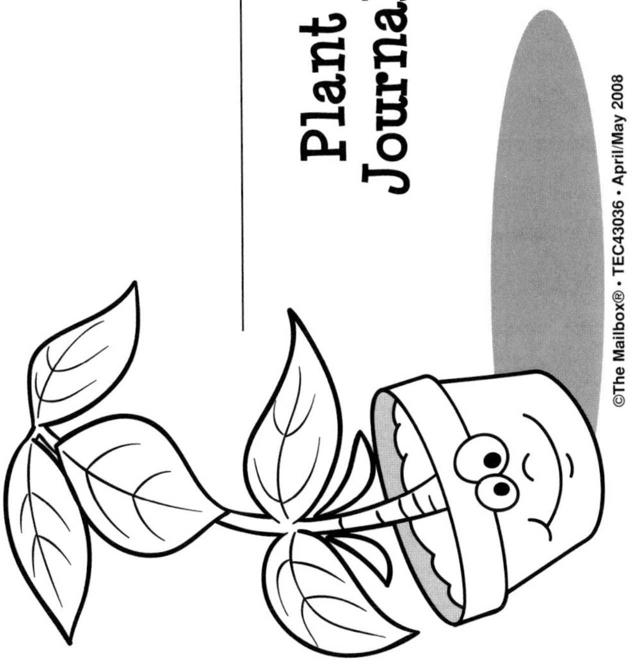

Plant
Journal

Date: _____

Materials I used: _____

What I did: _____

Date: _____

What I observe: _____

Date: _____

What I observe: _____

Name _____

Get to Work

Write the type of simple machine shown. Use the word bank.
Hint: Some words are used more than once.

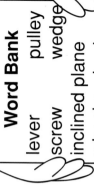

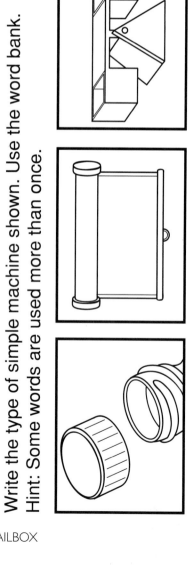

1 _ _ _ _ _

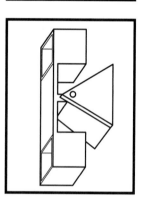

2 _ _ _ _ _

3 _ _ _ _ _

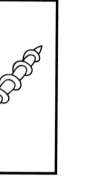

4 _ _ _ _ _

5 _ _ _ _ _

6 _ _ _ _ _

7 _ _ _ _ _

8 _ _ _ _ _

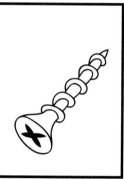

9 _ _ _ _ _

10 _ _ _ _ _

Why did the chicken cross the playground?

To find out, write each letter from above on the matching numbered lines below.

To __ __ __ to __ __ot
   6 10   7 8   7 8

__ __ __ __ __ __ __ __ "__ __ ."
7 8 3   1 2 4 5 9

©The Mailbox® • TEC43032 • Aug./Sept. 2007 • Key p. 311

WRITE ON!

Write On!

What can I write in my journal?

Stories
Realistic, fantasy, historical, scary, funny, exciting

Rhymes and Poems
About nature, friends, animals, family

Songs
New words to a tune I know well

Personal Ideas
How I feel, what my friends are like, what my weekend plans are

Letters
Thank-you, good news, invitation

Reyshawn

Little Red Writing Helper

Motivating to write

This simple tool provides students with ideas to jump-start their writing. Make a class supply of the bookmark patterns on page 190 on red paper and write each child's name on one. If desired, laminate the bookmarks for durability. Then have each child paper-clip his bookmark onto the first page of his writing journal. Review the different kinds of writing listed on the bookmark and explain to students that they can refer to the list when they need an idea for writing. Also tell students that as they complete an entry, they can move the bookmark to the next available page. Finding their place and finding a writing idea will be a snap each time they write.

adapted from an idea by Kelli Higgins, P. L. Bolin Elementary, East Peoria, IL

Ear to Ear
Peer editing

To help students identify changes that need to be made in their writing, try this partner activity. First, have student pairs place their chairs next to each other, but facing opposite directions. Next, have each student attach her rough draft to a clipboard before exchanging it with her partner. One student softly reads her partner's paper aloud, stopping when needed to clarify or ask questions before making suggestions for improving the paper. Then the other student repeats the process. Not only will this technique keep the noise level down, students will easily be able to hear how their own writing flows and how their stories progress.

Toni Brooks, Peachland Avenue Elementary, Newhall, CA

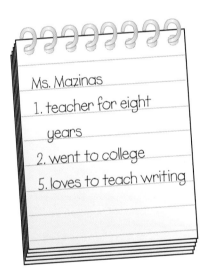

Ms. Mazinas
1. teacher for eight
   years
2. went to college
5. loves to teach writing

Junior Journalists
Expository writing

Here's a great way for students to get to know more about you and your job while practicing their expository-writing skills! To begin, share examples of personal interviews from local newspapers or the Internet and explain to students how it's a reporter's job to ask questions. Next, have students brainstorm a list of questions that they would like to ask about your job while you write the questions on a sheet of chart paper, numbering each one as you go. Then tell the class that they will act as reporters; if desired, give each child a small spiral notebook for taking notes. Call on one child at a time to ask a question from the class list. After you give your answer, students write the number of the question on their paper and jot down a few ideas related to the answer next to it. When each child has had a chance to ask a question, he reviews his notes and chooses the information he wants to share in his report. Then he writes a short report about you and your job. Post the completed reports on a display titled "Just the Facts About [your name]."

Lisa Mazinas, Bay Point Magnet Elementary, St. Petersburg, FL

Timely Prompts
Journal writing

Invite students to respond to one of the prompts below. Then have students share their responses with the class.

- Write a description of the perfect friend.
- Think about what makes you a good friend to others. Write an advertisement naming the qualities that make you a good friend.
- A good friend is fun to have around. A good friend can also make you feel better when you're down. Write a letter to a friend. Thank your friend for a time when he or she helped you when you were down.

Turkey Tim drove to the lake.
He drove so fast and didn't brake.
Then he tried with all his might
To stop the car at the red light!

by Drew

A Turkey's Tale

Writing couplets

Word families help students write silly poems about turkeys! Post several student-generated lists of word family words. Ask each student to refer to the lists to write pairs of sentences (couplets) that end with rhyming words. Direct him to include a different word family in each couplet. After the student proofreads his work, have him rewrite his poem on a copy of the turkey pattern on page 191. Then have each student cut out his turkey and color the details. Have each student read aloud his poem and invite his classmates to name the word families in each couplet.

Dr. Jennifer L. Kohnke, St. Charles, IL

Picture This!
Creative writing

No doubt students love to see pictures of their teachers, so why not use photographs as writing inspiration! Show students an interesting photo of yourself dressed in a costume, standing in a funny pose, or engaging in an activity such as riding a bike. Then ask each student to write a creative story about the photo, being sure to tell what happened before, during, and after the photo was taken. Display the photo and students' papers for all to see!

adapted from an idea by Ruthie Jamieson Titus, Union Elementary, Poland, OH

Ms. Titus wanted to know what it was like to be a clown. One day she went to clown school to learn everything there is to know about being a clown. After studying really hard, she graduated and got her costume. She was such a funny clown! She sang, danced, and did tricks. After a year of being a clown, she decided that she was tired of people laughing at her all day. So she gave back her costume and became my third-grade teacher!

by Ellen

C = Check for capital letters.
L = Look at spelling.
A = Ask whether each sentence makes sense.
P = Put punctuation marks where they are needed.

Clap and Edit
Editing

This editing acronym is so simple, students will want to give it a round of applause! Write on the board the acronym CLAP and its explanation as shown. Have each student trace his hand twice and cut out the tracings. Then direct him to copy the acronym on one of the hand cutouts. Show him how to glue the hands together to resemble a pair of hands clapping. Before a student turns in a piece of writing, tell him to "clap" and refer to his hand cutouts as an editing reminder.

Barclay Marcell, Roosevelt School, Park Ridge, IL

Timely Prompts
Journal writing

Have each student respond to a prompt below. Then have students share their responses with the class.

- Imagine you are a scarecrow. Describe what you look like and what you are wearing.
- Why do farmers need scarecrows? List three different reasons.
- A scarecrow's job—standing in the field all day—seems pretty boring. Pretend that a scarecrow could leave the field and go on a journey. Where would it go? What would it do?

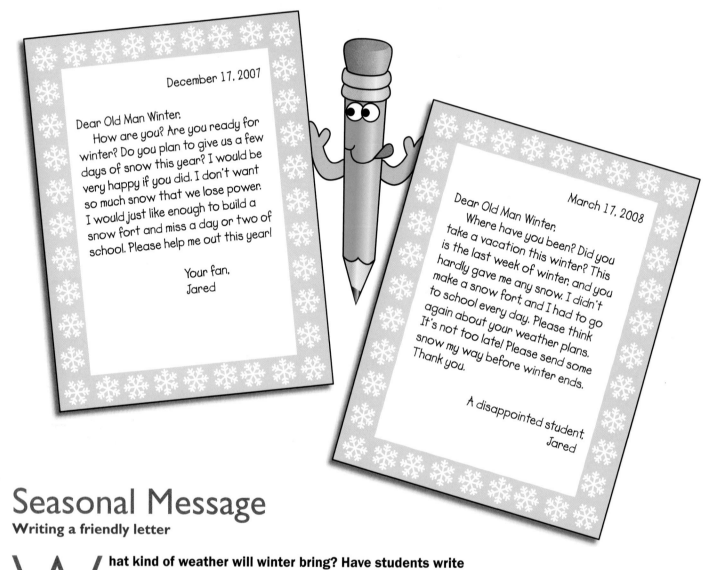

December 17, 2007

Dear Old Man Winter,
How are you? Are you ready for winter? Do you plan to give us a few days of snow this year? I would be very happy if you did. I don't want so much snow that we lose power. I would just like enough to build a snow fort and miss a day or two of school. Please help me out this year!

Your fan,
Jared

March 17, 2008

Dear Old Man Winter,
Where have you been? Did you take a vacation this winter? This is the last week of winter, and you hardly gave me any snow. I didn't make a snow fort, and I had to go to school every day. Please think again about your weather plans. It's not too late! Please send some snow my way before winter ends. Thank you.

A disappointed student,
Jared

Seasonal Message
Writing a friendly letter

What kind of weather will winter bring? Have students write a letter to Old Man Winter before the season starts to find out! First, have students generate a list of questions they would like answered about the upcoming winter season. Write the questions on the board. Next, have each student write a letter to Old Man Winter, including a few of the questions from the board and sharing his own wishes for winter weather. Provide time for students to share their letters aloud. Then, at the end of the winter season, have each student write another letter, this time telling Old Man Winter how he feels about the previous months' weather.

Christina Bainbridge, Centreville, MI

A Snowpal's Life
Planning a character

This prewriting activity brings snowpals to life! To prepare, have each student draw a snowpal on a sheet of paper or make a snowpal craft. Direct each student to imagine her creation is real as she completes a copy of the planning sheet on page 192. Guide the student to use her planning sheet to write a story with her snowpal as the main character. Bind the final drafts in a class book and place it at your reading center.

Laura Johnson, South Decatur Elementary, Greensburg, IN

Wacky Weather
Descriptive writing

Give each group of three students a large sheet of paper and have one student divide the paper into three equal sections. Direct each child to draw a cloud at the top of a different section. Next, have each group member cut out an interesting picture from a magazine or catalog and glue it under his cloud. Then have each student write a descriptive paragraph about a day of wacky weather, using the order of the pictures to sequence the weather events. Display the completed projects with the corresponding paragraphs.

Joslyn Cleary Matelski, Concord Academy Boyne, Boyne City, MI

Timely Prompts
Journal writing

- When you think of winter, what food or drink comes to mind? Describe it.
- How do you think your favorite holiday food is prepared? Write a list of steps to explain. Use words like *first, next, then,* and *finally* to keep your list in order.
- What food is missing from your family's holiday menu? Write a paragraph to explain why you think this food would make a holiday meal even better.

Write On!

Name **Ryan** _____ Expository Writing

How to Be a Professional **Chili Dog Eater**

Prompt: You are the expert! Teach a friend to become an expert like you.

Plan

What is the first thing an expert does?

pick a very juicy hot dog

What is the next thing an expert does?

put the hot dog on a bun

What is another thing an expert does?

add 2 or 3 spoonfuls of chili to make it taste better

What is the last thing an expert does?

roll the hot dog to spread the chili all over the bun

Write: Write a paragraph telling your friend how to be a professional.

Being an expert chili dog eater takes years to learn. The first thing to do before eating a chili dog is to pick the juiciest hot dog from the pot. Next, put it in a soft fresh bun. Then pour two or three spoonfuls of hot chili on top of the dog. The last trick is to roll the hot dog inside the bun. This makes the chili spread all over the bun and keeps it from falling off. Now that's the way to eat a chili dog!

Be a Professional

Writing a paragraph

Use your students' expertise to jump-start their expository writing. First, have students brainstorm a range of everyday things they do well, such as tying shoes, making ice cream sundaes, raking leaves, or washing dishes. Next, direct each student to complete a copy of the organizer on page 193 and then use it to write a brief paragraph. After he revises his writing, have the student write the final paragraph on an index card, drawing a picture of himself as a professional on the back of the card and writing the title "How to Be a Professional [__]." Provide time for each student to share his work. Then, bind the cards together and place the collection in the classroom library.

Anna Annunziata, East Orange, NJ

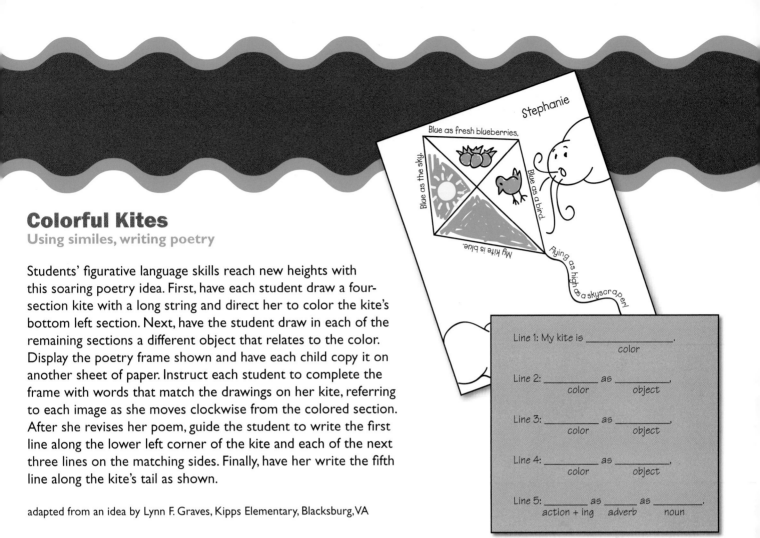

Colorful Kites
Using similes, writing poetry

Students' figurative language skills reach new heights with this soaring poetry idea. First, have each student draw a four-section kite with a long string and direct her to color the kite's bottom left section. Next, have the student draw in each of the remaining sections a different object that relates to the color. Display the poetry frame shown and have each child copy it on another sheet of paper. Instruct each student to complete the frame with words that match the drawings on her kite, referring to each image as she moves clockwise from the colored section. After she revises her poem, guide the student to write the first line along the lower left corner of the kite and each of the next three lines on the matching sides. Finally, have her write the fifth line along the kite's tail as shown.

adapted from an idea by Lynn F. Graves, Kipps Elementary, Blacksburg, VA

Line 1: My kite is _____.
             color

Line 2: _____ as _____,
             color   object

Line 3: _____ as _____.
             color   object

Line 4: _____ as _____,
             color   object

Line 5: _____ as _____ as _____.
        action + ing   adverb   noun

Story Starters
Writing narratives

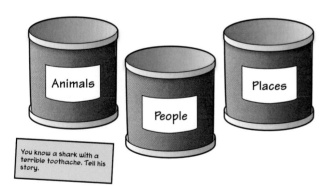

To inspire students to write, label three empty containers as shown. Cut out the prompt cards from several copies of page 194, place each card in the corresponding can, and put the cans at a writing center. If a student has difficulty starting a story, he pulls a strip from one of the cans and has an instant idea right at his fingertips!

Marciava Harris, Flora Macdonald Academy, Red Springs, NC

Timely Prompts
Journal writing

- Imagine following a rainbow. Where does it take you? What do you find at the end? Write about the events that take place.
- What are your three favorite colors of the rainbow? Explain.
- Pretend that the water droplets in a rainbow can talk. What would they say to each other? Write about the conversation that takes place between two water droplets. Be sure to use correct punctuation, including quotation marks.

Write On!

Soccer
Running hard
Kicking to teammates
Cheering for each other
Scoring goals
The thrill of victory!

Spring Into Action!
Writing poetry

Lead students to brainstorm a list of spring activities. Then guide each child to choose one activity as the topic of his poem. Next, have the child write a list of action verbs that relate to his topic. To write his poem, direct the child to write his topic on the first line of his paper. On each of the next four lines, have the child refer to his verb list as he writes a phrase that begins with an action verb and tells about his activity. On the last line, have him wrap up his poem by writing an exclamatory statement about his topic. Have the child illustrate his work; then bind the completed poems into a book and display it in the class library.

Julie Hays, Alcoa Elementary, Alcoa, TN

Everybody Needs One
Persuasive writing

Students set the stage for this cooperative activity by answering the question, "What could this be?" Give each small group of students an unusual or unfamiliar object, such as a kitchen or garden gadget. Then have the group make a three-column chart and label each column as shown. Direct the group to investigate its object and work together to complete each column of the chart. Next, have each group member use the completed chart as a resource as she writes a paragraph that describes the possible benefits of the object and convinces others that they need it. Invite each child to read aloud her final paragraph.

Heidi Harrell, Hackberry Elementary, Frisco, TX

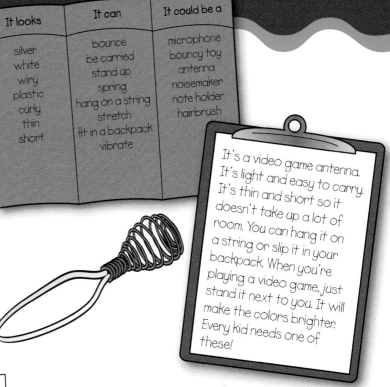

It looks	It can	It could be a
silver	bounce	microphone
white	be carried	bouncy toy
wiry	stand up	antenna
plastic	spring	noisemaker
curly	hang on a string	note holder
thin	stretch	hairbrush
short	fit in a backpack	
	vibrate	

It's a video game antenna. It's light and easy to carry. It's thin and short so it doesn't take up a lot of room. You can hang it on a string or slip it in your backpack. When you're playing a video game, just stand it next to you. It will make the colors brighter. Every kid needs one of these!

From "First" to "Finally"
Using transition words

This orderly graphic organizer provides students with words and phrases that keep their writing flowing smoothly. When a child is ready to create a plan for a narrative piece, give her a copy of page 195. On the numbered lines, guide the child to write the events of her story in the order in which they happen. Next, have her cut apart the transition cards at the bottom of the page, read each one, and choose an appropriate one to glue in each box. When she is ready to write, direct the student to work from her prepared organizer.

Amy Barsanti, Pines Elementary School, Plymouth, NC

Name **Trisha**   Transition words
From "First" to "Finally"

1. [First] We wanted a cat.
2. [In a little while] We went to the pet store.
3. [Then] We went to the animal shelter.
4. [Soon] We looked at all the cats.
5. [Before long] We found our new furry friend, Lily!

Timely Prompts
Journal writing

- Pretend that you are an earthworm. Describe what you do during the day.
- If you were an earthworm, would you rather live in someone's yard or in the forest? Explain your choice.
- Write a letter to an earthworm, telling how you think it helps your community.

Write On!

People pick plump pastel peach.

My buddy bought bumpy bubble gum.

Both boys beg for basic blueberry.

Choosy chums chew chocolate chip.

My parents prefer pure pistachio.

Cool, Creamy Word Collections

Alliteration

Brainstorm with students a variety of ice cream flavors; then assign one flavor to each student pair. Each pair makes a list of alliterative words for its assigned flavor, referring to a dictionary as necessary. Then the students choose words from their list to use in an alliterative sentence. Next, one student cuts an ice cream scoop from construction paper scraps; then his partner copies the pair's edited sentence onto the scoop. The pair works together to decorate the scoop and then adds it to a display with a large ice cream bowl cutout.

Laura Wagner, Bais Menachem Hebrew Academy, Austin, TX

Five-Pointed Prompt
Letter writing

This simple star is a shining reminder of the parts of a friendly letter! Make a class supply of the star pattern from page 196 on yellow paper and give one to each student. Direct each student to cut out her star and encourage her to refer to it each time she writes a friendly letter to ensure that she includes each part. After writing a letter, have the student clip the star inside her writing journal so it will be handy for her next letter-writing assignment.

Sue Fleischmann, Catholic East Elementary, Milwaukee, WI

1. Date
2. Salutation
3. Body
4. Closing
5. Signature

A Passport to Review
Parts of speech

On the board, write a list of the parts of speech students have studied during the year. Give each child copies of the passport pages from the bottom of page 196 so she has one page for each item on the list. Have her cut apart the pages, stack them, and staple them inside a folded 4½" x 8" construction paper cover. A child titles and personalizes the cover, and then copies a different item from the list on each of her pages. Then, for each page, she completes the information, draws a stamp in the box, and signs the page.

Kristen Priola, Hickory Day School, Hickory, NC

Topic: __Pronouns__
I learned __that pronouns take the place of nouns.__

Some examples are __he, she, it, they, we, us, you and I.__

Here are some tips that will help me: __Use a pronoun instead of repeating the noun over and over.__

Signature __Rachael__

Timely Prompts
Journal writing

- Imagine you are going on a picnic. What will you need to pack?
- Would you rather go on a picnic in the mountains or at the beach? Explain your choice.
- Pretend you are a picnic basket. Write a story about the best picnic you have ever been taken to.

Bookmark Patterns

Use with "Little Red Writing Helper" on page 178.

What can I write in my journal?

Stories
Realistic, fantasy, historical, scary, funny, exciting

Rhymes and Poems
About nature, friends, animals, family

Songs
New words to a tune I know well

Personal Ideas
How I feel, what my friends are like, what my weekend plans are

Letters
Thank-you, good news, invitation

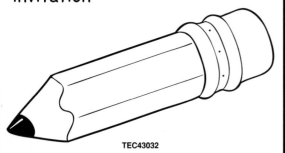

TEC43032

What can I write in my journal?

Stories
Realistic, fantasy, historical, scary, funny, exciting

Rhymes and Poems
About nature, friends, animals, family

Songs
New words to a tune I know well

Personal Ideas
How I feel, what my friends are like, what my weekend plans are

Letters
Thank-you, good news, invitation

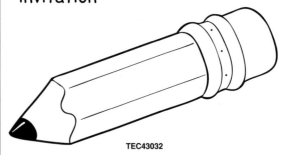

TEC43032

Turkey Pattern

Use with "A Turkey's Tale" on page 180.

TEC43033

Introducing...

My snowpal's name: _____

My snowpal's age: _____

Names of my snowpal's family members:

_____

_____

My snowpal's best friends:

_____

_____

My snowpal is

brave	fun	helpful	kind
shy	silly	smart	strong

Other words to describe my snowpal: _____

_____

My snowpal likes to

snowboard	ski	build snow forts
ice skate	fish with penguins	play with polar bears

Other things my snowpal likes to do: _____

_____

©The Mailbox® • TEC43034 • Dec./Jan. 2007–8

How to Be a Professional _____

Prompt: You are the expert! Teach a friend to become an expert like you.

Plan

World's Best Chef

What is the first thing an expert does?

What is the next thing an expert does?

What is another thing an expert does?

What is the last thing an expert does?

Write: Write a paragraph telling your friend how to be a professional.

Prompt Cards

Use with "Story Starters" on page 185.

Write a story titled "My Week on an Alien Spaceship." TEC43035	You go on an undersea adventure. Tell about it. TEC43035	Write about the interesting events from a class trip. TEC43035
Write a story titled "The Day I Ran the School." TEC43035	Tell about a visit to a new place. TEC43035	Where is your favorite place to be in school? Use this place as a setting in a story. TEC43035
Tell about a special day with someone in your family. TEC43035	Write about a time when someone in your family helped you solve a problem. TEC43035	You wake up to find that you have become your teacher. What happens? TEC43035
You and your friends find a million dollars. What do you do? TEC43035	Write a story titled "How I Met My Best Friend." TEC43035	You are a member of a winning team. Write a story about a big game. TEC43035
You are an animal. Describe your day. TEC43035	Write a story about two different animals that are friends. TEC43035	Write a story titled "Bear's Big Surprise." TEC43035
You know a shark with a terrible toothache. Tell his story. TEC43035	Write a story titled "Why the Hyena Can't Stop Laughing." TEC43035	Write a story about your first day with a new pet. TEC43035

©The Mailbox® • TEC43035 • Feb./Mar. 2008

Transition words

From "First" to "Finally"

1. ▬▬▬▬▬▬▬▬▬▬▬▬▬▬▬▬▬▬

_____

2. ▬▬▬▬▬▬▬▬▬▬▬▬▬▬▬▬▬▬

_____

3. ▬▬▬▬▬▬▬▬▬▬▬▬▬▬▬▬▬▬

_____

4. ▬▬▬▬▬▬▬▬▬▬▬▬▬▬▬▬▬▬

_____

5. ▬▬▬▬▬▬▬▬▬▬▬▬▬▬▬▬▬▬

_____

©The Mailbox® • TEC43036 • April/May 2008

Next	Suddenly	In a little while
Later	Then	First
Soon	Finally	Before long
Afterward	When that happened	After

Note to the teacher: Use with "From 'First' to 'Finally'" on page 187.

THE MAILBOX **195**

Star Pattern
Use with "Five-Pointed Prompt" on page 189.

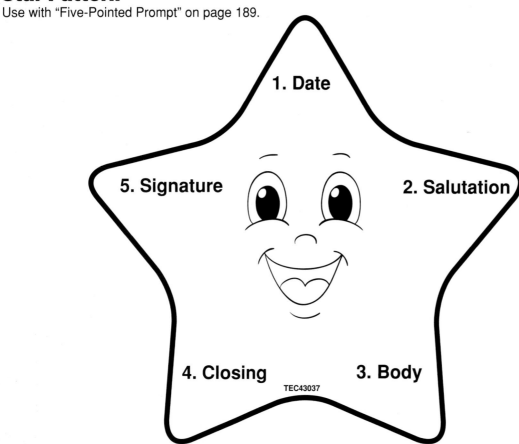

1. Date

5. Signature

2. Salutation

4. Closing

3. Body

TEC43037

Passport Pages
Use with "A Passport to Review" on page 189.

Topic: _____	Topic: _____
I learned _____	I learned _____

Some examples are

Here are some tips that will help me:

☐ Signature _____

Some examples are

Here are some tips that will help me:

☐ Signature _____

LANGUAGE ARTS UNITS

Filling Up on
Phonics Games

WELCOME TO FILL 'N GO!

	ft		
gr	ay		eed
	st	ake	spr
	ore		

Team 1	Team 2	Team 3
greed spray	flake	store

FILL 'N GO

UNDERCOVER SOUNDS
Using blends and word families

To prepare this whole-class game, copy the grid on page 200 onto an overhead transparency. Program each of eight squares with a different blend and each of the other eight squares with a different word family that makes a word with at least one of the chosen blends. Cover each grid square with a small sticky note and place the transparency on the overhead.

To play, divide the class into teams and call on a team to choose two grid squares. Reveal the word parts on two those squares. If the team uses the two parts to make a word, shade in each corresponding gas gauge (to show that the word part cannot be reused) and write the word under the team's name on the board. If the two parts do not make a word, re-cover the spaces with the sticky notes. Continue until all spaces are revealed or no more words can be made. The team with the most words listed wins. If desired, wipe the shading from the gas gauges, re-cover the squares, and challenge students to use the grid to make words not already listed on the board.

Molly Alvine, Van Allen Elementary, Mount Pleasant, IA

TALKING NONSENSE
Identifying vowel patterns in nonsense words

This game for two is a variation on Go Fish! Write on a separate index card each of the nonsense words shown, underlining the vowel sound as shown. Then make a second set of cards and shuffle the two sets together. To play, Player 1 deals five cards to both players and stacks the remaining cards facedown. Each player locates any matching cards in his hand and places them on the workspace. Next, Player 2 asks for a card that matches one in her hand, using the format "Do you have the [underlined sound] pattern as in [word]?" If Player 1 has the card, he gives it to Player 2. If not, Player 1 responds with "You're talking nonsense" and Player 2 draws a card from the pile. Players take turns in this manner until one player has matched all his cards.

Elizabeth Lilley, Parkway Elementary, Radcliff, KY

Do you have the *ar* pattern as in *zarn*?

z<u>ar</u>n   w<u>oo</u>t
bl<u>ay</u>   fl<u>ai</u>n
br<u>y</u>   f<u>ea</u>m
p<u>oa</u>t   z<u>ee</u>p
fl<u>oy</u>   tr<u>oi</u>l
pl<u>ir</u>d   j<u>ou</u>t

TIC-TAC-TOE TIMES FOUR
Writing blends, digraphs, and vowel pairs

This fun game has the whole class working in pairs. To prepare, have each duo fold a sheet of construction paper in fourths, unfold it, and then draw a tic-tac-toe grid in each section. Also give each pair a mini white-board and a dry-erase marker. To play, call out the sound of a blend, digraph, or vowel combination in a whole word, using an instruction such as "Show the /er/ sound in *teacher*." Have Player 1 write the letters that make the sound in that word on the mini whiteboard; then announce the correct answer. Have Player 2 check the answer for correctness. If the answer is correct, Player 1 puts an X on the first grid. If incorrect, he does not make a mark. Player 2 then takes a turn in a similar manner, drawing an O on the grid if she is correct, and the game continues until tic-tac-toe is achieved or all the spaces on the grid are filled and the game ends in a tie. When one game has ended, the student pair starts a new game on another grid. Continue play in this manner until a duo completes all four grids or time is called.

Adrienne Ambrose, Ormond Beach Elementary, Ormond Beach, FL

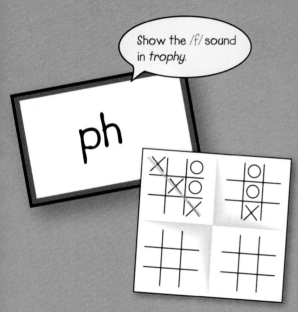

Show the /f/ sound in *trophy*.

ph

RIGHT ON TRACK
Identifying rhymes, words with long vowels, and blends

Give each student pair a coin and two different-colored linking cubes. Also give each duo a copy of page 201 and have one partner cut apart the answer keys. Next, have each player choose a word bank and write her name on the corresponding line. Each player then takes the answer key for her partner's word bank and turns it facedown. To play, Player 1 flips the coin and then moves her cube one space for heads or two spaces for tails. She names the word from her word bank that matches the clue. Player 2 turns over the answer key and checks her work. If Player 1 is correct, she crosses the word off of her list. If incorrect, she returns to the space where she began her turn. Play continues in this manner until one player reaches the finish.

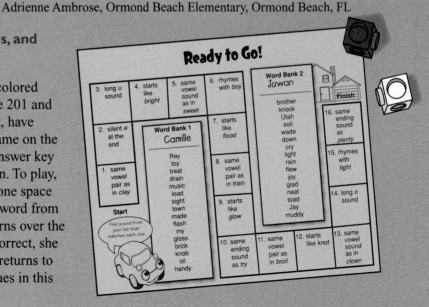

Ready to Go!

3. long *u* sound
4. starts like *bright*
5. same vowel sound as in *sweet*
6. rhymes with *boy*

Word Bank 2
Juwan

brother
knock
Utah
soil
wade
down
cry
light
rain
flew
joy
glad
neat
toad
Jay
muddy

Finish

2. silent *e* at the end

Word Bank 1
Camille

Ray
toy
treat
drain
music
load
sight
town
made
flash
my
gloss
brick
knob
oil
handy

7. starts like *flood*

8. same vowel pair as in *train*

9. starts like *glow*

16. same ending sound as *plenty*

15. rhymes with *tight*

14. long *o* sound

Start

Find a word from your list that matches each clue.

10. same ending sound as *try*

11. same vowel pair as in *broil*

12. starts like *knot*

13. same vowel sound as in *clown*

	A	B	C	D
1				
2				
3				
4				

©The Mailbox® • TEC43032 • Aug./Sept. 2007

Ready to Go!

Finish

16. same ending sound as *plenty*	
15. rhymes with *tight*	
14. long *o* sound	
13. same vowel sound as in *clown*	

Word Bank 2

brother
knock
Utah
soil
wade
down
cry
light
rain
flew
joy
glad
neat
toad
Jay
muddy

12. starts like *knot*	
11. same vowel pair as in *broil*	

6. rhymes with *boy*
7. starts like *flood*
8. same vowel pair as in *train*
9. starts like *glow*
10. same ending sound as *try*

5. same vowel sound as in *sweet*
4. starts like *bright*
3. long *u* sound
2. silent *e* at the end
1. same vowel pair as in *clay*

Start

Word Bank 1

Ray
toy
treat
drain
music
load
sight
town
made
flash
my
gloss
brick
knob
oil
handy

Find a word from your list that matches each clue.

©The Mailbox® · TEC43032 · Aug./Sept. 2007

Note to the teacher: Use with "Right on Track" on page 199.

Tackling Texts With
Reading Strategies

Dr. Jennifer L. Kohnke, St. Charles, IL

STAYING IN BOUNDS
Generating questions and answers from expository texts

Have each student label the top of a sheet of paper with the title of an expository text; then have him preview the text. Next, have him place four sticky notes on his paper so that the sticky portions are on the bottom. Then guide the student to use text features—such as titles, boldfaced words, and diagrams—to write one text-related question on each sticky note. After he reads the story, have him refer back to the text to answer his questions. Direct him to write the page number where the answer can be found and his response on the back of each sticky note as shown. Then encourage the student to refer to his work when discussing the book with a small group.

MAKING GAINS
Making predictions, monitoring comprehension

To start, preview a fictional story and then have each child make and record a prediction on a copy of page 204. After reading the story, have the student go back to the organizer and mark whether her prediction was accurate or not. Then have the child follow the arrow to the corresponding box to record evidence from the story that supports her accurate prediction or to tell what happened instead. As an alternative, allow the student to read the story up to a designated page. Then have the student complete the organizer using her knowledge of the story's events to make a prediction about what happens next.

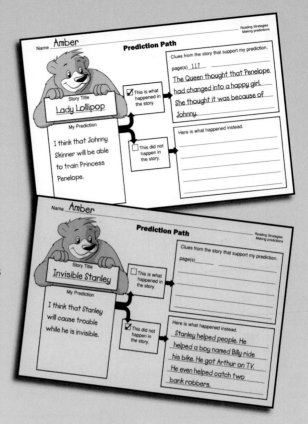

FLAG IT!
Identifying problem and solution

Before reading, remind students that story characters often make many attempts to solve their problems before finding solutions or reaching their goals. Provide each student with a supply of small sticky notes and have him read a fictional story. When he finds the problem of the story, have him label a sticky note with a *P* and place the note on that page. Next, he writes an *A* on a sticky note for each attempt the character or characters makes to solve the problem and places each sticky note on the corresponding page. Then he places one last sticky note, labeled with an *S*, on the page that shows the solution. When he has finished reading the book, he refers to the flagged pages to complete a copy of page 205.

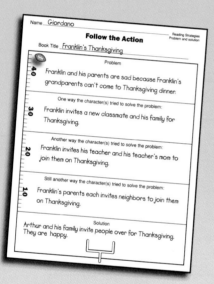

TEAMWORK
Generating questions

To begin this paired-reading activity, make a class supply and one transparency of a science or social studies textbook page. Read the text aloud as students read along silently. Next, display the transparency and reread the first paragraph aloud. As you read, model how to respond to the text by asking questions; then paraphrase your questions near the text as shown. As you continue to read, underline any answers you find to your questions. Pair students and direct each pair to reread the remainder of the passage, recording questions about the text as modeled. Provide time for students to share their questions and whether the answers were found in the passage. Encourage students to repeat this strategy when working on reproducible reading passages.

Soil

People cannot live without air or water. It would be hard for people to live without soil too. Why? Soil contains important minerals that people and other living things need.

Prediction Path

Story Title

My Prediction

☐ This is what happened in the story.

☐ This did not happen in the story.

Clues from the story that support my prediction.

page(s) _____

Here is what happened instead.

©The Mailbox® • TEC43033 • Oct./Nov. 2007

Note to the teacher: Use with "Making Gains" on page 203.

Name_____

Follow the Action

Book Title _____

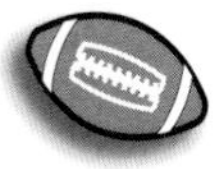

Problem

40

One way the character(s) tried to solve the problem:

30

Another way the character(s) tried to solve the problem:

20

Still another way the character(s) tried to solve the problem:

10

Solution

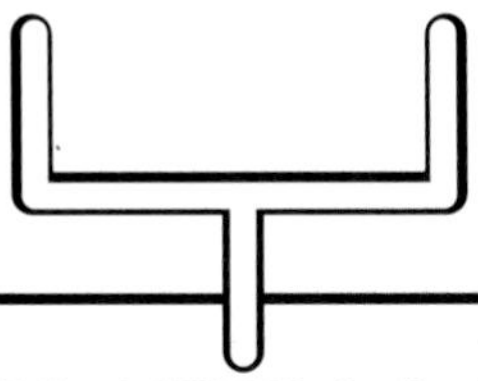

On the Lookout for
Main Idea and Details

Dr. Jennifer L. Kohnke, St. Charles, IL

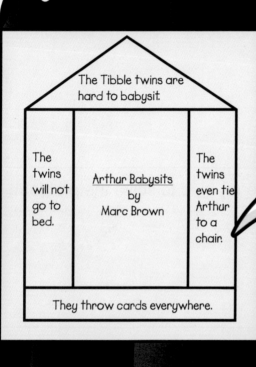

The Tibble twins are hard to babysit.

The twins will not go to bed.

Arthur Babysits
by
Marc Brown

The twins even tie Arthur to a chair.

They throw cards everywhere.

BUILDING UNDERSTANDING
Fiction and nonfiction texts

Compare main idea and details to a roof being supported by a frame. After reading a story, draw an obtuse triangle on the board. Guide students to determine the main idea, or what the story is mostly about, and write a sentence about it inside the triangle. Next, draw four rectangles under the triangle as shown. Write the book's title and author's name in the center rectangle. Then ask students to consider what proof, or supporting details, from the story makes the main idea true. Record each idea in a rectangle; then lead students to understand that the details support the main idea of the story the way the frame of a house supports a roof. Encourage students to recreate the organizer on a sheet of paper after reading another story.

Maria Mastee, Trautmann Elementary, Laredo, TX

TYING IT TOGETHER
Nonfiction texts

When a student completes a nonfiction reading, direct him to record its main idea on a colored index card. Next, have him write supporting details with each detail on a different index card. Then have the student punch a hole on the right side of the main idea card and holes on both sides of the detail cards, placing the holes in the same location on each card. Starting with the main idea and first supporting detail card, have the student connect the cards by feeding a piece of yarn through each hole and tying the ends together. If desired, post the completed projects as a reminder that the main idea and supporting details are tied together.

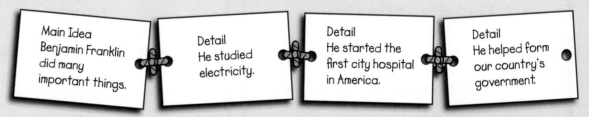

Main Idea
Benjamin Franklin did many important things.

Detail
He studied electricity.

Detail
He started the first city hospital in America.

Detail
He helped form our country's government.

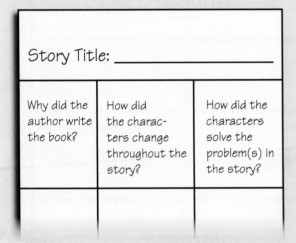

Story Title: _____

Why did the author write the book?	How did the characters change throughout the story?	How did the characters solve the problem(s) in the story?

DIGGING DEEPER
Fiction texts

After reading a fictional story aloud, post a piece of bulletin board paper labeled as shown. Guide students to provide information for each section and record the answers on the paper. Through the discussion of the book and completing the chart, lead students to name the main idea and details of the story.

FIND THREE
Categorizing

Have each child cut apart the cards from a copy of page 208. Then have the student arrange each set of cards on her workspace so the topic card is at the top and the three corresponding detail cards are arranged below it. Have her place the distracter cards aside. Provide time for each student to compare answers with a partner and explain why each distracter card doesn't belong with the other cards in the group. If desired, follow up the activity by having each child complete a copy of page 209.

adapted from an idea by Deborah Carlberg, Stewartsville Elementary Goodview, VA

storms

tornado

blizzard

thunderstorm

cloud

Category Cards

Use with "Find Three" on page 207.

holidays
TEC43034

New Year's Day
TEC43034

Valentine's Day
TEC43034

Thanksgiving
TEC43034

December
TEC43034

school subjects
TEC43034

reading
TEC43034

homework
TEC43034

writing
TEC43034

math
TEC43034

storms
TEC43034

tornado
TEC43034

blizzard
TEC43034

cloud
TEC43034

thunderstorm
TEC43034

parts of a computer
TEC43034

Internet
TEC43034

monitor
TEC43034

mouse
TEC43034

keyboard
TEC43034

Name_____

Fox on Rocks

Circle the main idea.
Underline each supporting detail.
Cross out the sentence that does not belong.

1. Farley Fox loves to watch other animals play. He laughs at the bear cubs. He smiles at the rabbits. Farley giggles when he sees the birds. He even looks at the mountains and the trees.

2. Farley's friend Faye is great at sports. Faye likes to draw pictures. She plays soccer. She also plays football. Faye was even the MVP of her swim team!

3. Farley Fox has lived in dens in many states. His first den was in California. Then he moved to a den in New Mexico. His brother lives in Canada. Now Farley lives in a den in Utah.

Building Vocabulary Skills

IN THE HOT SEAT
Whole class

To review vocabulary words and their meanings, place a chair in front of the board and designate it as "the hot seat." Select a student to sit in the hot seat facing the rest of the class. Write a vocabulary word on the board, ensuring that the child in the hot seat cannot see it. Then announce the meaning of the featured word. Invite the child in the hot seat to choose three student volunteers to, in turn, each give him a clue about the featured word. After hearing the last child's clue, ask the student in the hot seat to guess the word. If he is correct, have him choose a different child to sit in the hot seat and then repeat the process with a new word. If he is incorrect, offer more clues until he is able to name the word.

Suzanna White, Sycamore Elementary, Cookeville, TN

It is a compound word.

landform

STUCK ON WORDS
Partners

Have each child label several sticky notes, each with a different vocabulary word. Direct each student to trace around a sticky note on a blank sheet of paper to make a square for each vocabulary word. Have her look up each word in a dictionary or glossary and write its definition in a square. Next, invite students to trade papers with a partner. Have each child attach her sticky notes to the corresponding squares on her partner's paper. Then have the twosome trade papers again to check each other's work. The student with the higher number of correct matches wins.

Carrie Osterman, Sally K. Ride Elementary, The Woodlands, TX

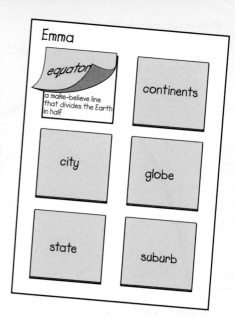

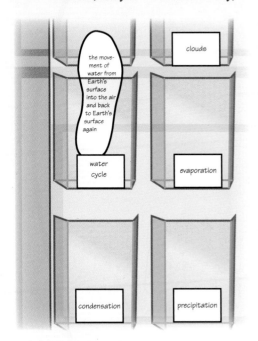

SORTING SHOES
Individual center

To prepare, place a card labeled with a different vocabulary word in each pocket of a plastic shoe organizer. For each word, use one of the patterns on page 212 to make a shoeprint cutout labeled with a corresponding definition. Place the shoe organizer and cutouts at a center. A child visits the center and sorts each shoeprint into the appropriate pocket.

Ashley Lovette, Warsaw Elementary, Warsaw, NC

MATCHING CRITTERS
Whole class

This versatile idea can be used with a variety of vocabulary skills. Copy the animal cards on page 213 to make a class supply. (If you have an odd number of students, copy a card for yourself and plan to participate in this activity.) Program matching pairs of animals with words that correspond with a chosen skill, such as *strong* and *weak* for antonyms or *quick* and *speedy* for synonyms. Cut apart and distribute the cards. Announce the skill; then ask a student volunteer to read the word on his card aloud. Have the child with the corresponding card stand and read her word aloud. Depending on the animal pictured on their card set, guide the children to "fly," "hop," or "swim" to each other to match their cards. Continue in this manner until each pair has been matched.

April Lewis, Warsaw Elementary
Warsaw, NC

Shoeprint Patterns
Use with "Sorting Shoes" on page 211.

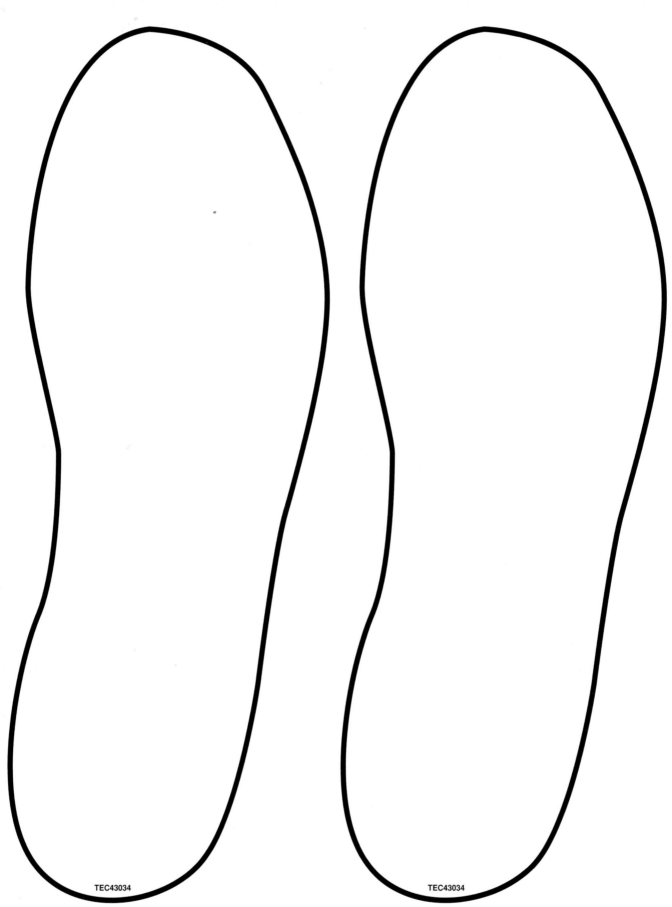

TEC43034

TEC43034

TEC43034

TEC43034

TEC43034

TEC43034

TEC43034

TEC43034

TEC43034

TEC43034

TEC43034

TEC43034

TEC43034

TEC43034

Serving Up Ideas for
Reading Fluency

does it cost

was the best

have an idea

FUN WITH PHRASES
Small group

This easy-to-prepare game uses common phrases to increase students' fluency. Cut out the cards from a copy of page 216, glue each one to a wide craft stick, and place the sticks word-side down in a cup. To play, each child, in turn, selects a stick from the cup. He reads the phrase on the stick aloud, rereading the phrase if needed to achieve accuracy and smoothness. Then he places the stick in a discard pile. If a child selects a "Blurb!" card, he reads each phrase in the discard pile before returning the sticks to the cup. Play continues until time is called.

Brooke Beverly, Dudley Elementary, Dudley, MA

POEMS ON THE MENU
Whole class

Motivate students to increase their oral-reading fluency with a poetry café! Have each student choose a poem to practice reading orally. Make a copy of the poem for the child to practice at home as well. Then use the invitation on page 217 to invite other classes, parents, or staff members to your classroom on a specified date to hear the poetry readings. On the day of the presentations, arrange desks in groups; then cover them with butcher paper tablecloths. If desired, serve snacks. Provide time for each child to read her poem. For extra fun, have audience members snap rather than clap to show appreciation for each reading.

Linda Groce, Hood Avenue Primary, Fayetteville, GA

You're Invited to the Poetry Café!

Please plan to visit room __12__ on __March 14__ at __1:30__ PM. We will serve up a fun assortment of well-read poems. We can't wait to share them with you!

Sincerely,

Ms. Groce's Class

Save the date and don't be late!

ON POINT
Independent

Provide a student with a plastic novelty finger and have him wear it on his pointer finger. Direct the student to use the finger to follow the text while he listens to a recorded reading. Then have him silently reread the story before reading it aloud to an adult or another student, each time using the novelty finger to guide and track his reading.

adapted from an idea by Dana Vaughan
Cypress Ridge Elementary, Clermont, FL

WHAT'S NEXT?
Small group

As students follow along, read a passage aloud, modeling expressive reading and pausing for punctuation. Then select a student to reread the passage aloud. Direct the child to periodically pause to allow her group members to read the next word in the passage. Remind group members to follow along with the reader to continue her flow when she pauses. When the first reader has completed the passage, choose another student to repeat the process with the same text.

Deborah Carlberg, Stewartsville Elementary, Goodview, VA

hungry

Phrase Cards

Use with "Fun With Phrases" on page 214.

what do you TEC43035	**again and again** TEC43035	**was the best** TEC43035
upon a time TEC43035	**most of all** TEC43035	**before you go** TEC43035
do you know TEC43035	**have an idea** TEC43035	**in the family** TEC43035
was her name TEC43035	**left all alone** TEC43035	**he would do** TEC43035
look at that TEC43035	**meet me at** TEC43035	**high in the** TEC43035
where it was TEC43035	**went down** TEC43035	**does it cost** TEC43035
should we do TEC43035	**by myself** TEC43035	**then she said** TEC43035
about it TEC43035	**Blurb!** TEC43035	**Blurb!** TEC43035
along the way TEC43035	**Blurb!** TEC43035	**Blurb!** TEC43035

You're Invited to the Poetry Café!

Please plan to visit room _____

on _____ at _____.

We will serve up a fun assortment of well-read poems. We can't wait to share them with you!

Sincerely,

_____

You're Invited to the Poetry Café!

Please plan to visit room _____

on _____ at _____.

We will serve up a fun assortment of well-read poems. We can't wait to share them with you!

Sincerely,

_____

Note to the teacher: Use with "Poems on the Menu" on page 215.

In the Spotlight With
Character Analysis

Laura Johnson, South Decatur Elementary, Greensburg, IN

Interview Questions

Do you like living in your house on the hill?

What do you like to wear?

What are some things you do as a Strega?

How did you feel when nobody came to your house?

Do you like to help people?

Book title:
Strega Nona
Meets Her Match

I am interviewing
Strega Nona

ASK AND TELL
Identifying character traits

Have each pair of students reread a familiar book that includes more than one important character. Then have each partner take the role of a different character. Direct each student to cut out a copy of the microphone pattern on page 220 and have him write interview questions directly related to his partner's chosen character traits. After a predetermined amount of time, have partners take turns asking and answering questions as they talk into their microphones. Encourage students to refer to the book to help them answer questions.

Heather Wynne, Tobyhanna Elementary
Pocono Pines, PA

WHAT HAPPENED?
Analyzing a character's response to events

Place at a center a variety of books students have previously read and student copies of page 221. When a student visits the center, she writes the title and the name of a character from a chosen book at the top of her paper. Then she finds five important story events involving the character. For each event found, she completes a row on the chart. If time permits, the student repeats the activity with a different character from the same book and then compares her charts.

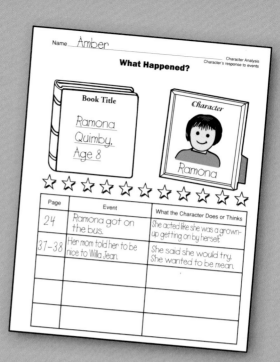

POST IT!
Comparing and contrasting characters' traits

Write the name of a familiar book character on a sheet of chart paper. Have each child write on a sticky note a word or phrase that describes the character and post the note on the chart. Then review the chart with students and stack any repeated words or phrases. Next, write on another sheet of chart paper the name of a different character. Remove one sticky note at a time and ask students if that trait would describe the character on the second chart. If it does, move it; if not, place it back on the original chart. Then provide each student with another sticky note of a different color to record additional traits for the second chart. After all the traits have been discussed, guide students to compare and contrast the characters.

WHO SAID WHAT?
Identifying characters' points of view

Make available several books students have previously read in which two or more of the characters have different points of view. To begin, a child chooses from one of the books two characters with differing viewpoints. She illustrates each character on a sheet of paper, labels them, and then cuts out each character and its label. Next, on separate speech bubble cutouts, she writes what each character would say about a story event. After completing her project, each child trades projects with a partner. The partner reads each speech bubble and places the correct character near each speech bubble. Students continue trading projects with different partners as time allows.

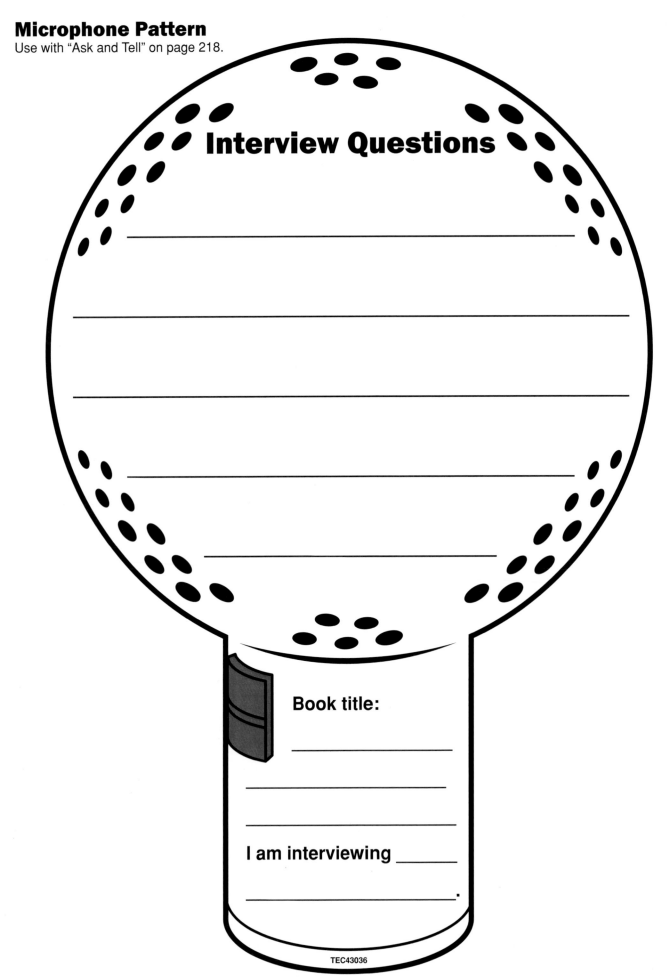

Interview Questions

_____

_____

_____

_____

_____

Book title:

_____

_____

_____

I am interviewing _____

_____.

TEC43036

What Happened?

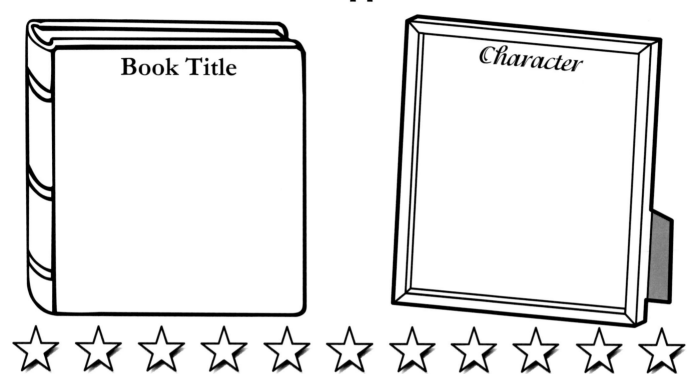

Page	Event	What the Character Does or Thinks

In the Spotlight

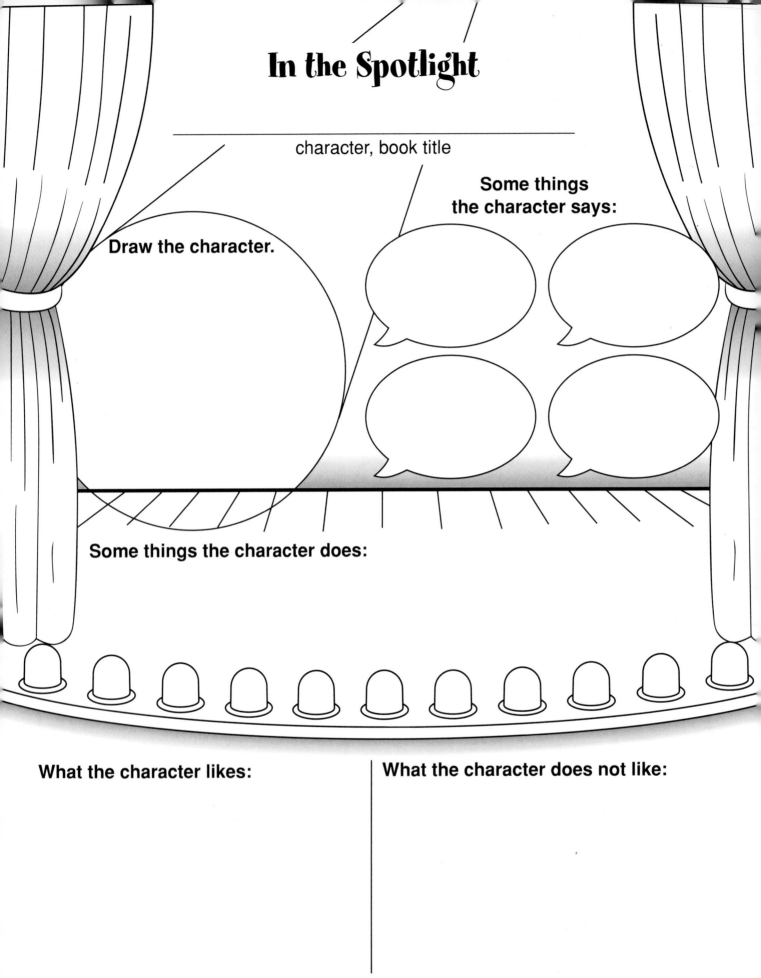

character, book title

Draw the character.

Some things
the character says:

Some things the character does:

What the character likes:

What the character does not like:

Note to the teacher: Use this sheet to help students analyze any character.

Building Stronger Reading Skills

Barclay Marcell, Theodore Roosevelt Elementary
Park Ridge, IL

Name Oliver

Making inferences

Here's what
I just read.

I just read how Wilbur spends all his time with Fern when she's home.

Here's what's in my head.

I already know that people who like other people or animals spend a lot of time together.

So I can infer that Wilbur likes being with Fern. Fern is very fond of Wilbur and she will make sure he stays safe.

Charlotte's Web

STRETCH YOUR THINKING
Making inferences

Use this simple technique to guide students to a better understanding of how to make inferences. First, read aloud a short passage from a current class reading. While referring to an overhead transparency of page 225, tap the passage or book and say, "Here's what I just read." Next, tap your head, say, "Here's what's in my head," and summarize what you already know about the subject. Tell students how you used the reading and your prior knowledge to lead you to a good guess or inference. Then clap your hands and say, "I infer that…" and reveal your inference. When students are familiar with making inferences, have each student read a passage and complete a copy of page 225.

CHARTING PROGRESS
Making predictions, determining an author's purpose

Before reading, have a student make a prediction about the story and record it in the first column on a copy of page 226. Also have the student predict the author's purpose for writing. As the student reads, guide her to respond to the reading by writing questions about the text. When she's finished reading, have the student answer her questions and then use her chart as a reference during a discussion of the book.

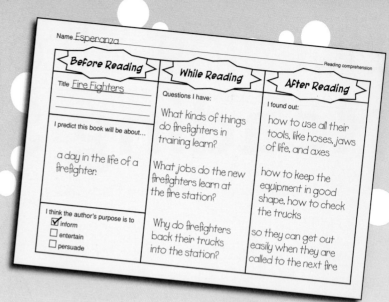

Name Esperanza

Reading comprehension

Before Reading

Title Fire Fighters

I predict this book will be about...

a day in the life of a firefighter.

I think the author's purpose is to
- ☑ inform
- ☐ entertain
- ☐ persuade

While Reading

Questions I have:

What kinds of things do firefighters in training learn?

What jobs do the new firefighters learn at the fire station?

Why do firefighters back their trucks into the station?

After Reading

I found out:

how to use all their tools, like hoses, jaws of life, and axes

how to keep the equipment in good shape, how to check the trucks

so they can get out easily when they are called to the next fire

Victoria

Cause

A man yelled at the barking dog.

Effect

The man's yelling woke up his baby.

GETTING RESULTS
Identifying cause and effect

Share an eventful story, such as *The Rain Came Down* by David Shannon. Have students retell examples of causes and effects from the story as you write the examples on the board. Direct each student to choose a different pairing; then have her fold a sheet of paper in half. Guide her to write and illustrate at the top of her paper the cause statement and then write and illustrate at the bottom of her paper the effect. Bind the completed pages to match the order of events in the story and place the resulting book with the original in your class library.

Jennifer Cripe, James Bilbray Elementary, Las Vegas, NV

GETTING FUELED UP
Identifying fact and opinion

After explaining to students the difference between a fact and an opinion, give each small group an empty cereal box and have the students read the text on it. Next, direct each group to fold a sheet of paper in half and unfold it. Then have the students make a list of facts about the cereal in the left section and a list of opinions in the right section. When each group is satisfied with its list, have the students cut apart the statements and mix them in a pile. On your signal, have each group move to another group's location, read the text on the cereal box, and sort the statements. Provide time for each group to share its results.

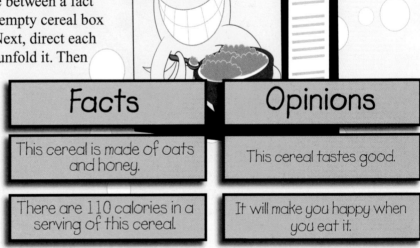

Oats & Honey

Facts

This cereal is made of oats and honey.

There are 110 calories in a serving of this cereal.

Opinions

This cereal tastes good.

It will make you happy when you eat it.

Name _____

Here's what's
in my head.

I already know that _____ _____ _____ _____ _____

Here's what
I just read.

I just read _____ _____ _____ _____ _____

So I can infer that _____ _____ _____ _____ _____

©The Mailbox® · TEC43037 · June/July 2008

Note to the teacher: Use with "Stretch Your Thinking" on page 223.

Name _____

After Reading

I found out:

While Reading

Questions I have:

Before Reading

Title: _____

I predict this book will be about...

I think the author's purpose is to

☐ inform

☐ entertain

☐ persuade

©The Mailbox® • TEC43037 • June/July 2008

Note to the teacher: Use with "Charting Progress" on page 224.

Name _____

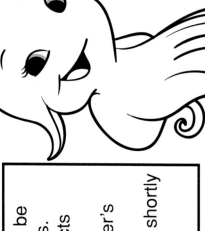

Read.

Life Cycle in the Sea

There are many kinds of octopuses swimming in the seas. They are different colors and different sizes. But each octopus goes through the same basic life cycle.

After mating, a female octopus may lay thousands of eggs. The eggs are often laid inside a safe den. The female tends to her eggs for a few weeks or months until they hatch. The female spends her time cleaning and protecting her eggs. She is so busy that she does not eat.

The eggs hatch and soon the female dies. The larvae that come from the eggs are on their own. They swim up toward the water's surface. Here they eat and grow bigger. Most of these young octopuses will become food for other sea animals. The few that survive move back toward the bottom of the ocean. They make a den of their own. Then each finds a mate, and the life cycle begins again.

Eggs

Larva

Adult

Read each statement.
Find the matching cause or effect below.
Write the statement on the chart.

Cause	Effect
Eggs are laid inside a safe den.	
The female spends all her time cleaning and protecting her eggs.	
Cause	Effect
	The larvae grow bigger.
Cause	Effect
	They will not become adults.

- Most young octopuses will be eaten by other sea animals.
- The female octopus protects them.
- The larvae feed at the water's surface.
- She does not eat and dies shortly after the eggs hatch.

Bonus Box: Why do you think the female octopus lays so many eggs? Write your answer on the back of this paper.

©The Mailbox® • TEC43037 • June/July 2008 • Key p. 312

Sizing Up Punctuation

I love tacos, burgers, and cookies.

"Do you have my phone number" asked Autumn?

Quinn said, "You are a good f

I won a million dollars!

PUNCTUATION POLICE
Identifying correct punctuation

Have each child write a different sentence on each of two sentence strips—one sentence with correct punctuation and another with incorrect punctuation. Put students in teams and have each team sort its sentence strips into two piles; correct and incorrect. Next, choose two students from one team to serve as the punctuation police and have them step outside the classroom. While the pair is out of the room, choose one group to place an incorrect sentence in a pocket chart. Have each of the other groups place one of its correct strips in the chart. Then invite the police back into the room. Challenge the pair to determine which sentence has incorrect punctuation. If the pair is correct, the students earn a point for their team. Continue playing in a similar manner, choosing pairs of students from different groups to serve as the police.

adapted from an idea by Jolyn Haye, Peach Hill Academy, Moorpark, CA

END OF THE LINE
Using correct end marks

To provide independent practice using end marks, copy
the cards on page 230 and cut them out. Mount the cards
on construction paper and laminate them for durability.
Also program two clothespins with periods, two with
question marks, and two with exclamation points. Place
the cards and clothespins at a center with a supply of
paper. A child chooses a card, reads a sentence, and clips
the correct clothespin at the end of the sentence. When
each sentence on the card has been punctuated, he copies
the sentences onto his paper and writes the correct end
marks.

adapted from an idea by Bonnie Gaynor, Franklin, NJ

CUTTING, GLUING, AND WRITING
Using commas in a series

Before starting this partner activity, make and post
a list of general categories, such as those shown,
listing one category for every two students. To
begin, have each student pair select a different category from the list. The students cut from magazines
and catalogs three examples of items from that category and glue the pictures to a sheet of construction
paper. Then the duo writes a sentence that includes
the names or descriptions of the items in the order
they appear. The pair separates the words by gluing
on macaroni commas. Provide time for each student
pair to share its work; then post the completed projects around the room.

Bonnie Gaynor

JUST JOKING
Punctuating dialogue

Review with students the correct placement of commas, quotation
marks, and end marks when setting off a speaker's exact words.
Next, have students share familiar knock-knock jokes. Then give
each child a copy of page 231 and have her write the words to her
favorite knock-knock joke in the speech bubbles at the top. Next,
direct her to rewrite each line of the joke in order at the bottom
of the page, adding character names and inserting correct punctuation where needed. Bind the completed pages in a class book
titled "Knock-Knock Quotes."

Laura Johnson, South Decatur Elementary, Greensburg, IN

Punctuation Cards

Use with "End of the Line" on page 229.

Card 1

1. Missy Mouse is a pastry chef

2. She measures all day long

3. Watch out for that falling bowl

4. Uh-oh. What did Missy do now

5. It seems she made a big mess

TEC43032

Card 2

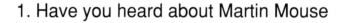

1. Have you heard about Martin Mouse

2. He loves to build fun mazes

3. He has become famous for them

4. Martin can build a maze in just five minutes

5. What do you think his secret is

TEC43032

Comic Quotes

Write each part of a knock-knock joke in a speech bubble.

Write each part of the joke as dialogue.
Use quotation marks, commas, and end marks as needed.

_____

_____

_____

_____

_____

Note to the teacher: Use with "Just Joking" on page 229.

THE MAILBOX **231**

Loading Up on Sentence Skills

Laura Johnson, South Decatur Elementary, Greensburg, IN

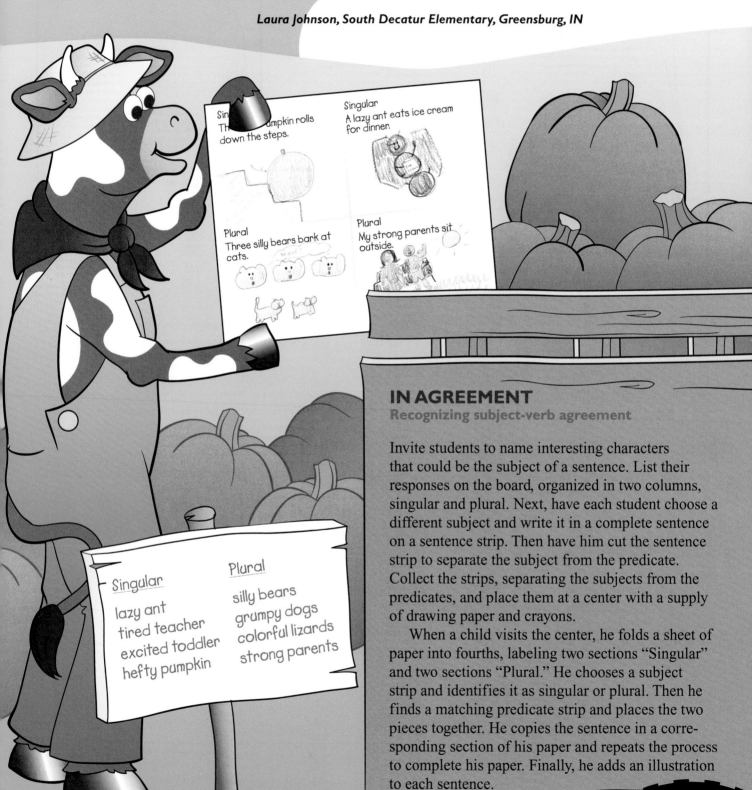

The hefty pumpkin rolls down the steps.

Singular
A lazy ant eats ice cream for dinner.

Plural
Three silly bears bark at cats.

Plural
My strong parents sit outside.

Singular	Plural
lazy ant	silly bears
tired teacher	grumpy dogs
excited toddler	colorful lizards
hefty pumpkin	strong parents

IN AGREEMENT
Recognizing subject-verb agreement

Invite students to name interesting characters that could be the subject of a sentence. List their responses on the board, organized in two columns, singular and plural. Next, have each student choose a different subject and write it in a complete sentence on a sentence strip. Then have him cut the sentence strip to separate the subject from the predicate. Collect the strips, separating the subjects from the predicates, and place them at a center with a supply of drawing paper and crayons.

When a child visits the center, he folds a sheet of paper into fourths, labeling two sections "Singular" and two sections "Plural." He chooses a subject strip and identifies it as singular or plural. Then he finds a matching predicate strip and places the two pieces together. He copies the sentence in a corresponding section of his paper and repeats the process to complete his paper. Finally, he adds an illustration to each sentence.

KEEP ON TRUCKING
Determining complete and incomplete sentences

To begin this independent activity, review what makes a sentence complete. Next, give each student a copy of page 234 and a sheet of paper. Have him cut out the trucks and glue each one to the bottom of his paper. Then have him read each sentence, cut it out, and glue it above the corresponding truck bed. As an additional challenge, have each student rewrite the incomplete sentences as complete ones on the back of his paper.

Sue Fleischmann, Sussex, WI

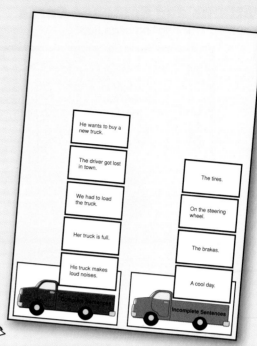

The word is *scarecrow.* The scarecrow stood alone in the field. *Scarecrow* is a noun.

scarecrow

WORDS IN MOTION
Identifying nouns and verbs

Prepare for this class game by having each student write a noun on a slip of paper and a verb on another slip. Collect the papers and place them in a bag. Next, divide students into teams and select a student to pull a slip from the bag. She silently reads the word on the slip then hands it back to you. The student has one minute to pantomime clues related to the noun or verb on the slip. If one of her teammates correctly identifies the word, he gets the chance to earn two points for his team. Award the team one point for correctly using the word in a sentence and another point for naming the word's correct part of speech in that sentence. If the word is not correctly named within the allotted time frame, return the paper to the bag. Then select a student from another team to repeat the process.

For practice with recognizing subject-verb agreement, check out the reproducible on page 235.

Truck Patterns and Sentence Cards

Use with "Keep on Trucking" on page 233.

Complete Sentences

TEC43033

Incomplete Sentences

TEC43033

A cool day.	His truck makes loud noises.	The brakes.
TEC43033	TEC43033	TEC43033
Her truck is full.	On the steering wheel.	Unloads the truck.
TEC43033	TEC43033	TEC43033
We had to load the truck.	Went for a ride.	The driver got lost in town.
TEC43033	TEC43033	TEC43033
The tires.	He wants to buy a new truck.	It's old.
TEC43033	TEC43033	TEC43033

All in a Day's Work

Underline each subject.
Circle each verb.
Color the pumpkin in the "Yes"
    column if the subject and
    verb agree.
Color the pumpkin in the "No"
    column if the subject and
    verb do not agree.

	Yes	No
1. The farmers start their work at dawn.		
2. Fred and Frank picks the crops.		
3. Fran loads the truck.		
4. Fran work hard!		
5. Her helpers takes a lunch break at noon.		
6. Then Fran drives the crops to the market.		
7. The boys nap for a while.		
8. They waits for Fran.		
9. The boys serve dinner when she returns.		
10. Then the boys cleans the truck.		

Bonus Box: On another sheet of paper, rewrite each sentence whose subject and verb do not agree, replacing the incorrect verb with the correct one.

On Board With
Writing Paragraphs

Stacie Stone Davis, Livonia Primary School, Livonia, NY

The first train engines were powered by steam.

Main Idea
What is the most important idea you want to share?

Details
What does the reader need to know about this idea?

Conclusion
How will you wrap up this idea?

FULL STEAM AHEAD
Creating a paragraph with a topic sentence, details, and a conclusion

These easy-to-make trains guide students to successful paragraph writing. First, have each child cut out a copy of the train cards on page 238 and glue each one to the front of an envelope. Next, guide him to choose the main idea for a given paragraph, write it on an index card, and place the card in the corresponding envelope. Then have the child write at least three details on separate cards and a conclusion on another card; have him place the cards in the corresponding envelopes. When his plan is complete, direct the student to refer to his cards while he writes his paragraph.

    For multiparagraph assignments, have the child record notes about his introductory paragraph on an index card and place it in the first envelope, place cards related to his supporting paragraphs in the middle envelope, and place a card for his concluding paragraph in the last envelope.

RIGHT ON TRACK
Sequencing how-to paragraph events

Here's a hands-on activity to use each time students write a how-to paragraph. To begin, brainstorm with students a list of how-to topics and write them on the board. Then have each student choose a topic, write it on a sticky note, and put the sticky note at the top of a sheet of construction paper. Next, direct the student to draw two parallel lines on the construction paper to represent rails. Then have her write each step of the process on individual 1" x 8½" paper strips and place them in order on the rails. Check her work for accuracy; then lead the child to use her completed railroad organizer to write her how-to paragraph. When she's finished, have the child remove the sticky note and paper strips and keep her organizer for another time.

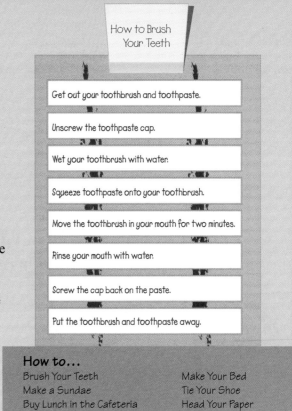

How to Brush Your Teeth

Get out your toothbrush and toothpaste.

Unscrew the toothpaste cap.

Wet your toothbrush with water.

Squeeze toothpaste onto your toothbrush.

Move the toothbrush in your mouth for two minutes.

Rinse your mouth with water.

Screw the cap back on the paste.

Put the toothbrush and toothpaste away.

How to...
Brush Your Teeth   Make Your Bed
Make a Sundae   Tie Your Shoe
Buy Lunch in the Cafeteria   Head Your Paper

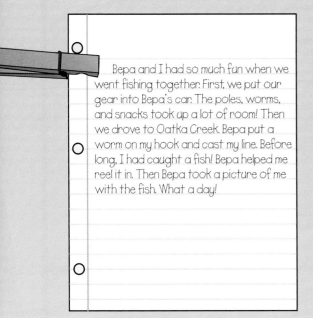

Bepa and I had so much fun when we went fishing together. First, we put our gear into Bepa's car. The poles, worms, and snacks took up a lot of room! Then we drove to Oatka Creek. Bepa put a worm on my hook and cast my line. Before long, I had caught a fish! Bepa helped me reel it in. Then Bepa took a picture of me with the fish. What a day!

NEXT STOP
Indenting paragraphs

Use clothespins to help students remember to indent each paragraph. After a student plans her work on a graphic organizer, help her determine the number of paragraphs she will need to write. Then give the student one clothespin for each paragraph and direct her to clip the pins to her organizer. As she begins a new paragraph, have her move a clothespin to that line on her paper and indent. When she has completed the paragraph, have her move the clothespin to her workspace.

Deb Emelander, East Kelloggsville Elementary, Kentwood, MI

THAT'S THE TICKET
Editing for paragraph form

This editing checklist is just the ticket for ensuring editing success! After a student writes a paragraph, give him a copy of the top ticket on page 239 and have him punch a hole next to each completed task on the ticket. Then have the student revisit his paragraph to complete tasks left unpunched before turning in the assignment. **For a multiparagraph assignment,** give the student a copy of the bottom ticket on page 239.

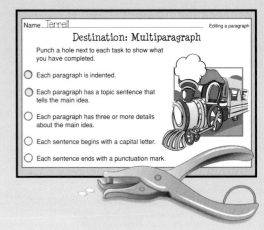

Name Terrell   Editing a paragraph

Destination: Multiparagraph

Punch a hole next to each task to show what you have completed.

○ Each paragraph is indented.

○ Each paragraph has a topic sentence that tells the main idea.

○ Each paragraph has three or more details about the main idea.

○ Each sentence begins with a capital letter.

○ Each sentence ends with a punctuation mark.

Train Cards

Use with "Full Steam Ahead" on page 236.

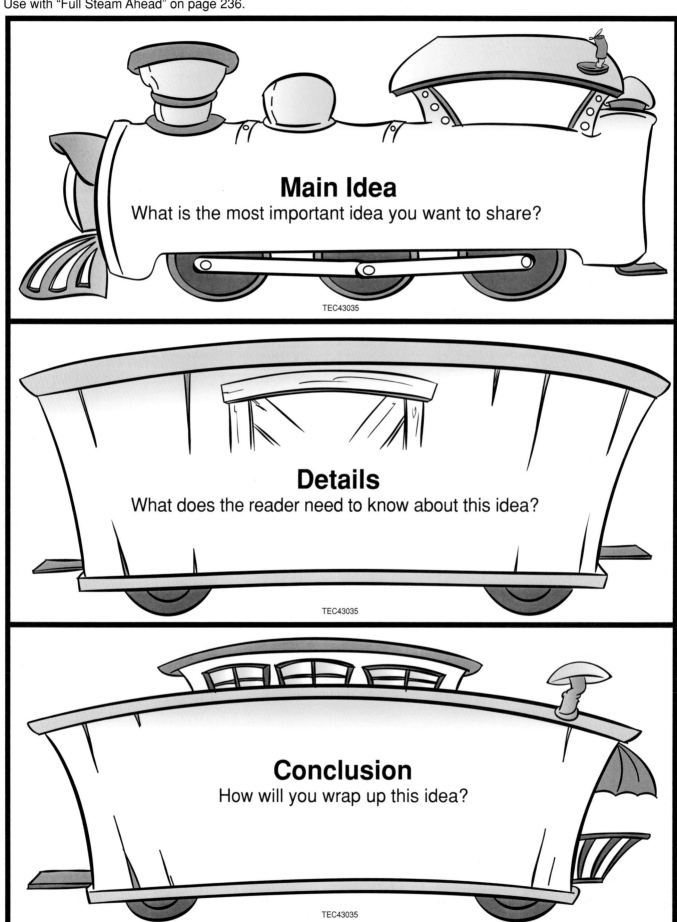

Main Idea
What is the most important idea you want to share?

TEC43035

Details
What does the reader need to know about this idea?

TEC43035

Conclusion
How will you wrap up this idea?

TEC43035

Name _____

Destination: Single Paragraph

Punch a hole next to each task to show what you have completed.

○ The paragraph is indented.

○ There is a topic sentence that tells the main idea.

○ There are three or more details about the main idea.

○ Each sentence begins with a capital letter.

○ Each sentence ends with a punctuation mark.

Name _____

Destination: Multiparagraph

Punch a hole next to each task to show what you have completed.

○ Each paragraph is indented.

○ Each paragraph has a topic sentence that tells the main idea.

○ Each paragraph has three or more details about the main idea.

○ Each sentence begins with a capital letter.

○ Each sentence ends with a punctuation mark.

Name _____

Animal Express

Cut the sentence cards apart.
Glue a topic sentence on each train engine.
Glue each supporting detail on its matching train car.

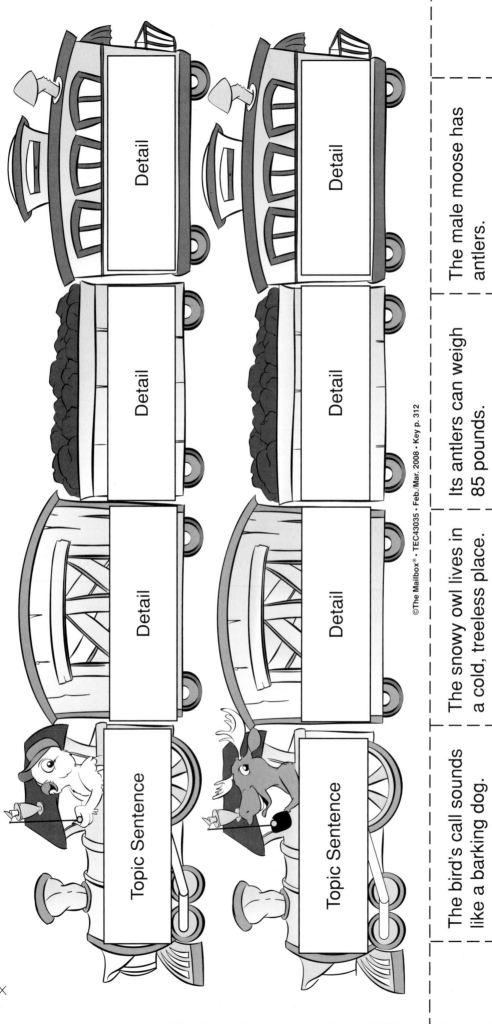

| Topic Sentence | Detail | Detail | Detail |

| Topic Sentence | Detail | Detail | Detail |

©The Mailbox® • TEC43035 • Feb./Mar. 2008 • Key p. 312

| The bird's call sounds like a barking dog. | The snowy owl lives in a cold, treeless place. | Its antlers can weigh 85 pounds. | The male moose has antlers. |
| The antlers can be up to six feet wide. | The snowy owl is a unique bird. | The moose sheds them every winter. | Its feathers are mostly white. |

A Bunch of Ideas for Writing Reports

Dr. Jennifer L. Kohnke, St. Charles, IL

Name: Jack   Writing reports

TOPIC: Sloth

Subtopic: Where it lives
1. South America
2. trees
3. tropical rain forests

Subtopic: What it eats
1. leaves
2. fruit
3. twigs

Subtopic: How it looks
1. almost no tail or ears
2. hooked claws on long arms
3. brown or gray hair

Subtopic: Its enemies
1. jaguar
2. anaconda
3. harpy eagle

SOUTH AMERICA

SLOTH

FOUR SQUARES TO SHARE
Organizing research

Have each student label a copy of page 243 with his research topic. Next, guide him to write in each square a subtopic and three related facts. Then have him glue his paper to the front of a sheet of construction paper and add an illustration to the back. Bind the completed projects to make a class book and place it in your classroom library. Then, to extend the activity, have each student choose an organizer to review and use it to write a complete report.

GET STARTED
Recounting facts, reporting information

As an introduction to report writing, present a topic to students through a book, magazine article, or video. Next, guide students to share information they learned as you write each fact on a separate sentence strip. Repeat the activity after other lessons on the same topic. Then help students organize the strips into categories, and model how to use the facts to write a report. If desired, write each report category on a separate sheet of chart paper for small groups to illustrate; then display the pages together as a class report.

How Humans Help the Environment	How Humans Hurt the Environment
plant trees	cut down trees for farming or building
set aside land for parks	put waste in rivers and lakes
recycle	burn waste

Where did she live?
When was she born?
What was she like as a child?
Where did she go to college?
What did she study in college?
Why was she important?
What kinds of jobs did she have during her life?
How did she help her community?

Name __Morgan__   Writing reports

☆ TOPIC: Mae Jemison ☆

☆ Question 1: When was she born?

☆ Question 2: Where did she go to college and what did she do?

☆ Question 3: Why was she important?

☆ Question 4: What kinds of jobs did she have during her life?

LOOKING FOR FACTS
Preparing questions for investigation

After reading a nonfiction text, such as a biography, have students share what they learned as you record their responses in question form. Tell students that they will read a similar nonfiction text and direct them to refer to the prepared list to write their own list of questions on a copy of page 244. Then at another time, provide research materials and have students answer their questions.

IN ORDER
Presenting information in a sequenced manner

Use this simple organizer to help students record information for a book report or order factual events. First, direct each student to draw on a copy of page 245 pictures of the four most important events. Then have him write a brief summary of each event on the corresponding lines. Have the student refer to his organizer as he writes his detailed report.

Name __Jamie__   Writing reports
TOPIC OR STORY TITLE __Two Bad Ants__

First, the ants went out to find tasty crystals for the queen.

Next, they found the crystals. Two ants secretly stayed behind.

Then the two ants went on a wild adventure around the kitchen.

Finally, the ants decided they wanted to go home, so they did.

TOPIC:

Subtopic:

1.

2.

3.

Subtopic:

1.

2.

3.

Subtopic:

1.

2.

3.

Subtopic:

1.

2.

3.

©The Mailbox® • TEC43036 • April/May 2008

Note to the teacher: Use with "Four Squares to Share" on page 241.

THE MAILBOX **243**

TOPIC:

★ Question 1:

★ Question 2:

★ Question 3:

★ Question 4:

Note to the teacher: Use with "Looking for Facts" on page 242.

TOPIC OR STORY TITLE

First,

Next,

Then

Finally,

©The Mailbox® • TEC43036 • April/May 2008

Note to the teacher: Use with "In Order" on page 242.

Far-Out Ideas for Using Reference Books

Jean Erickson, Grace Christian Academy, West Allis, WI

BLAST OFF
Recognizing reference materials and their parts

For this partner game, have each player label a rocket on a copy of page 248 with his name. Next, direct each pair to cut apart the game cards from a copy of page 249, shuffle the cards, and stack them facedown. To play, Player 1 takes the top card and reads aloud the clues. He locates the term that matches the clues, colors the space on his rocket, and returns the card to the bottom of the stack. If the term is already colored on his rocket, he returns the card to the bottom of the stack. Then Player 2 takes a turn in the same manner. The first player to color all eight sections of his rocket wins.

AROUND THE WORLD
Using an atlas

Students work in pairs to explore this reference book. First, write on the board a list of world locations. Give each student pair a number of sticky notes equal to the number of locations listed and have the pair write each location on a different sticky note. On your signal, have each pair use an atlas to find each location and flag the page with the corresponding sticky note. After a predetermined length of time, have the pairs stop and share their findings with the class. If desired, provide a small prize to the duo that correctly flagged the most locations.

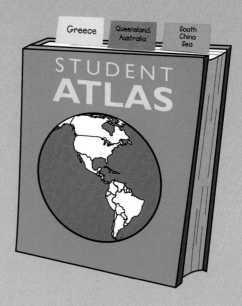

NEW WORLDS OF INFORMATION
Recognizing parts of a reference book

Give each small group of students a reference book and a sheet of construction paper. Direct the group to review the book's contents and write its type (such as atlas, dictionary, encyclopedia, or thesaurus) on the paper. Draw a chart on the board with different reference books and characteristics as shown. Announce an action, such as, "Stand if your book is organized in ABC order." If the characteristic is found in a group's book, direct one student in the group to hold the paper displaying the type of book, while the rest of the group completes the action. Verify students' responses and check off the reference materials the characteristic applies to. If desired, ask a follow-up question for each characteristic.

	atlas	dictionary	encyclopedia	thesaurus
organized in ABC order		✓	✓	✓
has an index	✓			
pages have guide words		✓	✓	✓
has a table of contents	✓			
has a glossary	✓			

Actions and Follow-up Questions

Hop on one foot if your book has a table of contents.
How can the table of contents help you?
Touch your nose if there are guide words on your book's pages.
What do you think guide words are used for?
Stand if your book is organized in ABC order.
How can this order help you?
Place your book on the floor if it has a glossary.
How can a glossary help you?
Wave a hand if your book has an index.
What do you notice about how the index is organized?

A FUN FIND
Using a thesaurus

Each student directs a classmate on a scavenger hunt with this fun activity! First, a child refers to a thesaurus as he fills in the blanks on a copy of the scavenger hunt form from page 250. Then he exchanges papers with a classmate and uses a thesaurus to complete her scavenger hunt form. If time allows, the student turns the paper over and writes four tasks for the classmate to complete before returning the paper to her.

adapted from an idea by Heather Schumacher, Coronado Village Elementary, Universal City, TX

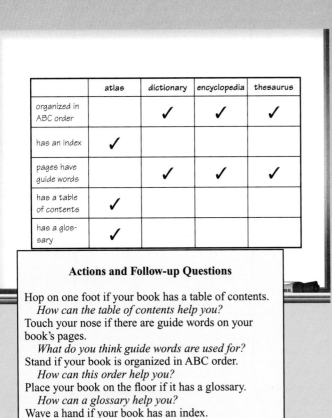

Name Carlos
Partner Macy
Using a thesaurus

Find a synonym for look.
observe
page 116

Find a word that starts with w and means the same as eat.
wolf
page 68

Find the page the entry word healthy is on.
page 94

Find a word that means the opposite of object.
agree
page 131

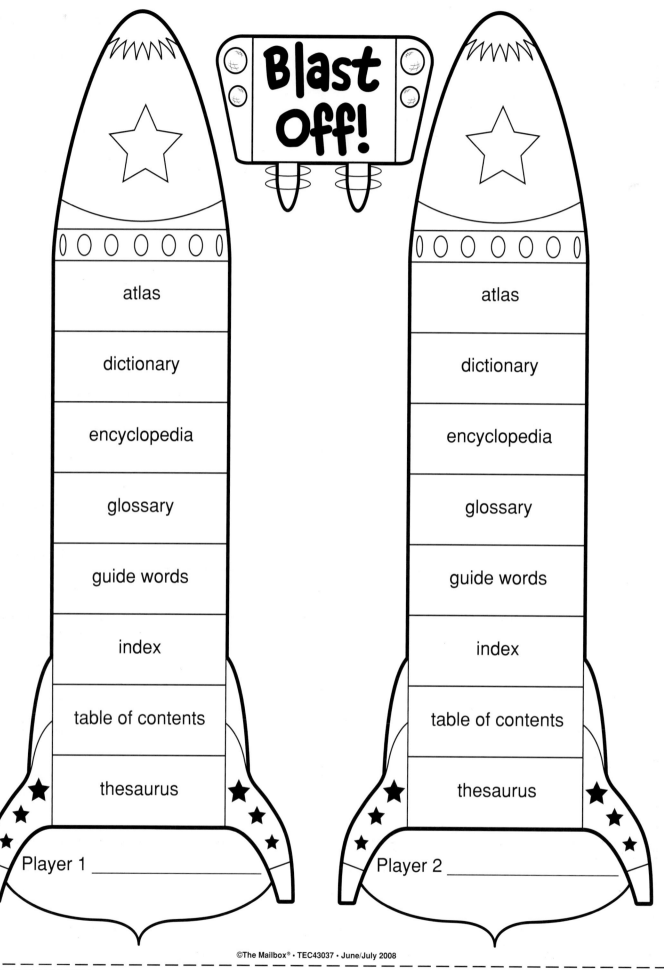

Blast Off!

atlas

dictionary

encyclopedia

glossary

guide words

index

table of contents

thesaurus

Player 1 _____

atlas

dictionary

encyclopedia

glossary

guide words

index

table of contents

thesaurus

Player 2 _____

Note to the teacher: Use with "Blast Off" on page 246.

Blast Off!
- It is a book.
- It has maps.
- It tells about places on Earth.

TEC43037

Blast Off!
- It is a book.
- It has maps.
- It tells about places on Earth.

TEC43037

Blast Off!
- It is a book.
- It is arranged in ABC order.
- It tells the meaning of many different words.

TEC43037

Blast Off!
- It is a book.
- It is arranged in ABC order.
- It tells the meaning of many different words.

TEC43037

Blast Off!
- It is a book.
- It is arranged in ABC order.
- It tells about each subject listed.

TEC43037

Blast Off!
- It is a book.
- It is arranged in ABC order.
- It tells about each subject listed.

TEC43037

Blast Off!
- It is a book.
- It is arranged in ABC order.
- It names synonyms for each listed word.
- It may also list antonyms for each word.

TEC43037

Blast Off!
- It is a book.
- It is arranged in ABC order.
- It names synonyms for each listed word.
- It may also list antonyms for each word.

TEC43037

Blast Off!
- It is part of a book.
- It lists key words found in the book.
- It also tells each word's meaning.
- It is often in the back of the book.

TEC43037

Blast Off!
- It is part of a book.
- It lists key words found in the book.
- It also tells each word's meaning.
- It is often in the back of the book.

TEC43037

Blast Off!
- These are part of a book page.
- There are two words.
- The first word tells the first entry word on the page.
- The second word tells the last entry word on the page.

TEC43037

Blast Off!
- These are part of a book page.
- There are two words.
- The first word tells the first entry word on the page.
- The second word tells the last entry word on the page.

TEC43037

Blast Off!
- It is part of a book.
- It is a list of key words in the book.
- It also tells the page number each word is on.

TEC43037

Blast Off!
- It is part of a book.
- It is a list of key words in the book.
- It also tells the page number each word is on.

TEC43037

Blast Off!
- It is part of a book.
- It is found at the beginning of the book.
- It shows the chapters or sections of the book.
- It is ordered from the beginning of the book to the end.

TEC43037

Blast Off!
- It is part of a book.
- It is found at the beginning of the book.
- It shows the chapters or sections of the book.
- It is ordered from the beginning of the book to the end.

TEC43037

Name _____

Partner _____

Find a word that starts with _____ and means the same as _____.

Find a synonym for _____.

page _____

Find a word that means the opposite of _____.

page _____

Find the page the entry word _____ is on.

page _____

©The Mailbox® • TEC43037 • June/July 2008

Name _____

Dig In

Circle the reference book you are using.

dictionary   encyclopedia   thesaurus

The first entry in this book is _____.

Word: _____

This word is on page(s) _____.

The guide words on this page are _____ and _____.

From this entry, I learned _____
_____
_____.

©The Mailbox® • TEC43037 • June/July 2008

MATH UNITS

Stepping Into
Number Sense

with ideas by Stacie Wright, Millington School, Millington, NJ

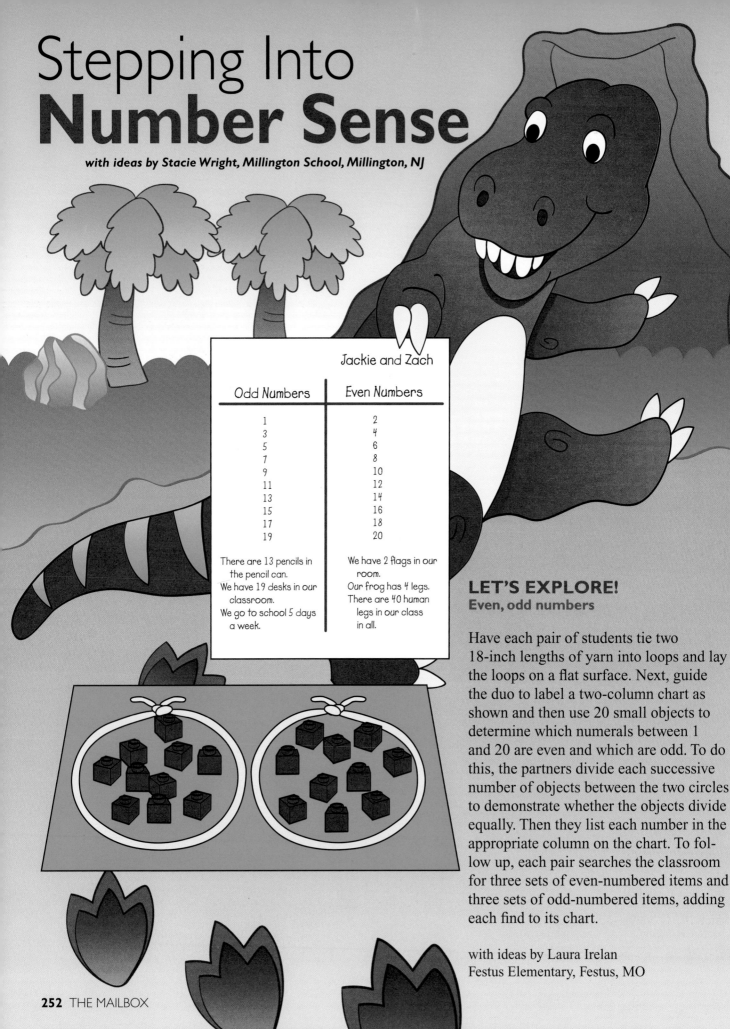

Jackie and Zach

Odd Numbers	Even Numbers
1	2
3	4
5	6
7	8
9	10
11	12
13	14
15	16
17	18
19	20

There are 13 pencils in the pencil can.
We have 19 desks in our classroom.
We go to school 5 days a week.

We have 2 flags in our room.
Our frog has 4 legs.
There are 40 human legs in our class in all.

LET'S EXPLORE!
Even, odd numbers

Have each pair of students tie two 18-inch lengths of yarn into loops and lay the loops on a flat surface. Next, guide the duo to label a two-column chart as shown and then use 20 small objects to determine which numerals between 1 and 20 are even and which are odd. To do this, the partners divide each successive number of objects between the two circles to demonstrate whether the objects divide equally. Then they list each number in the appropriate column on the chart. To follow up, each pair searches the classroom for three sets of even-numbered items and three sets of odd-numbered items, adding each find to its chart.

with ideas by Laura Irelan
Festus Elementary, Festus, MO

"GRRRR-EATER" OR LESS
Comparing numbers

To begin, have each student cut out a copy of the dino-saur shapes at the top of page 254. Guide him to tape a half chenille stem to the back of each cutout and then wrap the bottom of the stems around his index fingers to wear as rings. Explain to students that the dinosaurs will always try to eat the bigger number, so the open ends of the greater than and less than symbols should always face the larger numbers. Then write two numbers on the board and guide students to show you the dinosaur with the correct symbol. Repeat with additional numbers as time allows. Then have each student keep his dinosaurs handy as he completes a copy of page 256.

WHAT'S MY NUMBER?
Place value

Before setting up this partner center, make a class supply of the recording sheet at the bottom of page 254. Then lami-nate and cut out the cards and mat on page 255. At the center, each player, in turn, draws two cards, places them on the mat to make the greatest possible number, and writes the number on his recording sheet. The players compare their numbers and the player with the larger number circles it. Students continue playing in this manner as time allows, reshuffling the cards as necessary. The child who has more circled numbers wins. For practice with larger numbers, have the players take up to six cards each turn.

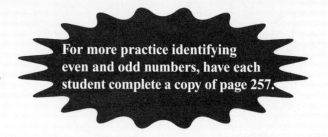

REMIND 'EM
Even, odd numbers

Point out to students that the word *even* has four letters, which is an even number of letters, and the word *odd* has three letters, which is an odd number of letters.

Pat Biancardi, Homan Elementary, Schererville, IN

For more practice identifying even and odd numbers, have each student complete a copy of page 257.

Dinosaur Patterns

Use with "'Grrrr-eater' or Less" on page 253.

less than

greater than

TEC43032

TEC43032

Recording Sheet

Name _____

What's My Number?

1. _____
2. _____
3. _____
4. _____
5. _____
6. _____
7. _____
8. _____
9. _____
10. _____
11. _____
12. _____

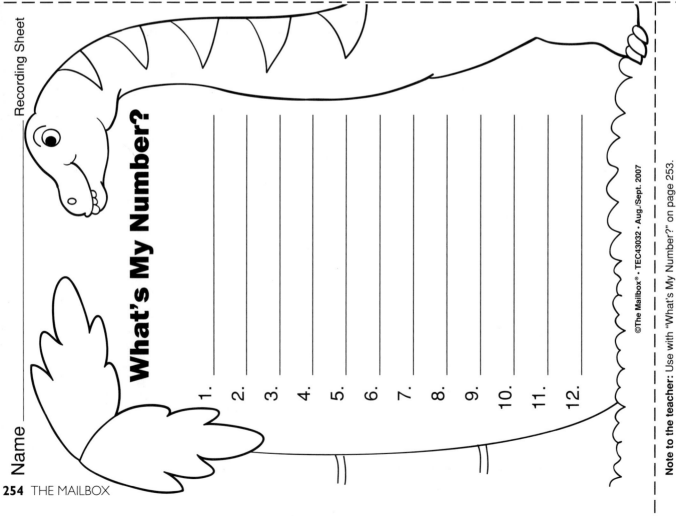

©The Mailbox® • TEC43032 • Aug./Sept. 2007

Note to the teacher: Use with "What's My Number?" on page 253.

9	8	7	6	5	4	3	2	1	0
TEC43032	TEC43032	TEC43032	TEC43032	TEC43032	TEC43032	TEC43032	TEC43032	TEC43032	TEC43032
9	8	7	6	5	4	3	2	1	0
TEC43032	TEC43032	TEC43032	TEC43032	TEC43032	TEC43032	TEC43032	TEC43032	TEC43032	TEC43032

ones

tens

hundreds

ones

tens

hundreds

thousands

TEC43032

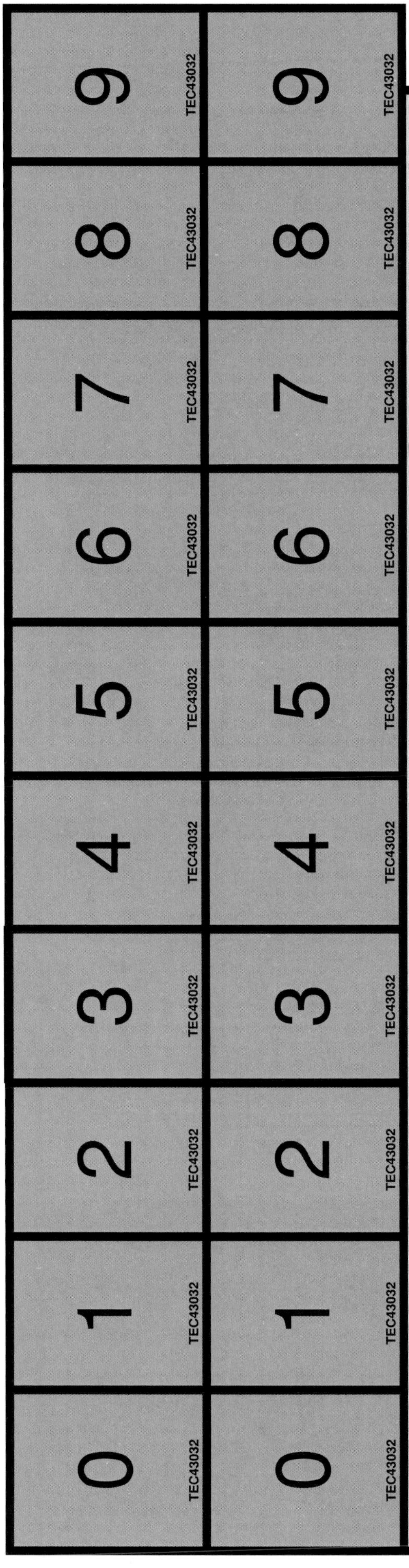

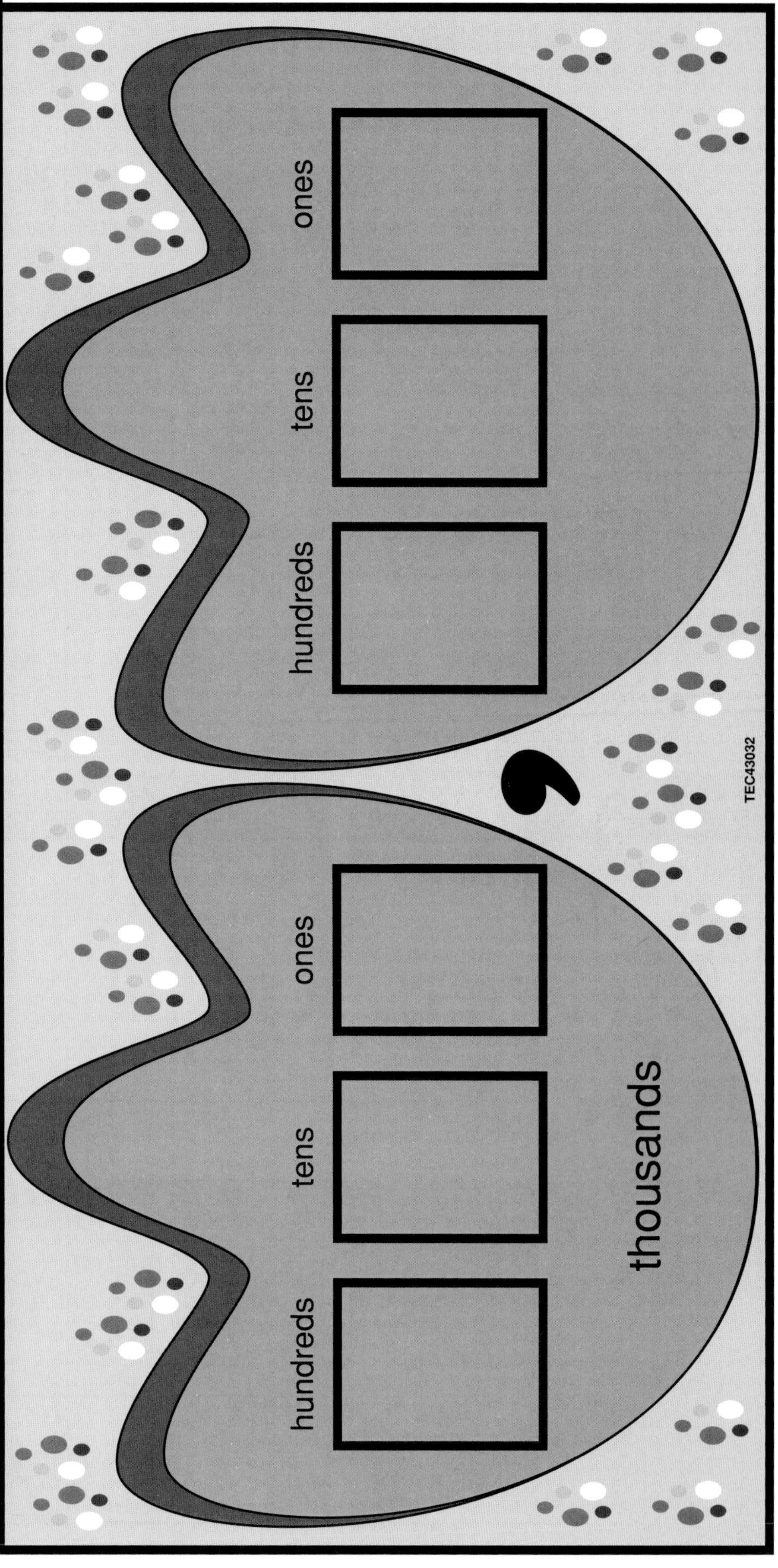

Big Steps

Write < or > to complete each sentence.
Color a matching symbol.

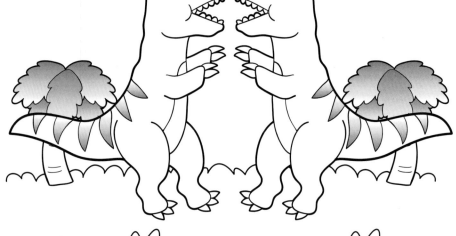

1. 13  16

2. 7  4

3. 9  11

4. 20  21

5. 19  16

6. 33  37

7. 38  27

8. 41  40

9. 50  75

10. 62  59

11. 58  59

12. 83  38

Bonus Box: Write a number on each line below that makes the number sentence true.

12 > ___   ___ < 55   100 > ___

©The Mailbox® • TEC43032 • Aug./Sept. 2007 • Key p. 312

256 THE MAILBOX   **Note to the teacher:** Use with " 'Grrrr-eater' or Less" on page 253.

Odd, even numbers

Dino Details

Color by the code.

Color Code
odd number = green
even number = orange

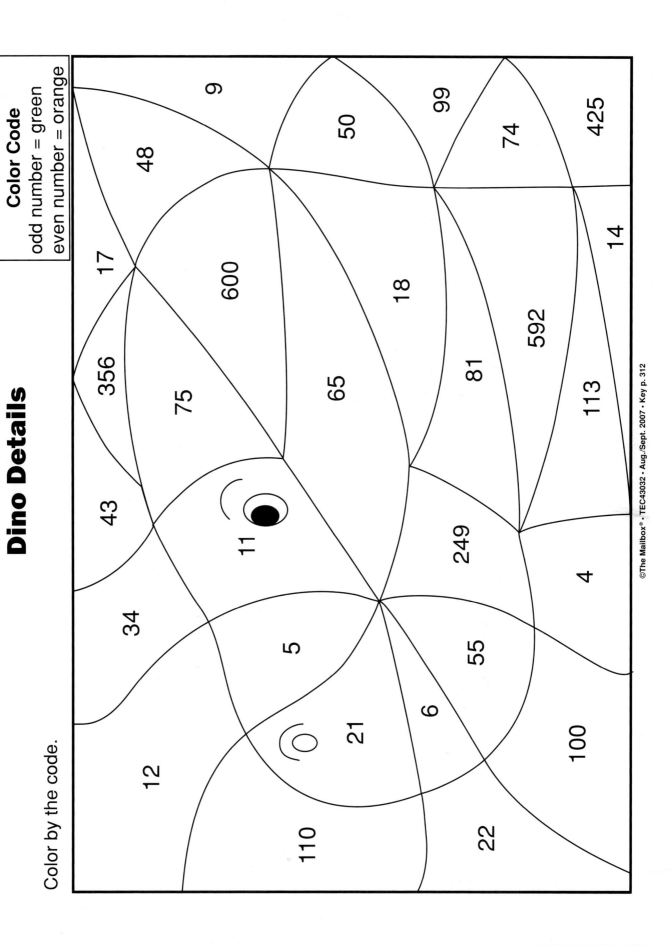

9		
48	50	99
		74
17		425
356	600	14
75	18	
43	65	592
34	81	113
11		
	249	4
12	5	55
21	6	
110		100
	22	

On a Roll With
Rounding and Estimating!

Carolyn M. Burant, St. John Vianney School, Brookfield, WI

SHOW-AND-TELL
Rounding

Help students see what rounding is all about by giving each small group of students a meterstick, three clothespins, and a marker. Have the group draw an arrow on each clothespin as shown. Next, announce a number less than 100 and have each group clip a clothespin onto its meterstick so the arrow points to the number. Lead the group to clip the other two clothespins on the multiples of ten just before and just after the number. Then guide students to round the number to the multiple of ten that's closer. Repeat as time allows, having students show and tell how to round each number. To follow up, have each student complete a copy of page 261.

TIC-TAC-ROUND
Rounding

For this twist on a childhood favorite, have each student draw on a sheet of paper a tic-tac-toe grid and then program each space with a multiple of ten from 10 to 90. Next, announce a number and have each student draw an X over the multiple of ten to which that number should be rounded. (Jot down the number for later verification.) Repeat with other numbers until a student marks three in a row. Confirm the student's win and have each student draw another grid for a new round of play. To practice rounding to hundreds, have students program their grids with multiples of 100 from 100 to 900.

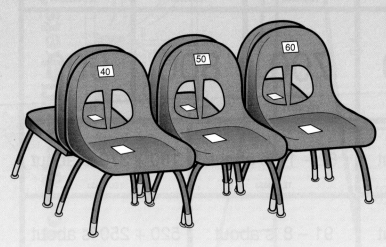

STICK WITH IT!
Estimating sums and differences

Before a math assignment, have each child draw on a sticky note a space for each problem from the assignment and stick the note to her paper. Then, for each equation, the student estimates the sum or difference, jots her estimate on the sticky note, solves the equation, and compares her answer and estimate. If the numbers aren't similar, she checks her work and corrects her answer as necessary before moving to the next problem.

TUNEFUL CALCULATIONS
Estimating sums and differences

For a few rounds of musical estimating, set up a CD or tape player with lively music. Also copy and cut apart the estimate cards and equation strips on page 260. Next, arrange two rows of chairs back-to-back, making sure there is a chair for every student. Tape an estimate card to each chair as shown; then place each equation strip facedown on a chair. Next, have each student stand in front of a chair and wait for the music. When the music starts, each student takes a strip from the nearest chair and estimates the answer. As the music plays, students rotate in a clockwise direction around the chairs. When a student finds the estimate card that matches his strip, he sits in that chair. After a few minutes, stop the music and have seated students read their equations and estimates. Then collect the equation strips and spread them out again for another round!

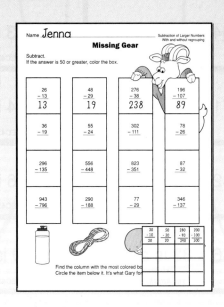

Ticket Tally

Estimate each sum or difference.

A. 17
  + 28

B. 66
  + 12

C. 37
  − 15

D. 22
  + 84

E. 91
  − 56

F. 51
  + 72

G. 45
  + 94

H. 63
  − 29

I. 420
  + 280

J. 630
  + 540

K. 860
  − 710

L. 150
  + 370

M. 930
  − 290

N. 510
  + 450

Voilà! Regrouping Practice

Carolyn M. Burant, St. John Vianney School, Brookfield, WI

THE MAGIC OF THE HAT
Addition with regrouping

For this activity, have each student cut apart the ones and tens cards on a copy of page 265 and draw and label a two-column chart on a sheet of paper as shown. To begin, post an addition problem that requires regrouping. Have each child place ones and tens cards on the chart to equal each of the problem's numbers. Guide students to determine they need to regroup by reminding them that they cannot put more than nine ones or nine tens in each place. Then lead students to regroup their pieces and solve the problem. If desired, have students save their cards to practice subtracting with regrouping at another time.

NUMBER EXCHANGE
Regrouping with three or more digits

In advance, program two sets of index cards with the numbers 10 through 19. Also program four sets of index cards with the numbers 0 through 9, one card with a minus sign, and one card with a plus sign. Next, slide index cards into a pocket chart to display an addition or subtraction problem. Then guide students to regroup the ones, tens, or hundreds as necessary, exchanging regrouped numbers for the original ones to solve the problem. After several demonstrations, post the chart at a center along with copies of a practice page to give students hands-on regrouping practice.

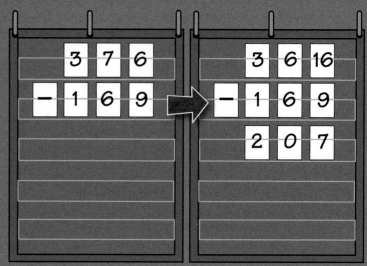

REVIEW RELAY
Subtraction with regrouping

Have each small group of students sit one behind the other in a line. Give the first student in each line a whiteboard with a dry-erase marker. Then post two subtraction problems and guide each group to follow the steps below. When the board reaches the end of the line, the final child takes it back to the first child to continue the race. The first group to finish both problems correctly wins!

Steps:
1. The first student in line records the problem and passes the board and marker to the next student.
2. The next student makes sure the problem has been copied correctly and passes the board and marker to the next student.
3. The next student determines whether the number in the ones place should be regrouped and, if needed, regroups it. She subtracts the numbers in the ones place, then passes the board and marker to the next student.
4. The next student checks the previous step and subtracts the numbers in the tens place. Then he passes the board and marker to the next student.
5. The next student checks the problem's answer and passes the board and marker to the next student.
6. Students repeat steps 1 through 5 for the second problem.

OFF TO A GOOD START
Starting with the ones place

Here's a quick chant to help students remember to start solving problems in the ones place. Before beginning a page of addition or subtraction, have each student point to the ones place in the first problem and then say, "Right is right!"

Jessica Keller, Columbia Academy, Columbia, MD

TEC43034	TEC43034	TEC43034	TEC43034	TEC43034	TEC43034	TEC43034	TEC43034	TEC43034
TEC43034	TEC43034	TEC43034	TEC43034	TEC43034	TEC43034	TEC43034	TEC43034	TEC43034
TEC43034	TEC43034	TEC43034	TEC43034	TEC43034	TEC43034	TEC43034	TEC43034	TEC43034
TEC43034	TEC43034	TEC43034	TEC43034	TEC43034	TEC43034	TEC43034	TEC43034	TEC43034

Razzle-Dazzle!

Subtract.
Show your work.
Cut out the matching answer below and glue it in place.

A.   354
    − 138

B.   671
    − 223

C.   283
    − 257

D.   530
    − 418

E.   178
    − 94

F.   921
    − 380

G.   764
    − 573

H.   458
    − 196

I.   832
    − 643

541	26	216	191	84
112	189	448	262	

Hit It Big With Multiplication

Laura Wagner, Bais Menachem Hebrew Academy, Austin, TX

Home of the World Famous
GOLDEN EGGS

14 36 10

1 10

JACKPOT!
Building knowledge of facts

For this partner center, program a supply of paper strips with three different products on each. Also write each number from 1 to 10 on two sets of index cards and store them in a paper lunch bag. Place the bag and strips at a center with a supply of game markers and a calculator. To play, Player 1 takes a strip and randomly selects two cards from the bag. She multiplies the numbers together and names the product. Player 2 confirms Player 1's answer, using the calculator as needed. If Player 1 is correct and her product matches one of the numbers on the strip, she covers it with a game marker before placing the cards back in the bag. Then Player 2 takes a turn in a similar manner. The player to cover the last number says "jackpot" and wins the round. Then the duo plays again with another strip.

adapted from an idea by David Green, North Shore Country Day School, Winnetka, IL

A WEALTH OF PRACTICE
Using charts to determine multiples

Use a different-colored crayon or marker to write
each number from 1 to 10 on a separate index card.
Shuffle the cards and place them in a stack. Give each
child a copy of a hundred chart; then choose a card
and reveal the number to the class. Have each student
use a crayon color that matches the number on the
card to lightly circle the multiples of that number on
his hundred chart. Then have him refer to the circled
numbers to write corresponding number sentences
on another sheet of paper. After a designated amount
of time, have students share their answers. Have
each child award himself one point for each correct
multiple and one point for each correct number
sentence. Then reveal a new number and play again.

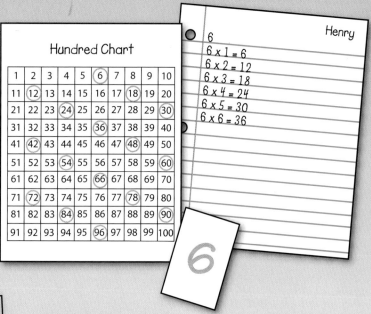

A GOLDEN ARRAY
Using arrays and number sentences

Fill each of a supply of resealable plastic bags with a
different number of same-colored Unifix cubes. Place the
prepared bags along with a supply of paper at a center. A
child chooses a bag and removes the cubes. She counts the
cubes, then arranges them in an array. The student copies
the array onto her paper and writes a corresponding number
sentence. She rearranges the cubes to form another array
and records the new information on her paper. When all
possible arrays have been recorded for that number, the
student repeats the process with another bag of cubes.

PRODUCTS APLENTY
Memorizing facts

Invite students to sit in a large circle. Present a small object, such as a
stuffed toy or rubber ball; then announce a number between two and
ten. Pass the object to one student and have him name the first multiplication fact for that number. Repeat the fact (restating it
correctly, if needed) and then direct the other students to
repeat the fact in unison. Have the child pass the object to
his right; then continue the activity in this manner, with
each child naming the next successive fact.
Challenge students to continue moving the
object around the circle until they reach
or just pass a predetermined product. For
an added twist, play instrumental music in
the background to encourage a rhythm for
students to follow.

Golden Products

Cross out the number that does not belong.
Write a multiplication sentence using the three other numbers.

A.
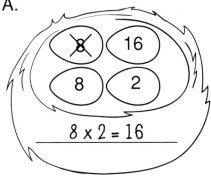

8 × 2 = 16

B.
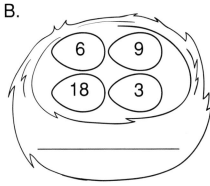

_____

C.
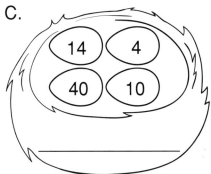

_____

D.
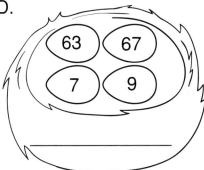

_____

E.
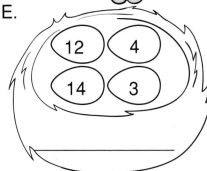

_____

F.
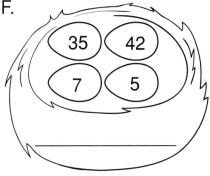

_____

G.
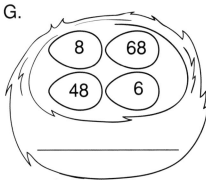

_____

H.
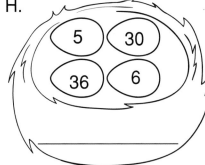

_____

I.
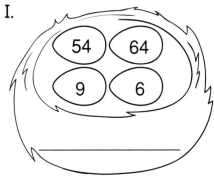

_____

J.
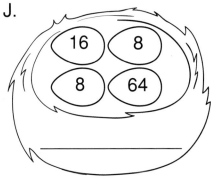

_____

K.

_____

Sharing the Wealth

Write each product.
Cut out the eggs.
Glue each egg in the correct nest.

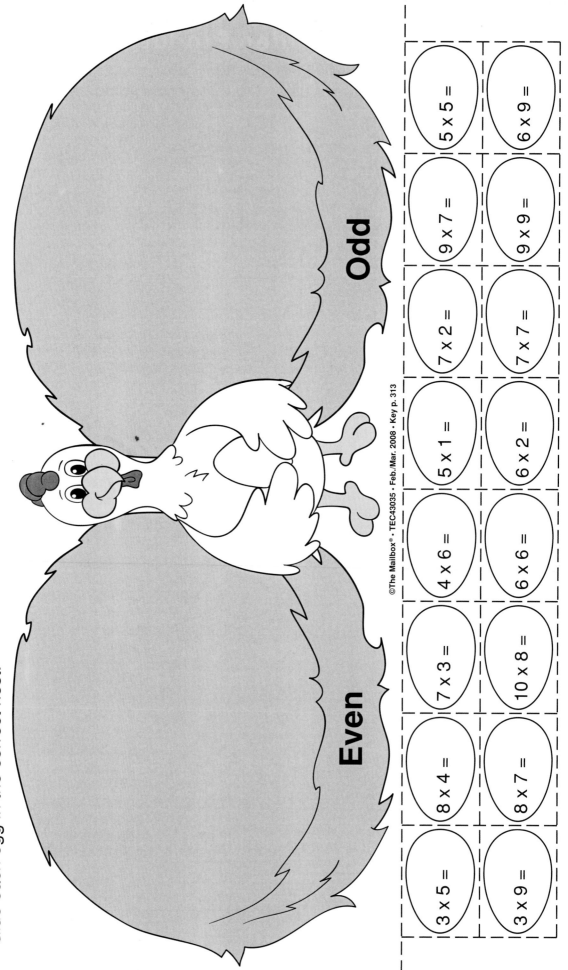

Odd

Even

| 5 x 5 = | 9 x 7 = | 7 x 2 = | 5 x 1 = | 4 x 6 = | 7 x 3 = | 8 x 4 = | 3 x 5 = |
| 6 x 9 = | 9 x 9 = | 7 x 7 = | 6 x 2 = | 6 x 6 = | 10 x 8 = | 8 x 7 = | 3 x 9 = |

©The Mailbox® • TEC43035 • Feb./Mar. 2008 • Key p. 313

Ready to Score With **Division**

DIVISION DELIVERIES
Basic division facts

To prepare for this whole-class review, program a supply of seasonal cutouts with basic division problems. Also, label a different mailing envelope with each quotient and post the envelopes around the room. To complete the activity, give each student a supply of cutouts and, at your signal, have him deliver the cutouts to the corresponding envelopes. When all cutouts have been delivered, remove them from one envelope at a time and determine with students if the cutouts were correctly placed. Then review any misplaced problems.

Rebecca Conroy, The Peck School
Morristown, NJ

63 ÷ 7

9

81 ÷ 9

27 ÷ 3

108 ÷ 12

DUPLICATE ANSWERS
Division concepts

To prepare this class game, write a division problem on the board; then assign each student one of two strategies to solve it, such as repeated subtraction or drawing a picture. On your signal, direct students to use their assigned strategies to solve the problem and then turn their papers over. When all students appear to be done, call on one student from each strategy group to reveal her results to the class. If both students reveal the same correct quotient, award the class a point. Write a new problem on the board and continue in this manner until a predetermined number of points have been awarded.

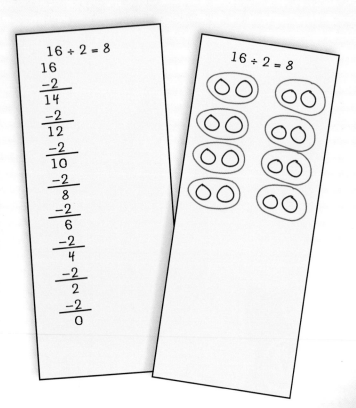

HELPFUL HINTS
Multidigit dividend, single-digit divisor

Share the mnemonic device "Division Monsters Smell Bad" to help students remember to divide, multiply, subtract, and bring down. Then provide time to sing this catchy tune.

Ashley Lovette, Warsaw Elementary, Warsaw, NC

The Division Song
(Sung to the tune of "London Bridge")

Division Monster first divides,
First divides, first divides.
Division Monster first divides.
It's not finished.

Then the monster multiplies,
Multiplies, multiplies.
Then the monster multiplies.
It's not finished.

Next the monster must subtract,
Must subtract, must subtract.
Next the monster must subtract.
It's still not finished.

Now the monster should bring down,
Should bring down, should bring down.
Now the monster should bring down.
Start all over!

DIVIDE AND CONQUER
Equal sharing

To begin this small-group activity, share a division-related story, such as *One Hundred Hungry Ants* by Elinor J. Pinczes, aloud. Next, give each child a small box of raisins and direct her to combine her raisins with the students in her small group so they have 100 raisins to work with. Reread the story and pause periodically to allow the small groups to model each division example shared in the story.

Heather Hopkins, Balfour Elementary
Asheboro, NC

Practice Shots

x	1	2	3	4	5	6	7	8	9
1	1	2	3	4	5	6	7	8	9
2	2	4	6	8	10	12	14	16	18
3	3	6	9	12	15	18	21	24	27
4	4	8	12	16	20	24	28	32	36
5	5	10	15	20	25	30	35	40	45
6	6	12	18	24	30	36	42	48	54
7	7	14	21	28	35	42	49	56	63
8	8	16	24	32	40	48	56	64	72
9	9	18	27	36	45	54	63	72	81

Multiply.
Write a related division fact.

A. $6 \times 3 =$ ____   ____ $\div$ ____ $=$ ____

B. $2 \times 8 =$ ____   ____ $\div$ ____ $=$ ____

C. $5 \times 7 =$ ____   ____ $\div$ ____ $=$ ____

D. $9 \times 4 =$ ____   ____ $\div$ ____ $=$ ____

E. $3 \times 5 =$ ____   ____ $\div$ ____ $=$ ____

F. $8 \times 6 =$ ____   ____ $\div$ ____ $=$ ____

G. $7 \times 2 =$ ____   ____ $\div$ ____ $=$ ____

H. $4 \times 6 =$ ____   ____ $\div$ ____ $=$ ____

I. $9 \times 3 =$ ____   ____ $\div$ ____ $=$ ____

J. $8 \times 8 =$ ____   ____ $\div$ ____ $=$ ____

K. $6 \times 7 =$ ____   ____ $\div$ ____ $=$ ____

L. $4 \times 5 =$ ____   ____ $\div$ ____ $=$ ____

Use Your Head

Divide.

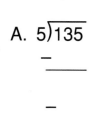

A. 5)135
___
___

B. 7)483
___
___

C. 6)138
___
___

D. 4)252
___
___

E. 3)195
___
___

F. 8)344
___
___

G. 3)249
___
___

H. 5)320
___
___

©The Mailbox® • TEC43036 • April/May 2008 • Key p. 313

Getting Cozy With
Multidigit
Multiplication

AT HOME WITH MULTIPLYING
Whole class

Cut out an enlarged copy of page 277 and laminate
it. Use a dry-erase marker to program the second floor of the
house shape with a two- or three-digit number and the first floor with
a one-digit number. Explain to students that the products will be stored in
the basement, but if the basement gets too crowded, regrouped numbers will
be held in the "add-ic." Then demonstrate how to multiply with several sample
problems, being sure to stress the importance of adding the numbers in the
"add-ic."

Tricia Sharkey, Immaculate Heart of Mary, Philadelphia, PA

CHECK, CHECK
Independent

Display a list of the products shown and have each student write the numbers on a piece of paper. Next, write on the board one of the multiplication problems shown and direct each student to rewrite the problem in a column format on her paper and solve it. When the problem is solved, have her place a check by the matching product on her list. (If she cannot find the product, direct her to try to solve the problem again.) Then have the student break the problem into the following three steps to solve it again: she multiplies the digits in the ones place; she writes the tens digit with a zero and multiplies it by the multiplier; and she adds the two resulting products. Guide her to confirm her answer by making another check next to the matching product. Write the remaining problems on the board; then have each student solve and check her work.

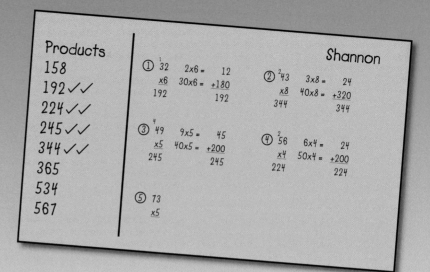

Products
158
192 ✓✓
224 ✓✓
245 ✓✓
344 ✓✓
365
534
567

Shannon

① ¹32   2x6 =   12
   x6   30x6 = +180
   192   192

② ²43   3x8 =   24
   x8   40x8 = +320
   344   344

③ ⁴49   9x5 =   45
   x5   40x5 = +200
   245   245

④ ²56   6x4 =   24
   x4   50x4 = +200
   224   224

⑤ 73
   x5

32 × 6   73 × 5
43 × 8   79 × 2
49 × 5   81 × 7
56 × 4   89 × 6

Angelo

¹213   ¹231   ¹215
x 5   x 5   x 3
1,065   1,155   645

¹251   ¹153   123
x 3   x 2   x 5
753   306

0 7 4

6 5

3 2

1 1

1 2 3

X 5

6 1 5

NEW ARRANGEMENTS
Independent

For this tactile activity, a child cuts out the grid and the number cards from a copy of page 278. He arranges three boldfaced cards across the second row of the grid to make a three-digit number and places a single bold-faced card in the ones place on the third row. Starting with the ones place, the child multiplies the numbers and places a card in the fourth row for the product. If he needs to regroup, he places the corresponding card in the top row. He continues in this manner with the remaining numbers. When he's finished, the student writes the problem and its answer on another sheet of paper and then clears the cards from the grid. He continues making and solving problems as time allows or until he has recorded 24 different problems.

adapted from an idea by Bonnie Gaynor
Franklin, NJ

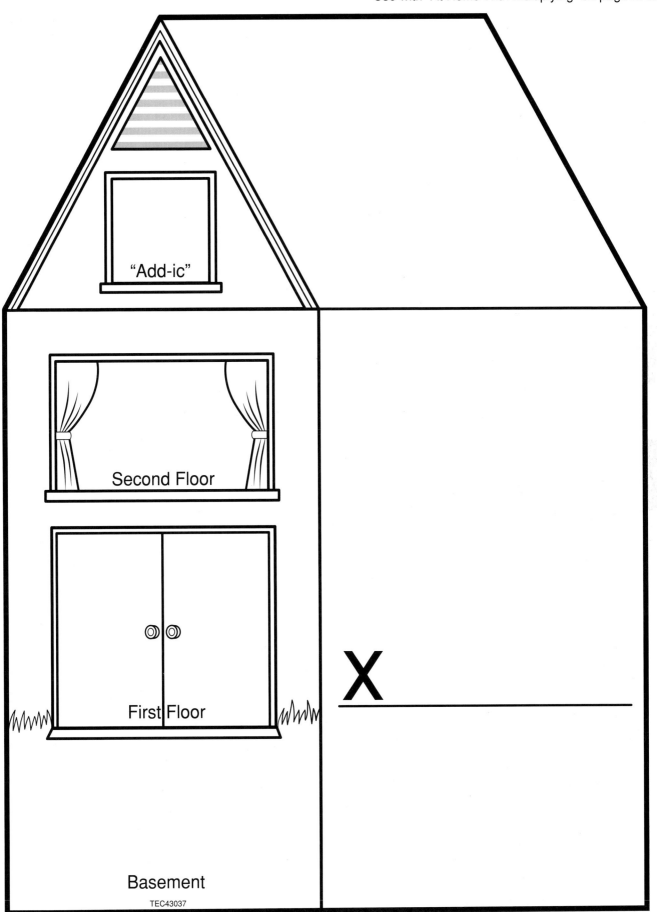

"Add-ic"

Second Floor

First Floor

X
_____

Basement

TEC43037

Grid and Number Cards

Use with "New Arrangements" on page 276.

	ones	ones	TEC43037
	tens		
	hundreds	X	

3 TEC43037	**1** TEC43037	**5** TEC43037	**7** TEC43037
2 TEC43037	**1** TEC43037	**4** TEC43037	**6** TEC43037
5 TEC43037	**1** TEC43037	**3** TEC43037	**6** TEC43037
1 TEC43037	**0** TEC43037	**2** TEC43037	**5** TEC43037

Geared Up for Problem Solving

Laura Wagner, Hebrew Academy Day School, Austin, TX

WRITE.

Steven spent 8 more minutes cleaning his room than Brandon. Together they spent 28 minutes cleaning. How many minutes did each boy spend cleaning?

REWRITE.

Steven spent 8 more minutes cleaning his room than Brandon. Together they spent 28 minutes cleaning. Brandon rode his bike for 15 minutes. How many minutes did each boy spend cleaning?

SWITCH AND SOLVE.

Steven spent 8 more minutes cleaning his room than Brandon. Together they spent 28 minutes cleaning. Then Brandon rode his bike for 15 minutes. How many minutes did each boy spend cleaning?

Steven spent 18 minutes cleaning. Brandon spent 10 minutes cleaning.

TOO MUCH!
Solving problems with extra information

To start this partner activity, have each student write a word problem. Next, have partners exchange problems and rewrite each other's problem by adding a sentence of extra information. After reviewing students' work, direct the pair to exchange problems with another duo. Have each pair work together to draw a line through the extra information in their partners' problems; then have the pair solve the problems.

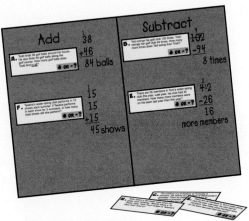

IN ITS PLACE
Choosing the appropriate operation

To complete this independent activity, a child divides a sheet of paper into two sections and labels each section as shown. He cuts apart the word problem cards from a copy of the top of page 281, reads each card, and underlines the key words that signal the appropriate operation. He glues each card in the corresponding column of his paper and uses the space beside the card to solve the problem. **To complete the activity using multiplication and division word problems,** the child labels his columns with those two terms and completes the activity with the cards from the bottom of page 281.

TEAMWORK
Solving multiple-step problems

Students team up for extra problem-solving practice in this small-group activity. To begin, provide each student group with a multiple-step word problem and several different-colored highlighters. Direct the group members to read the problem and determine the different steps involved. Then have the students highlight each step with a different color. Lead the students to work together to solve the problem; then provide time for groups to explain their thinking with the rest of the class.

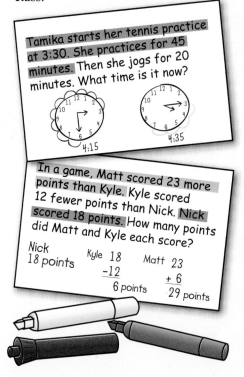

Julian does not go first.
Chelsea goes last.
Alondra goes after Cole but before Julian.

Teeing Order	1st	2nd	3rd	4th
Julian	X		✓	
Alondra		✓		
Cole	✓			
Chelsea				✓

GETTING ORGANIZED
Acting it out, making a table to solve

Draw on the board a 5 x 5 table, like the one shown, and label four of the columns with different ordinal numbers. Also place on the floor four pieces of paper, each labeled with a different ordinal number. To complete the activity, invite four students to stand at the front of the room; write each child's name on the table. Replace the underlined names in the clues shown with the names of the students selected and then read each clue aloud. After each clue is read, have the student or students involved stand at the corresponding paper and then use what is known or confirmed to complete a row on the table. Continue in this manner until each child is in the correct position and the table is complete.

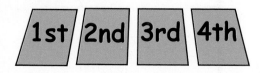

A. Todd finds 38 golf balls around his house. He also finds 46 golf balls along the golf course. How many golf balls does Todd find in all?

✚ OR – ?

TEC43037

B. Ted swings his golf club 102 times. Trish swings her golf club 94 times. How many more times does Ted swing than Trish?

✚ OR – ?

TEC43037

C. Tim strikes out 6 batters at Tuesday's practice. He strikes out 7 batters at Wednesday's practice. Then he strikes out 5 batters at Thursday's practice. How many total batters does he strike out on those three days?

✚ OR – ?

TEC43037

D. Tilly throws 44 pitches on Monday. She throws 69 pitches on Friday. How many more pitches does she throw on Friday than on Monday?

✚ OR – ?

TEC43037

E. There are 26 members in Tom's water-skiing club this year. Last year, his club had 42 members. How many more members were on his team last year than this year?

✚ OR – ?

TEC43037

F. Teesha's water-skiing club performs in 15 shows each summer. If Teesha performs in each show for 3 summers, in how many total shows will she perform?

✚ OR – ?

TEC43037

G. The Thomas family takes 9 tents when they go camping. The Taylor family takes 7 tents, and the Tanner family takes 5 tents. How many tents do they take in all?

✚ OR – ?

TEC43037

H. Tyler takes a 55-meter rope when he goes rock climbing. Teesha takes a 70-meter rope. How much longer is Teesha's rope than Tyler's?

✚ OR – ?

TEC43037

A. Todd loses 3 golf balls each time he plays golf. He plays golf 7 times. How many golf balls does Todd lose in all?

X OR ÷ ?

TEC43037

B. Ted swings his golf club the same number of times for each hole he plays. He plays 9 holes and swings a total of 54 times. How many times does he swing at each hole?

X OR ÷ ?

TEC43037

C. Tim strikes out 4 batters each game. He plays 4 games. How many total batters does he strike out?

X OR ÷ ?

TEC43037

D. Tilly throws 18 pitches. Half of the pitches are fastballs. How many pitches are not fastballs?

X OR ÷ ?

TEC43037

E. Teesha's water-skiing club performs 9 shows each month. The club performs for 3 months. How many shows do they perform in all?

X OR ÷ ?

TEC43037

F. The water-skiing team competes in 24 total events. There are 8 team members, and each member competes in the same number of events. In how many events does each team member compete?

X OR ÷ ?

TEC43037

G. The Thomas family takes 2 gallons of water for each person when they go camping. There are 6 family members. How many gallons of water do they take when they go camping?

X OR ÷ ?

TEC43037

H. Tyler goes camping every 7 days for 49 days. How many times does Tyler go camping?

X OR ÷ ?

TEC43037

Name_____

Taking Inventory

Solve each problem.
Check the matching number sentence.

A. Tim had 12 golf clubs. He lost four of them. How many golf clubs does Tim have now?

_____ golf clubs

B. Tara has 5 pairs of water skis. How many water skis does she have in all?

_____ water skis

C. Tim has 3 tennis rackets. Each racket weighs 6 ounces. How much do Tim's rackets weigh altogether?

_____ ounces

D. Tina's family has 10 baseball gloves. If Tina and her brother each store the same number of gloves in their rooms, how many gloves will each one store?

_____ gloves

E. Tim has 12 wet suits. His sister has 4 wet suits. How many wet suits do they have altogether?

_____ wet suits

F. There are 18 tennis balls in the closet. Tara puts 3 balls in each container. How many containers does she use?

_____ containers

☐ 12 + 4 = 16
☐ 12 − 4 = 8
☐ 5 x 2 = 10
☐ 10 ÷ 2 = 5
☐ 3 x 6 = 18
☐ 18 ÷ 3 = 6

©The Mailbox® • TEC43037 • June/July 2008 • Key p. 313

Time to Play Ball!

Name_____

Complete each table.
Circle the final answer.

A. Trent bats 4 times each game. How many times will he have batted after 4 games?

Game	1	2	3	4
At Bats	4			

B. Tasha catches 14 fly balls in the first game. In each game after that, she catches two fewer balls than the game before. How many fly balls does she catch in the fifth game?

Game	1	2	3	4	5
Fly Balls	14				

C. Tomas rotates positions. He plays pitcher in one game, second base in the next game, and then right field. If this order starts with the first game and stays the same, what position will he play in the seventh game?

Game	1	2	3	4	5	6	7
Position	P						

D. The Tigers score 3 runs in their first game. In each of the next 3 games, they score twice as many runs as the game before. How many runs do the Tigers score in the fourth game?

Game	1	2	3	4
Runs	3			

E. Every third game, the Tigers play on their home field. If their first two games are played away, when will they play their fourth home game?

Game	1	2	3	4	5	6	7	8	9	10	11	12	13	14	15	16
Home or Away?	A	A														

Falling for Patterns

with ideas by Stacie Stone Davis, Lima, NY

Show an AB pattern.

Show an ABBC pattern.

THE SPIN ON PATTERNS
Creating and extending patterns using pictures

Put a new twist on practicing patterns with this partner center. First, make a copy of page 286 and cut apart the strips. Wrap each strip around an empty, lidded chip can, as shown, and tape the ends of each strip together. Repeat the process to make another completed can. Next, program a supply of index cards with different pattern-related tasks. Then place the cans and cards at a center. To complete the activity, each student selects a can. Player 1 chooses a card and reads it aloud. Each student then manipulates his can's strips to complete the task. When each child has completed the task, he shares the pattern with his partner. Then Player 2 chooses a card. Students continue in this manner until all the tasks have been completed or time is called.

SWITCHEROO
Analyzing patterns using concrete objects

Keep students on their toes with this small-group game!
First, provide each group with a supply of pattern blocks,
counters, and a file folder. Player 1 uses the blocks to
create a pattern behind the file folder. Then, while still
working behind the folder, he switches the placement of two blocks. He softly announces, "One, two,
switcheroo!" and moves the file folder to reveal the pattern. The
other players study the pattern. When a student determines the misplaced blocks, he quickly
places a counter next to each one. The first child to correctly do this earns a point for the
round. Students alternate play and continue playing in this manner as time allows.

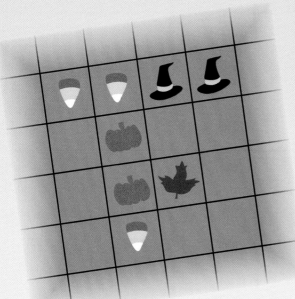

POSTED PRACTICE
Identifying, creating, and extending patterns using pictures

Here's a whole-class approach to building patterns. Draw a grid
of one-inch squares on a sheet of poster board and hang it in an
easily accessible area. Place a supply of multicolored stickers
nearby. During free time, invite students to visit the grid and use
the stickers to create a new pattern or extend an existing one.
Periodically refer to the poster, name a sticker combination
shown, and have students identify the pattern.

SCREENED-IN SHAPES
Identifying patterns using concrete objects

This partner game adds a mathematical slant to 20
Questions. First, give each student a matching supply
of pattern blocks. Pair students and have Player 1 fold a
piece of cardstock in half as shown. Next, have Player 1
create a pattern with her blocks, using the folded paper
as a workmat and a screen. Then challenge Player 2 to
determine the hidden pattern by asking a yes-or-no
question, such as "Is the first shape in the pattern
a triangle?" or "Is it an ABC pattern?" After
hearing Player 1's response, Player 2 uses his
pattern blocks to replicate the hidden pattern. He
shows his work to Player 1, who identifies which
blocks are placed correctly. Player 2 continues
in this manner until he determines the pattern
or until he has asked 20 questions. Then players
switch roles.

Pattern Strips

Use with "The Spin on Patterns" on page 284.

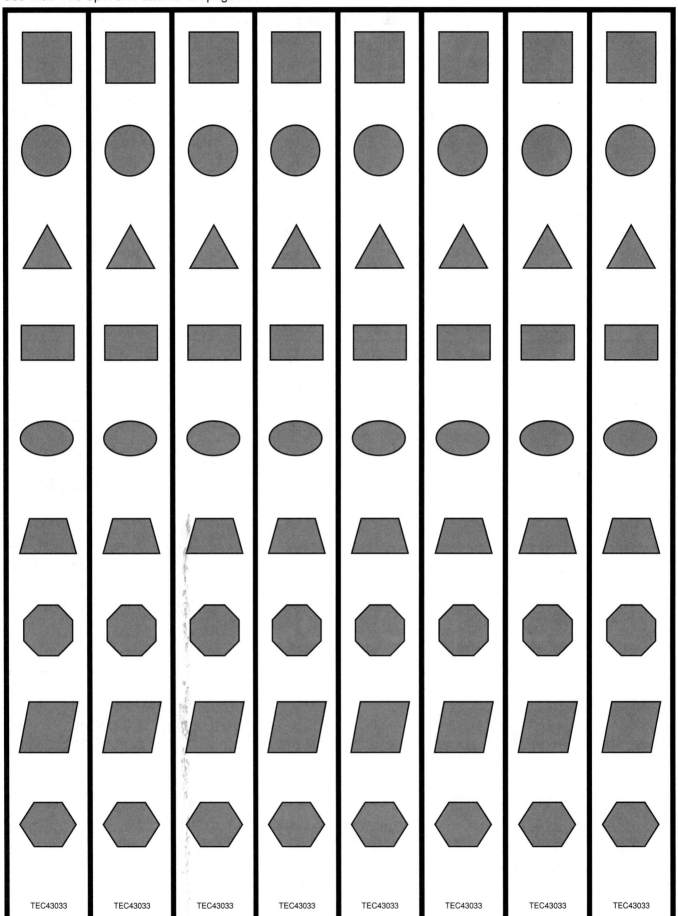

TEC43033 TEC43033 TEC43033 TEC43033 TEC43033 TEC43033 TEC43033 TEC43033

Leaves on the Loose

Two leaves in each row are out of order.
Label the pattern.
Circle the two misplaced leaves.
The first one has been done for you.

1.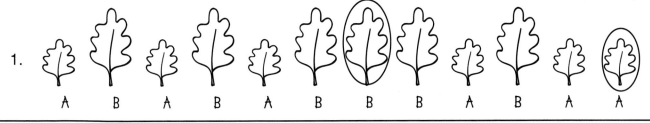

A B A B A B B B A B A A

2.

3.

4.

5.

6.

Clock Patterns

Use with "Time Travelers" on page 288 and
"Time Flies..." on page 289.

TEC43034

Game Cards

Use with "Time Flies..." on page 289.

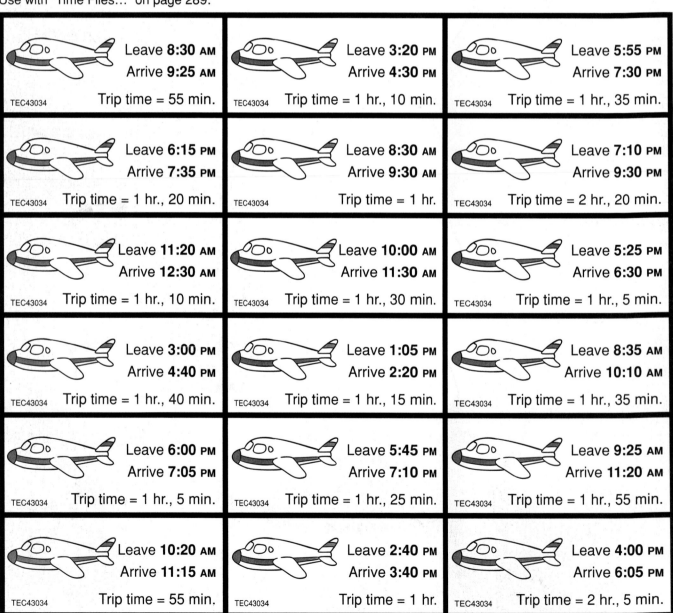

Leave **8:30** AM Arrive **9:25** AM Trip time = 55 min.	Leave **3:20** PM Arrive **4:30** PM Trip time = 1 hr., 10 min.	Leave **5:55** PM Arrive **7:30** PM Trip time = 1 hr., 35 min.
Leave **6:15** PM Arrive **7:35** PM Trip time = 1 hr., 20 min.	Leave **8:30** AM Arrive **9:30** AM Trip time = 1 hr.	Leave **7:10** PM Arrive **9:30** PM Trip time = 2 hr., 20 min.
Leave **11:20** AM Arrive **12:30** AM Trip time = 1 hr., 10 min.	Leave **10:00** AM Arrive **11:30** AM Trip time = 1 hr., 30 min.	Leave **5:25** PM Arrive **6:30** PM Trip time = 1 hr., 5 min.
Leave **3:00** PM Arrive **4:40** PM Trip time = 1 hr., 40 min.	Leave **1:05** PM Arrive **2:20** PM Trip time = 1 hr., 15 min.	Leave **8:35** AM Arrive **10:10** AM Trip time = 1 hr., 35 min.
Leave **6:00** PM Arrive **7:05** PM Trip time = 1 hr., 5 min.	Leave **5:45** PM Arrive **7:10** PM Trip time = 1 hr., 25 min.	Leave **9:25** AM Arrive **11:20** AM Trip time = 1 hr., 55 min.
Leave **10:20** AM Arrive **11:15** AM Trip time = 55 min.	Leave **2:40** PM Arrive **3:40** PM Trip time = 1 hr.	Leave **4:00** PM Arrive **6:05** PM Trip time = 2 hr., 5 min.

TEC43034

Move ahead one space.

Move 2 spaces.

Move 1 space.

Start

Finish

Go back one space.

Move ahead one space.

Time Flies

©The Mailbox • TEC43034 • Dec./Jan. 2007–8

Name

The Perfect Plan

Cut apart the cards on the left.
Put them in the correct order.
Glue them in place.

Answer the questions.

1. What time will Grace wake up?

   _____

2. How much time will Grace have before
   she leaves for the airport?

   _____

3. How long is her flight to Bird Beach?

   _____

4. What time will Grace check in at the hotel?

   _____

5. How much time will Grace spend at the
   beach? _____

From the Desk of Grace
8:00 AM   Time to wake up.
2:30 PM   Go to the beach to relax.

10:45 AM   Board flight to Bird Beach.

2:00 PM   Check in at the hotel and unpack.

9:15 AM   Leave for the airport.

4:45 PM   Come back to the hotel for dinner.

12:45 PM   Arrive in Bird Beach.

Head Over Heels for Linear Measurement

Stacie Wright, Millington School, Millington, NJ

SIZING UP
Measuring, comparing measurements

Direct each student to choose two numbers between 1 and 12 and have him write them on a piece of scrap paper. Next, give each student construction paper and a ruler and have him draw a rectangle, using his first number as the shape's height in inches and his second number as its width in inches. Then have him draw an object within the space, extending the object to touch all sides of the rectangle. The child cuts out his object and then repeats the process, using the same numbers but measuring in centimeters. When both objects are cut out, the child writes the name of the object on two index cards and records their measurements. Post the completed projects and their corresponding cards on a display titled "Sizing Up Similar Objects."

adapted from an idea by Sheri O'Quinn, Skyview Elementary, Lizella, GA

flower
height = 9 centimeters
width = 8 centimeters

flower
height = 9 inches
width = 8 inches

HOW LONG?
Estimating measurement

To begin, cut a 12-inch length of yarn and show it to the class. Compare the yarn's length to the lengths of objects in the room; then post the yarn in an easy-to-see location. Next, give each student pair a 24-inch length of yarn. Have one partner trim a piece from the yarn while her partner has his eyes closed. Direct the student to show her partner the cut yarn and have him estimate its length, referring to the posted yarn piece as needed. Encourage the duo to measure the length of yarn to check the accuracy of the estimate before switching roles.

MULTIPURPOSE MEASURING
Finding perimeter and area

Reinforce perimeter and area during spelling practice. Here's how! Have each child write her spelling words on a sheet of centimeter graph paper, placing one letter in each space. Then have the student trace around the word with a crayon, following the lines on the graph paper. Direct the child to use the graph paper's lines to determine the perimeter of each word or use the squares within the lines to determine the area of each word. Then have her write each answer on her paper.

Stacy Koerner, Bailey Elementary, Owasso, OK

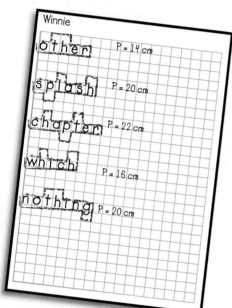

EVENTFUL PRACTICE
Using inches, feet, and yards

To prepare these interactive activities, designate in your classroom or multipurpose room areas for measuring a long jump, a ball toss, and a box slide. Tape off a starting line at each location. Then place at each starting line a copy of the corresponding task card from page 295 and the materials needed to complete the task. Direct small groups of students to travel to each area; then have each student complete the designated task. After the student measures his results, he writes them on a copy of the recording sheet from page 295. Then, at your signal, each group travels to the next location and repeats the process. **As an added challenge,** have students convert their measurements to another form, such as from inches to feet.

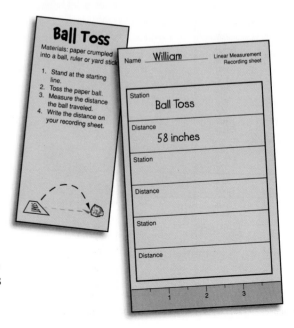

Long Jump

Materials: ruler or yard stick

1. Stand at the starting line.
2. Jump forward.
3. Have a partner measure the length of your jump.
4. Write the length on your recording sheet.

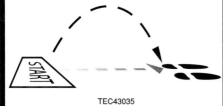

TEC43035

Ball Toss

Materials: paper crumpled into a ball, ruler or yard stick

1. Stand at the starting line.
2. Toss the paper ball.
3. Measure the distance the ball traveled.
4. Write the distance on your recording sheet.

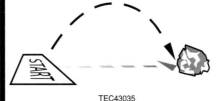

TEC43035

Box Slide

Materials: tissue box, ruler or yard stick

1. Stand at the starting line.
2. Slide the box forward.
3. Measure the distance the box slid.
4. Write the distance on your recording sheet.

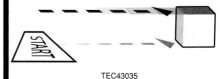

TEC43035

Linear Measurement
Recording sheet

Final Results

Name _____

Station	Distance	Station	Distance	Station	Distance

©The Mailbox® • TEC43035 • Feb./Mar. 2008

Measure Up

Circle the best unit to measure each object.

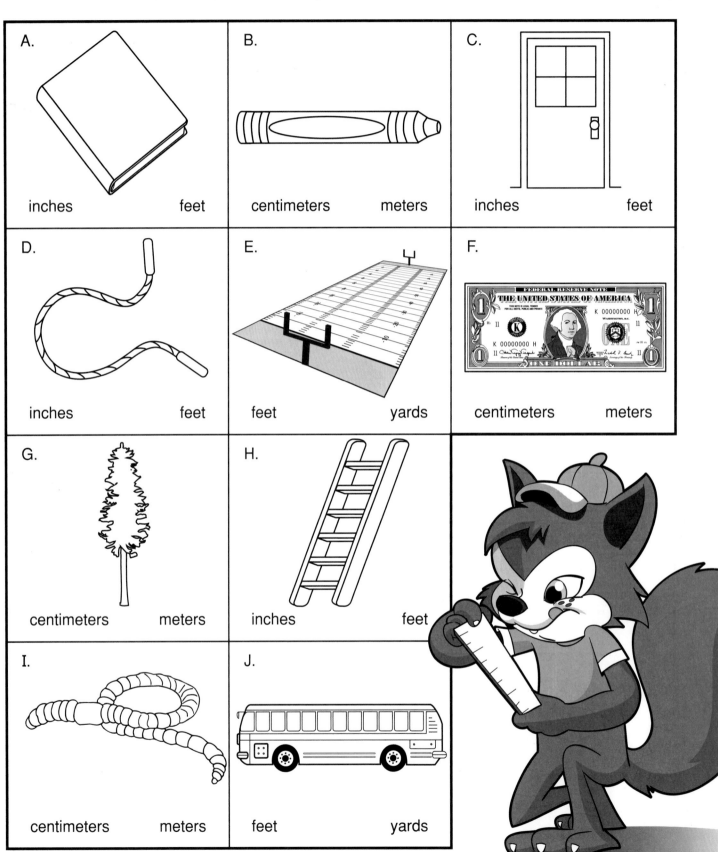

A.

inches   feet

B.

centimeters   meters

C.

inches   feet

D.

inches   feet

E.

feet   yards

F.

centimeters   meters

G.

centimeters   meters

H.

inches   feet

I.

centimeters   meters

J.

feet   yards

Name_____

Flipping for Centimeters

Use a centimeter ruler to measure each line.
Write the total length.

A. 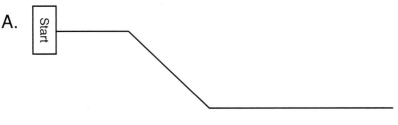 _____ cm

B.  _____ cm

C.  _____ cm

D. 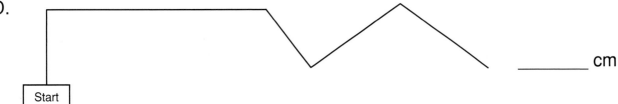 _____ cm

E. 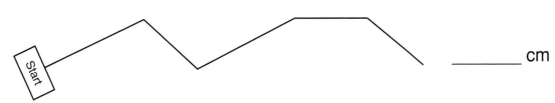 _____ cm

Having a Blast With Probability

by Stacie Stone Davis, Livonia Primary, Livonia, NY

COULD IT HAPPEN?
Recognizing whether an event is certain, possible, or impossible

For this activity, draw on the board three schoolhouse shapes and label each one as shown. Next, guide each student to think of an event that might or might not take place at school. Have the child write a sentence about the event on a sticky note. Then lead each student to read aloud his note and stick it on the corresponding shape.

SWEET SURPRISES!
Recording data

In advance, prepare a bag of jelly beans or other colorful candy for each small group of students. In each bag, place six candies of one color, three candies of another color, and one candy that is a third color. Give each group a bag and guide group members to complete section A on individual copies of the recording sheet from the bottom of page 300. Then have each child, in turn, draw a candy from the bag and announce its color. Direct each group member to record a tally for the color drawn before the student returns the candy to the bag. When each group member has had a turn, have students complete section B and discuss their sweet results!

PROBABLY PEPPERONI
Showing whether an event is certain, likely, unlikely, or impossible

To serve up this tasty lesson, make four copies of the pizza pattern from the top of page 300 for each pair of students. Next, guide each pair to color the slices on each pizza to show a different likelihood of being served a slice of pepperoni pizza. Have the pair flip each pizza and label it accordingly. Then have each pair trade its pizzas with another pair and check the pepperoni probability!

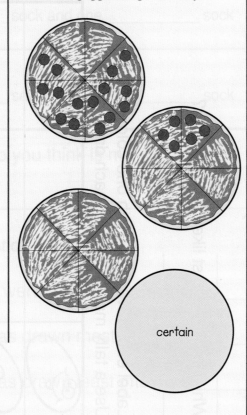

MATCHED PAIR?
Recording possible outcomes of an event

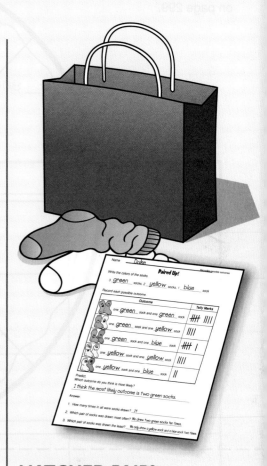

Collect six socks: three of one color, two of another color, and one of third color. Next, display the socks and lead students to identify the possible combinations of socks that could be pulled from a bag. (Be sure to note that the order of the colors pulled will not affect the number of combinations.) Have each child record the possibilities on a copy of the recording sheet on page 301 and then make a prediction about the most likely outcome. Put the socks in a bag and have a student draw two socks. Show the outcome and guide each student to mark a tally in the appropriate row. Then provide time for each child to have a turn. Finally, lead each student to evaluate the outcomes as guided by the questions on his recording sheet.

Pick a Crayon!

Color each set of crayons to match each statement.

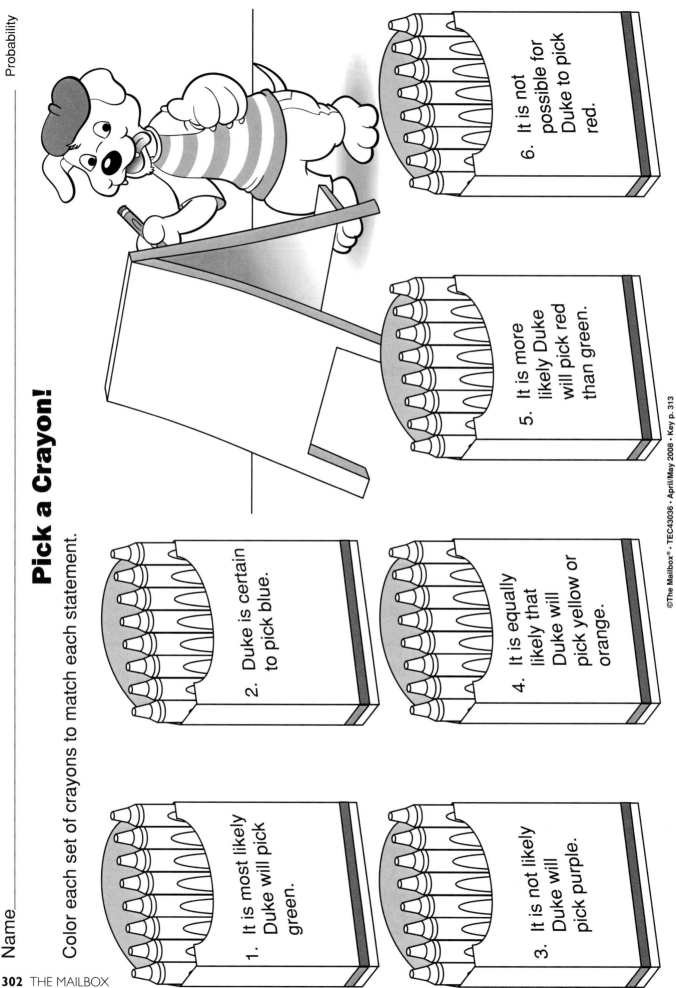

1. It is most likely Duke will pick green.

2. Duke is certain to pick blue.

3. It is not likely Duke will pick purple.

4. It is equally likely that Duke will pick yellow or orange.

5. It is more likely Duke will pick red than green.

6. It is not possible for Duke to pick red.

©The Mailbox® • TEC43036 • April/May 2008 • Key p. 313

Tune In to Math Songs and Chants

SING IT!
Rounding

Help students remember the steps for rounding with this clever song and the matching actions! Lead students to point to their eyes and step to the right each time they sing, "Look at the…" As children sing the first part of the chorus, they roll their arms clockwise and crouch down. Then, as students sing the second part of the chorus, they roll their arms counter clockwise and stand up straight. Rounding has never been so much fun!

Jolyn Haye, Peach Hill Academy, Moorpark, CA

Rounding Song
(sung to the tune of "If You're Happy and You Know It")

Verse
If you're rounding to the [tens] place, look at the [ones].
If you're rounding to the [tens] place, look at the [ones].
If you're rounding to the [tens] place, then always look at the [ones] place.
If you're rounding to the [tens] place, look at the [ones].

Chorus
If that digit's four or lower, you round down.
If that digit's four or lower, you round down.
If that digit's four or lower, then the number will be smaller.
If that digit's four or lower, you round down.

If that digit's five or higher, you round up.
If that digit's five or higher, you round up.
If that digit's five or higher, then the number will be bigger.
If that digit's five or higher, you round up.

For additional verses, replace the underlined words with the following pairs:
hundreds, tens
thousands, hundreds

READY? GO!
Place value

Reinforce place-value order with this active chant. For ones, each student holds his arms over his head, making a giant *o*. For tens, the child holds his arms straight out at his sides, forming a giant *t*. For hundreds, the child holds one arm straight up, bends the other arm, and holds the elbow of the outstretched arm, making a large *h*.

Rita Nierling, College Community School District
Cedar Rapids, IA

Place-Value Chant
Place value, how does it go?
Ones!
Tens!
Hundreds!

MY DIGITS MAKE A NUMBER
Standard form, expanded form

Before introducing this great rhyming reminder, have each student write a three- or four-digit number on one side of an index card. Next, guide the child to write the number in expanded form on the card's flip side. Then have the student hold up the appropriate side of the card as you lead the class in chanting or singing each verse.

Esther Fogle, Powdersville Elementary, Greenville, SC

Standard and Expanded Forms Song
(sung to the tune of "Miss Lucy")

My digits make a number.
We write them in this way.
We call it standard form.
And this is where they stay!

My digits make a number.
Expand is what we say.
We give each digit a value
And stretch and stretch away!

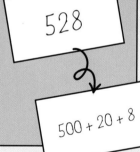

528

500 + 20 + 8

WHAT'S ON TOP?
Parts of a fraction

To clarify the parts of a fraction, sing this creative ditty.

Danielle Hinson
Clay Springs Elementary
Apopka, FL

Fraction Song
(sung to the tune of "On Top of Old Smokey")

On top of a fraction,
What will you find?
It's the numerator,
Up over the line.

Then, on the bottom,
Look and you'll see
The denominator,
Down where it should be.

TEACHER RESOURCE UNITS

Sharp Ideas for
Back-to-School

HANDY REMINDER

Discuss with students the many tasks in the classroom, such as keeping the classroom neat, taking
care of materials, and working as part of a team.
Guide students to understand that one of their most
important tasks at school is to learn. Reinforce the
importance of this task by having students create
visual reminders. First, have each student string an
elastic cord through decorative beads and alphabet
beads that spell *learn*, leaving some unbeaded cord
at each end. Then help each child tie the ends in a
knot, as shown, pulling the knot tightly. Each morning, direct students to put on their wristbands as a
reminder of the important task of learning.

Toni Brooks
Peachland Avenue Elementary
Newhall, CA

MAKING MEMORIES

On the first day of school, take a picture of each child. Then, on the second day, have students reflect on the previous day's events. Have students consider what they did, how they felt, and what they learned. Next, have each student write on lined paper a short description of the first day of school and cut around it to make a speech bubble. Direct her to glue her photo to a sheet of construction paper and glue the speech bubble above the photo. Bind the completed pages in a class book. Or, as an alternative, repeat the activity periodically throughout the year, keeping each child's completed pages to later bind in a yearlong memory book of her own.

Lisa Blackburn
Roberts Elementary

The first day of school was scary and fun. I was worried at first. After I met my new teacher and saw some old friends, I felt better. I really liked making learning wristbands. It was also fun to learn how to check out books from the class library.

Elizabeth 8-21-07

BACK-TO-SCHOOL SNACK

Show students how their individuality plays an important part in a class setting with this tasty idea. At the beginning of the week, give each child a resealable plastic bag with a short note inside, like the one shown. On Friday have each child name the snack he brought before he empties the bag's contents into a large bowl. (You may wish to have some bags prepared for students who forget.) When each child has had a chance to add his snack, mix the contents of the bowl. Explain to students that on its own, each food has its own unique qualities, just as each student in the class does. But when the foods are mixed, their unique qualities come together to form a more interesting snack, just as the students come together to form an interesting class. Then give each child a sample of the completed class snack to munch on while you lead the class in a discussion of the week's highlights.

Heather Leverett, Nashville, TN

This Friday, we will have a special snack. Please fill this bag with your favorite dry food, such as pretzels, cereal, or raisins (no nuts, please). Then send the bag back to school on Friday. Thanks for your help!

Ms. Leverett

GETTING TO KNOW YOU

The result of this project is a class supply of informational cubes that help students get acquainted with their classmates. To make a cube, a child cuts out a tagboard copy of the cube patterns on page 308. Next, he writes or illustrates his responses on each cube section. He also draws a self-portrait and writes his name on the individual section. The student folds the cutout along the dotted lines and applies glue to Tabs 1 and 2 to start his cube shape. Then he glues his self-portrait to the inside bottom of the cube before adding glue to the remaining tabs. After he completes his cube, he places it at a center. A student visits the center to read each cube and reveal the classmate named inside.

adapted from an idea by Rita Skavinsky, Minersville Elementary Center
Minersville, PA

Cube Patterns

Use with "Getting to Know You"
on page 307.

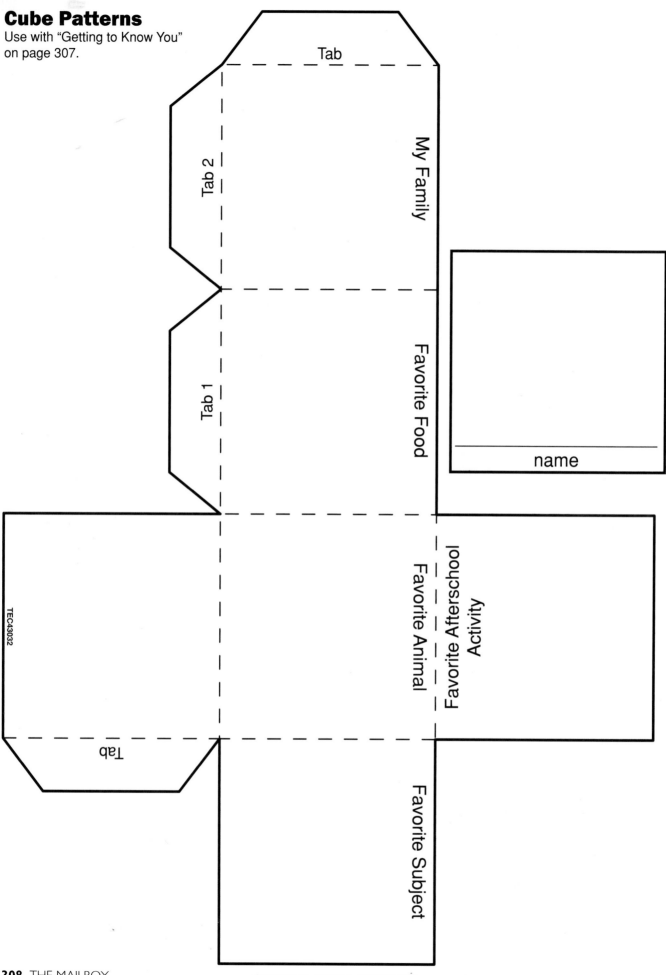

Tab

Tab 2

Tab 1

My Family

Favorite Food

name

Favorite Animal

Favorite Afterschool Activity

Tab

Favorite Subject

TEC43032

First-Class Tips for
Organizing
Differentiated Learning

CHALLENGE CENTER

Encourage higher-level thinking while building in student choice. Make a class set of three different challenge activities and place each set in a separate manila envelope. Put each original in a separate plastic sheet protector and tape it to the corresponding envelope. Then place the envelopes in an easily accessible area. When a child needs an extra challenge, he reviews the activities and selects one to complete. Periodically replace the activities with new ones to keep students motivated.

Stephanie Allen, Berlin Memorial School, Berlin, MA

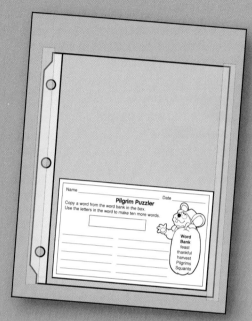

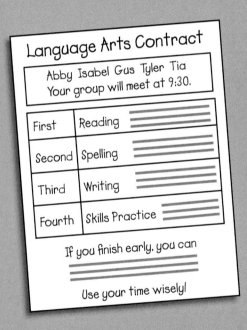

STUDENTS ON SCHEDULE

Keep students focused on learning while you work with small groups. For each student, create a contract that includes the order of each activity she should work on, when her small group will meet, and what she can work on if she completes her work early. If desired, have students ask a group member to help with any questions while you work with others. Not only will students know just what to work on, they'll know when to work on it too!

Gail Hollenshead, Heather Glen Elementary, Garland, TX

MAKING A MATCH

To provide differentiated center practice, organize students into groups and assign each group a color. Organize center work for each group by placing the directions and any needed supplies in a corresponding colored file folder. When a student visits a center, he simply locates the file folder that matches his assigned color and begins work.

Thea Clark, Indian Hollow Elementary, Winchester, VA

Answer Keys

Page 30
1. Earth Day
2. reduce
3. reuse
4. recycle
5. conserve

Page 34
1. Can you draw a snowball**?**
2. (h)ow big will your snowball be?
3. <u>Draw a snowman in the center of the box.</u>
4. My friend (C)arl likes to draw lots of snowmen.
5. He draws with crayons, pencils**,** and chalk.
6. <u>Draw eyes, a nose, and a hat on your snowman.</u>
7. I built a snowman on (b)lizzard (d)rive.
8. <u>Add snowflakes around your snowman.</u>
9. Maybe (i) will draw a snowpet.
10. <u>Now, color your snowman quickly!</u>
11. (d)o you like your picture?
12. <u>Draw another snowman on the back of this paper.</u>

Page 35
1. The third Monday in January is a U.S. holiday.
2. School was a big part of Dr. King's life.
3. How did Dr. King share his message of peace?

Page 36

February 14, 2008

Dear Daisy,

Did you know that you are a ___great___ friend? The
first time I met you, I knew that you were a ___kind___
dog. You shared your ___delicious___ bones with me. You
shared your ___snug___ blanket with me. You told me
___silly___ jokes. You let me see your doghouse, even though
you said it was ___cluttered___. I knew that you would be my
___pal___! Maybe someday we could ___stroll___
to the movies and get some ___frosty___ ice cream. I am
___glad___ you are my friend!

Your friend,
Digger

(word bank guides: good, nice, tasty, cozy, funny, messy, friend, walk, cold, happy)

Page 37
A. 139	B. 206	C. 125	D. 223
E. 288	F. 421	G. 322	H. 122
I. 779	J. 189	K. 305	L. 244
M. 252	N. 496	O. 393	

Page 38

Kyra works at the salon. Every day she gets to (meet)(new) customers and (see) old friends. As she styles (their)(hair)(some) customers tell interesting (tales). Kyra likes to (hear) the stories. In fact, Kyra loves her job! Many (days) she gets to the salon before anyone else. When they ask her how she does it, she laughs. "It's easy!" she says. "I (know) all the short cuts."

1. new		6. meet
2. tales		7. see
3. hear		8. hair
4. some		9. know
5. days		10. their

Page 82
A. 56	D. 139
B. 98	E. 2,772
C. 450	F. 3,508

Page 93

A
1. diagram
2. The Water Cycle
3. Precipitation falls.
4. the sun's heat
5. rain and snow

B
1. chart
2. This Week's Weather
3. sunny but windy
4. one
5. more sunny days

C
1. graph
2. Monthly Rainfall at Green Lake
3. inches; The graph is labeled "Rainfall in inches."
4. May
5. three inches

Page 94
5 = IT	40 = T
8 = IS	54 = I
10 = "T	70 = R
12 = W	74 = E
31 = O"	78 = D

<u>IT IS "TWO" TIRED.</u>

Page 96

Number	Start Time	Arrival Time	Length of Trip
1			1 hr. 15 min.
2			20 min.
3			3 hr. 55 min.
4			4 hr. 35 min.
5			1 hr. 25 min.
6			1 hr. 50 min.
7			1 hr. 10 min.
8			45 min.

Page 97

I love the Fourth of July! It is my favorite holiday.
My family spends this holiday at the beach, and I
love the beach. ^We Like to dress in red, white, and blue
clothes. we roast hot dogs and watch the colorful
fireworks. My mom lets me stay up late. i always
look forward to the Fourth of July!

Page 98
Order may vary.

Rule: Add 3.
7, 10, 13, 16, **19**
Rule: Add 4.
4, 8, 12, **16,** 20
Rule: Add 5.
22, 27, 32, 37, **42**
Rule: Add 10.
8, **18,** 28, 38, 48

Rule: Subtract 3.
37, 34, 31, **28,** 25
Rule: Subtract 4.
29, 25, **21,** 17, 13
Rule: Subtract 5.
60, 55, 50, **45,** 40
Rule: Subtract 10.
53, 43, 33, 23, **13**

Page 120
1. 47 students
2. 36 students
3. 21 students
4. 40 students
5. 7 students
6. yes; There are 16 extra cartons of milk.
7. 25 minutes
8. Answers will vary.

Page 123

A. 22	F. 24	K. 18	P. 14
B. 19	G. 16	L. 13	Q. 13
C. 21	H. 13	M. 23	R. 16
D. 15	I. 28	N. 39	S. 19
E. 41	J. 17	O. 19	T. 17

Page 127
1. 5
2. 3
3. 2
4. 7
5. markers
6. 5

Page 128

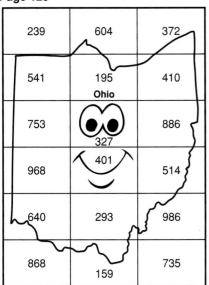

239	604	372
541	195 **Ohio**	410
753	327	886
968	401	514
640	293	986
868	159	735

Page 129

Q. 61	C. 197	E. 182	R. 76	K. 47	A. 304
I. 68	R. 76	S. 129	C. 197	W. 210	E. 182
U. 386	A. 304			I. 68	W. 210

Their classmate is a real "wise-quacker"!

Page 130
1. 2
2. 9
3. 12
4. 20
5. 25
6. 10
7. 4
8. 16

Page 131
A. cups (orange)
B. gallon (purple)
C. quarts (red)
D. pints (yellow)
E. pints (yellow)
F. quart (red)
G. gallons (purple)
H. cups (orange)
I. pints (yellow)
J. quarts (red)

Page 132
a dolphin

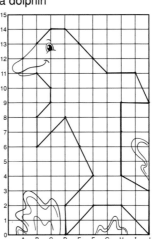

Page 161
1. 25
2. 24
3. pp. 18–20
4. the largest kind of bat
5. bats

Bonus Box: prey, nocturnal

Page 162

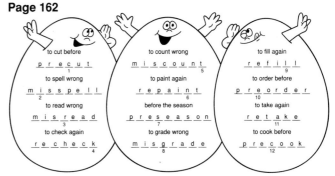

to cut before
p r e c u t
1
to spell wrong
m i s s p e l l
2
to read wrong
m i s r e a d
3
to check again
r e c h e c k
4

to count wrong
m i s c o u n t
5
to paint again
r e p a i n t
6
before the season
p r e s e a s o n
7
to grade wrong
m i s g r a d e
8

to fill again
r e f i l l
9
to order before
p r e o r d e r
10
to take again
r e t a k e
11
to cook before
p r e c o o k
12

"LET'S GET CRACKING!"

Page 176

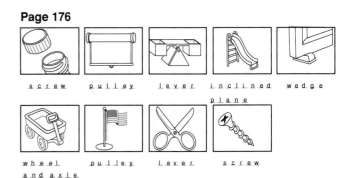

s c r e w   p u l l e y   l e v e r   i n c l i n e d
p l a n e

w e d g e

w h e e l   p u l l e y   l e v e r   s c r e w
a n d   a x l e

To get to the other "slide."

311

Page 209

1. (Farley Fox loves to watch other animals play.) He laughs at the bear cubs. He smiles at the rabbits. Farley giggles when he sees the birds. ~~He even looks at the mountains and the trees.~~

2. (Farley's friend Faye is great at sports.) ~~Faye likes to draw pictures.~~ She plays soccer. She also plays football. Faye was even the MVP of her swim team!

3. (Farley Fox has lived in dens in many states.) His first den was in California. Then he moved to a den in New Mexico. ~~His brother lives in Canada.~~ Now Farley lives in a den in Utah.

Page 227

Cause	Effect
Eggs are laid inside a safe den.	The female octopus protects them.
The female spends all her time cleaning and protecting her eggs.	She does not eat and dies shortly after the eggs hatch.
The larvae feed at the water's surface.	The larvae grow bigger.
Most young octopuses will be eaten by other sea animals.	They will not become adults.

Bonus Box: Answers will vary. The female lays so many eggs because so many larvae will be eaten. By laying thousands of eggs, she increases the chances of having offspring that will grow to be adults.

Page 230

Card 1
1. Missy Mouse is a pastry chef.
2. She measures all day long.
3. Watch out for that falling bowl!
4. Uh-oh. What did Missy do now?
5. It seems she made a big mess!

Card 2
1. Have you heard about Martin Mouse?
2. He loves to build fun mazes.
3. He has become famous for them.
4. Martin can build a maze in just five minutes!
5. What do you think his secret is?

Page 234

Order may vary.

Complete Sentences
His truck makes loud noises.
Her truck is full.
We had to load the truck.
The driver got lost in town.
He wants to buy a new truck.
It's old.

Incomplete Sentences
A cool day.
The brakes.
On the steering wheel.
Unloads the truck.
Went for a ride.
The tires.

Page 235

	Yes	No
1. The farmers (start) their work at dawn.	●	○
2. Fred and Frank (picks) the crops.	○	●
3. Fran (loads) the truck.	●	○
4. Fran (work) hard!	○	●
5. Her helpers (takes) a lunch break at noon.	○	●
6. Then Fran (drives) the crops to the market.	●	○
7. The boys (nap) for a while.	●	○
8. They (waits) for Fran.	○	●
9. The boys (serve) dinner when she returns.	●	○
10. Then the boys (cleans) the truck.	○	●

Bonus Box:
Fred and Frank pick the crops.
Fran works hard!
Her helpers take a lunch break at noon.
They wait for Fran.
Then the boys clean the truck.

Page 240
Order of supporting details may vary.

Page 256

1. <	5. >	9. <
2. >	6. <	10. >
3. <	7. >	11. <
4. <	8. >	12. >

Bonus Box: Answers will vary.

Page 257

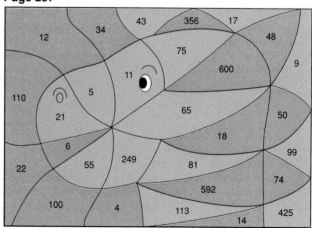

Page 260

30	140	70	600
50	150	80	800
90	120	60	200
110	20	500	300
160	10	900	100
130	40	700	400

Page 261

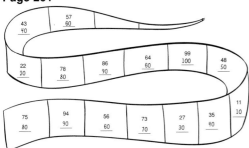

43/40		57/60			
22/20	78/80	86/90	64/60	99/100	48/50
75/80	94/90	56/60	73/70	27/30	35/40	11/10

Page 262

A. 50 E. 30 I. 700 M. 600
B. 80 F. 120 J. 1,100 N. 1,000
C. 20 G. 140 K. 200
D. 100 H. 30 L. 600

Page 266

A. 216 B. 448
C. 26 D. 112
E. 84 F. 541
G. 191 H. 262 I. 189

Page 269

Order of factors may vary.
A. 8 x 2 = 16 B. 6 x 3 = 18
C. 4 x 10 = 40 D. 7 x 9 = 63 E. 4 x 3 = 12
F. 7 x 5 = 35 G. 8 x 6 = 48 H. 5 x 6 = 30
I. 9 x 6 = 54 J. 8 x 8 = 64 K. 7 x 4 = 28

Page 270

Order in each set may vary.

Even
6 x 2 = 12
7 x 2 = 14
4 x 6 = 24
8 x 4 = 32
6 x 6 = 36
6 x 9 = 54
8 x 7 = 56
10 x 8 = 80

Odd
5 x 1 = 5
3 x 5 = 15
7 x 3 = 21
5 x 5 = 25
3 x 9 = 27
7 x 7 = 49
9 x 7 = 63
9 x 9 = 81

Page 273

A. 18
    18 ÷ 6 = 3 or 18 ÷ 3 = 6
B. 16
    16 ÷ 2 = 8 or 16 ÷ 8 = 2
C. 35
    35 ÷ 5 = 7 or 35 ÷ 7 = 5
D. 36
    36 ÷ 9 = 4 or 36 ÷ 4 = 9
E. 15
    15 ÷ 3 = 5 or 15 ÷ 5 = 3
F. 48
    48 ÷ 8 = 6 or 48 ÷ 6 = 8
G. 14
    14 ÷ 7 = 2 or 14 ÷ 2 = 7
H. 24
    24 ÷ 4 = 6 or 24 ÷ 6 = 4
I. 27
    27 ÷ 9 = 3 or 27 ÷ 3 = 9
J. 64
    64 ÷ 8 = 8
K. 42
    42 ÷ 6 = 7 or 42 ÷ 7 = 6
L. 20
    20 ÷ 4 = 5 or 20 ÷ 5 = 4

Page 274

A. 27 B. 69 C. 23
D. 63 E. 65
F. 43 G. 83
H. 64

Page 281

Addition
A. 84 golf balls
C. 18 batters
F. 45 shows
G. 21 tents

Subtraction
B. 8 times
D. 25 pitches
E. 16 members
H. 15 meters

Multiplication
A. 21 golf balls
C. 16 batters
E. 27 shows
G. 12 gallons

Division
B. 6 times
D. 9 pitches
F. 3 events
H. 7 times

Page 282

A. 12 – 4 = 8 D. 10 ÷ 2 = 5
B. 5 x 2 = 10 E. 12 + 4 = 16
C. 3 x 6 = 18 F. 18 ÷ 3 = 6

Page 283

A. 4 8 12 (16)
B. 14 12 10 8 (6)
C. P S R P S R (P)
D. 3 6 12 (24)
E. A A H A A H A A H A A (H) A A H A

Page 287

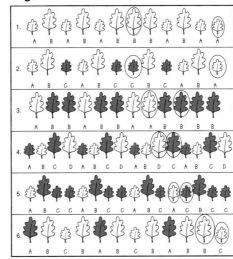

Page 292

8:00 AM Time to wake up.
9:15 AM Leave for the airport.
10:45 AM Board flight to Bird Beach.
12:45 PM Arrive in Bird Beach.
2:00 PM Check in at the hotel and unpack.
2:30 PM Go to the beach to relax.
4:45 PM Come back to the hotel for dinner.

1. 8:00 AM
2. 1 hour, 15 minutes
3. 2 hours
4. 2:00 PM
5. 2 hours, 15 minutes

Page 296

A. inches B. centimeters C. feet
D. feet E. yards F. centimeters
G. meters H. feet
I. centimeters J. yards

Page 297

A. 10 D. 16
B. 15 E. 12
C. 14

Page 302

1. At least five crayons are green.
2. All the crayons are blue.
3. Three or fewer crayons are purple.
4. Four crayons are yellow; four crayons are orange.
5. At least five crayons are red; three or fewer crayons are green.
6. No crayons are red.

INDEX